AMERICA'S
BOUNTIFUL WATERS

AMERICA'S BOUNTIFUL WATERS

150 YEARS OF FISHERIES CONSERVATION AND THE U.S. FISH & WILDLIFE SERVICE

EDITED BY CRAIG SPRINGER

STACKPOLE
BOOKS

Guilford, Connecticut

This book is humbly dedicated to the scores of men and women and their families who have worked to conserve America's fisheries since 1871 under the banners of the U.S. Fish Commission, the U.S. Bureau of Fisheries, and today's U.S. Fish and Wildlife Service.

Published by Stackpole Books
An imprint of The Rowman & Littlefield Publishing Group, Inc.
4501 Forbes Blvd., Ste. 200
Lanham, MD 20706
www.rowman.com

Distributed by NATIONAL BOOK NETWORK

British Library Cataloguing in Publication Information available

Library of Congress Cataloging-in-Publication Data available

ISBN 978-0-8117-3955-9 (cloth: alk. paper)
ISBN 978-0-8117-6954-9 (electronic)

♾™ The paper used in this publication meets the minimum requirements of American National Standard for Information Sciences—Permanence of Paper for Printed Library Materials, ANSI/NISO Z39.48-1992.

Contents

Note about photo credits: Historic images from the National Fish and Aquatic Conservation Archives are credited as USFWS NFACA and the National Conservation Training Center Museum as USFWS MA.

Prologue

Fish are special—or so I was always told. As the son of an extremely passionate fisheries biologist, my eight siblings and I were raised on a number of national fish hatcheries around the country. My father, Arden, worked for the Fish and Aquatic Conservation program of the U.S. Fish and Wildlife Service and was dedicated to the agency's mission. His contributions to the field, the fishery resources, and the outdoors helped to instill in me those same beliefs—so much so that I would eventually pursue a similar career of fighting for protection of natural resources.

It is fitting that fish started it all for me, because fish is what started it all for the U.S. Fish and Wildlife Service. Fish came first. One hundred and fifty years ago, on February 9, 1871, the U.S. Commission of Fish and Fisheries was born—our nation's very first federal conservation agency. Because in the big, grand scheme of the many varied landscapes across this glorious planet, one thing holds true in all of them—healthy landscapes and the species that depend on them all start with, and depend upon, healthy water sources and the aquatic life within them. The flashes of fish catching sunlight, fleeting glimpses of life beneath the translucent surface—if those are healthy then there is a strong chance the dependent ecosystems are too.

My parents may have played a hand in helping shape some of my interests but there was another aspect that contributed. My so-called "backyards" growing up were the grounds of the Spearfish, Gavins Point, and McNenny National Fish Hatcheries in South Dakota; New London National Fish Hatchery in Minnesota; Marion National Fish Hatchery in Alabama; and Senecaville National Fish Hatchery in Ohio. Every day was an opportunity to learn about bugs, squirrels, porcupines, and, of course, a variety of fish—sunfish and bass, trout and suckers, crappie and catfish. My siblings and I learned about habitats, the seasons and animal behavior, migrations and hibernation and, most importantly, how ecosystems and biodiversity are strong and resilient but yet so delicate.

Born in the 1960s on the Senecaville National Fish Hatchery, and then through my entire childhood, I was surrounded by fisheries biologists and scientists who were focused on understanding and stewarding our nation's natural resources and wildlife into the future. Their vision had no limits—and their desire and effort to create the next generation of conservationists unending. That is something I have come to admire about the work of the U.S. Fish and Wildlife Service—the unwavering dedication and passion of its employees, especially those who work in the field. Often the employees in the field have huge obstacles—budget shortfalls, too few employees on the ground, regulations, politics, and working through issues with partners. But they believe so wholeheartedly in their work that they figure out creative ways to achieve incredible results. Over the past 150 years, the passion of the employees has persisted. Commemorating this monumental milestone is as much about recognizing the fish and wildlife successes as it is about celebrating all the people who have given their talents, sweat, tears, and joys in service to fisheries conservation. Their contributions cannot be overstated and their work will continue to play a key role in fish and aquatic issues and management for the next 150 years and beyond.

As a "fish hatchery family," as we were always called, we were required by the U.S. Fish and Wildlife Service to relocate every few years to various research and rearing facilities around the country. This required an incredible partnership between my parents, with my mom, Sylvia, focused on every logistical detail, every child's need, and doing whatever was required to settle our family seamlessly into a new community. She was the rock that truly made it all possible for my family. During my childhood, I resided on five different national fish hatcheries and finally settled in Spearfish, South Dakota. That was my father's last duty station. Spearfish National Fish Hatchery, through his work, became the beloved D.C. Booth Historic National Fish Hatchery and the National Fish and Aquatic Conservation Archives. It

Spring Stocking honors workers of the past on the grounds of the D.C. Booth Historic National Fish Hatchery. The late Arden Trandahl modeled the figure on shore, overseeing the work of others. Trandahl was a visionary biologist and leader who established the National Fish and Aquatic Conservation Archives in Spearfish, South Dakota. COURTESY LES VOORHIS

is the U.S. Fish and Wildlife Service's official fisheries archives.

Fish was my family story: standing on the banks of a pond filled with thousands of trout, their sinuous movement would mesmerize me. Their shimmering colors in spangled light and their sudden bursts of speed faster than their shadow could keep up hooked me. My love for fish started early. My interests grew as I learned more about conservation and the purpose of my father's work.

And that love remains today. Growing up, I fished nearby lakes, ponds, and streams, especially when we lived in Spearfish. Nearly every day, I fished Spearfish Creek, a blue-ribbon trout stream that was the center of our community. It became an addiction. Today I own more than a hundred fly rods and love to restore old bamboo fly rods. It is a labor of love, something that I do in honor and in memory of all my older fishing buddies that have passed away over the years— friends that were always willing to share their fishing knowledge and love of our community with me.

Over the years, my father explained and ingrained in our entire family the importance of fish to the history of the United States. Fish possess food, commercial, and economic value, the latter, measurable: every one dollar in taxes invested into the federal fisheries program translates into twenty-eight dollars in economic impact. That equates to approximately $4 billion in annual contributions to the United States economy. The effect ripples outward, like the concentric rings of a floating bass plug landing on glassy water. The ripple effect contributes sixty-eight thousand jobs on a national scale. The fisheries program brings direct benefits to main street America with dozens of conservation offices, hatcheries, labs, and health and technology centers. The program's facilities and its employees are a significant economic force where they live and work.

Fish have intrinsic values not so easily expressed in words. But anglers who write have tried over the span of five centuries. Angling is the strongest connection to our history and heritage of fisheries conservation.

Fisheries conservation contributes to the human experience in ways that cannot be computed. What is the real worth of a parent's joy in introducing their child to fishing? What is the real worth of citizen's satisfaction in knowing local waters are clean enough to support sensitive species?

The Fish and Aquatic Conservation program and the joy of fishing are special to me because they touch everyone. Angling is available to nearly everyone: young, old, men, women, rich, and poor—all Americans are served. You enjoy angling as a family, alone, or with your friends. Fisheries conservation in many cases centers on saving our biodiversity and protecting native species—but it is also building community and connection among people and the outdoors.

As we try to capture the heritage of fisheries conservation in the pages that follow, it is important to know that this is not a book about the past, but truly about the future. Part of that proof lies in the fact that the original charges to the 1871 U.S. Fish Commission still reside in today's U.S. Fish and Wildlife Service. Then, as now, the workers in the field are dedicated, inventive, and resourceful.

The past is prologue. What has passed begets the future. The sacrifices of so many to shape and protect and conserve America's fisheries live on as consummate professionals face a future sure to be filled with new and emerging challenges over the next century and a half.

—Jeff Trandahl

A freshly harvested Atlantic sturgeon hangs outside the shingle of a wholesale market. Date unknown. Today's Virginia Fish and Wildlife Conservation Office monitors the species. USFWS MA

From the Headwaters to the Meanders—150 Years of Conservation

MARK MADISON, PH.D.

AMERICAN FISHERIES IN AN AGE OF EXPLOITATION

"But although we must, with respect to our land animals, be content to accept nature in the shorn and crippled condition to which human progress has reduced her, we may still do something to recover at least a share of the abundance which, in a more primitive state, the watery kingdom afforded."

—George Perkins Marsh, *Report on the Artificial Propagation of Fish* (1857)

From 1800 to 1871, the precipitous decline in American fisheries drove the creation of the American Conservation Movement and the U.S. Fish Commission, our nation's first federal conservation agency. Out of the wanton destruction of all American wildlife—furred, feathered, and finned—arose a new popular movement and a new agency to help ensure this age of exploitation would never be repeated.

Both marine and freshwater fishery resources began to noticeably decline in the eastern half of the United States by the 1850s. This led to the creation of the first state fish commissions to address the sport and food needs of their citizens. The most famous of these early fish commissioners was George Perkins Marsh, arguably America's first conservationist. A native of Vermont, Marsh witnessed firsthand the decimation of his state's freshwater fisheries through overfishing, destruction of waterways, and denuding of terrestrial habitats that affected fisheries. Marsh's visionary *Report on the Artificial Propagation of Fish* (1857) laid the foundations for a nationwide fisheries program. Marsh predicted that anglers and scientists could be the backbone of a new conservation movement to restock waterways and restore fish habitats. Marsh's dreams came true fourteen years later, when President Ulysses S. Grant appointed his longtime correspondent, Spencer Baird, as the first U.S. Fish Commissioner. Marsh had recommended hiring Baird initially as assistant secretary to the Smithsonian

while Marsh was a member of the Board of Regents, and then politicked to have Baird become the first U.S. fish commissioner. Baird repaid the favor in his 1872–1873 *Report of the Commissioner* by acknowledging Marsh's pioneering role in promoting fisheries conservation, noting: "The history of the efforts in the United States, looking especially toward the restoration of salmon to American waters, may perhaps be considered as dating from a report upon the artificial propagation of fish made in October 1857, to the general assembly of Vermont by the Hon. George Perkins Marsh. . . ."

Marsh's views were not unique. In neighboring New York, Robert Barnwell Roosevelt was an avid angler, a fly-fishing advocate, an author, ambassador, and congressman. The conservation-minded Roosevelt founded the New York State Fishery Commission in 1867 and served as a fish commissioner for two decades (1868–1888). He went on to serve from 1874–1882 as the president of the American Fish Culturists' Association (today's American Fisheries Society) and originated the congressional bill that created the U.S. Fish Commission in 1871. Perhaps his greatest legacy was in inspiring his nephew, Theodore Roosevelt, to join politics and conservation in a career. It was under his purview in 1903 that the U.S. Fish Commission became the U.S. Bureau of Fisheries. His conservation ethos would have a huge impact on the Bureau and what eventually became the U.S. Fish and Wildlife Service.

Robert Barnwell Roosevelt (1829–1906)

The only Roosevelt anyone knew during the nineteenth century was also the only one everyone has forgotten. Uncle to one president (Theodore), distant cousin to a second (Franklin), and great uncle to a first lady (Eleanor), Robert Barnwell Roosevelt was a writer, congressman, ambassador, naturalist, and activist for progressive causes. It is to our everlasting good fortune that the cause dearest to his heart was fishing.

"RBR," as his family called him, was born to a charmed life—and never looked back. The fourth son in a wealthy family, he grew up in a household of boys. He assumed the performativity characteristic of younger children and combined that with the dutifulness that was Roosevelt. Like each of his older brothers, RBR visited his mother every day until she died. That was one side.

The other was a hard-charging young man on the rise. He studied law, passed the bar in 1850, and cultivated an abiding interest in the outdoors, particularly fishing. He joined the New York Sportsmen's Club led by exiled Englishman William Henry Herbert (Frank Forester), a haunted, prolific writer, who introduced the idea of a conservation ethic to these shores before he committed suicide in 1858. Roosevelt later remembered Forester as "disagreeable" but "without equal in sporting matters." Many would say the same of RBR someday. But he was never much given to self-reflection—and, more to the point, he picked up the gauntlet of conservation and never set it down.

Roosevelt wrote the first American book on fishing, *The Game Fish of the Northern States of America and British Provinces* in 1862. With the book's success, his life course was set: RBR dedicated his privilege, erudition, and personality to improve the health and restoration of our stocks of fish. Period. And, there was nothing conflict averse about him; like his famous nephew who followed, he lived for the fray.

To be sure, Roosevelt picked his battles. For as exercised as he could become, he was also a master

ROBERT BARNWELL ROOSEVELT. COURTESY LIBRARY OF CONGRESS

at "compartmentalizing," as we might say today. Upon the outbreak of the Civil War, the Roosevelt family supported Lincoln and the Union; however, due to their upperclass New York City world and southern connections through marriage—men from Theodore Roosevelt's mother's family, for example, served with the South—most Roosevelt men of military age had a muted response to the call to arms. RBR's contribution was in this vein—he was involved for a while in a volunteer regiment from New York.

Roosevelt's more adroit segmenting came domestically. At the time, he was married with a family, lived in an adjoining brownstone next to his brother, Theodore Sr., and nephew, Theodore Jr., and presided over a bohemian household with his wife, Lizzie. Enter their home and you might encounter a German shepherd dressed for dinner or a monkey swinging from the chandelier. Look out the window and you would see a cow grazing in the backyard. It is said that the Victorians brought the outdoors in, and there is no better example. The embrace of the natural world left a lasting impression on young Theodore.

As always with RBR, another reality waited around the corner, and this one concerned his heading of a second household, just several blocks away. Its existence could well have prompted Theodore Sr.'s decision to move his family to another New York City location. In any case, the relationship resulted in a public distancing by the Roosevelt family, which appeared to have had little impact on RBR. When Lizzie died in 1879, he married the woman from the second household, Minnie Fortesque. Their four children, previously born, became his "stepchildren"—one of whom served as a Rough Rider with TR in the Spanish-American War. Through it all, TR and RBR maintained a cordial, affectionate relationship—very much alive in letters and private engagements, but seldom apparent in public interactions. TR understood political optics, but he maintained a genuine appreciation for the uncle who gave him a deep love for all things wild.

And, it is one of the wonderful coincidences of history that this was the time for these two particular Roosevelts to take their places on the American political stage. Because, by the late 1860s, populations of native fisheries were dropping like stocks in a bank run. Native brook trout, their habitat destroyed by tanning operations and deforestation, their numbers depleted by overfishing, were lucky to reach six inches long. Anglers "fished for count," as the saying of the day went. Commercial netting operations decimated salmon, shad, and other anadromous fish.

TR is the man we remember given all he did with his bully pulpit and preservation of land at century's turn. But the truth is, we would never have gotten there with fisheries had his uncle not come first. RBR was a progressive before there was a movement. He had fire and intelligence, but he also had money and influence. He was the most admired after-dinner speaker in New York, and at a time when this mattered. He took on Boss Tweed and Tammany Hall. He could work a room. He mobilized his fellow members of the American Fisheries Society in New York City and petitioned the New York State Legislature to take up the problem of declining fishes, most notably the shad in the Hudson. The legislature initiated an investigative committee in 1868, and the results led to the New York State Fish Commission of which RBR served as head for the next twenty years.

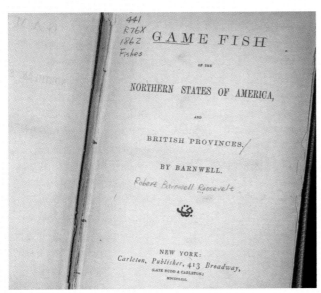

Robert Barnwell Roosevelt may well have been thinking about creating a federal fisheries agency when he published *Game Fish* in 1862.
BRETT BILLING, USFWS

He joined forces with the man generally considered the most famous fisherman in New York at the time, Seth Green, himself busy devising novel contraptions to propagate fish. Roosevelt also pushed for legislation to control harvest, through measures such as seasons and net sizes. He and Green went to war with netters and their financiers for the next twenty years. It was the first shot. The fight to save our national resources had begun.

In 1871, RBR caught this regional tailwind and ran for Congress from the 4th district with an agenda in mind—start a similar fisheries conservation agency on a federal level. He was elected and promptly wrote legislation for a bill to authorize the U.S. Fish Commission to propagate fish. Many congressmen, particularly those from interior states and those influenced by commercial interests, lampooned Roosevelt's efforts. But after five days' debate, the bill passed. Some, like Secretary of State Hamilton Fish, recognized Roosevelt's achievements. The secretary called RBR "The Father of all Fishes."

Eminent conservationist Spencer Baird headed the Commission. Both men were not simply interested in preserving what remained, but in restoring what had been. And, Roosevelt and other men dedicated to fisheries continued that fight. The rise of interest in fishing and the outdoors throughout the 1870s and '80s and the accompanying explosion of print journalism gave RBR and his allies an audience and a venue. And he treated the situation like it was a river that had never been fished—and he had a full weekend to do so.

Although it feels hyperbolic today, Roosevelt's emphasis on how fish conservation could reframe the larger society was just what was necessary to awaken the public to the disaster on their doorstep. As he explained in a speech to the American Fisheries Society, "There is light. There should be no fear. Waters will teem and feed all the poor." These are big ideas, nothing short of connecting the health of fisheries to the destiny of the republic. Now, to be clear, Roosevelt was delivering a speech to the Fish Culturist Association. So it's a bit like a coach talking at half time. But the natural world was in deep peril, with buffalo herds vanishing, bird species disappearing. Fisheries seemed destined to follow, but it didn't happen. There are a good many people to thank for the robust populations of fishes that we enjoy today, but we should start with the man they called the father of them all.

—Will Ryan

Having chronicled the decline in fisheries, these commissioner-conservationists also offered and demonstrated solutions. Aquaculture seemed the most pragmatic course of action; if there are too few fish, we should breed more of them. Around this time, early experiments in scientific aquaculture began. Theodatus Garlick and H. A. Ackley successfully fertilized captive brook trout eggs in the autumn of 1853. By 1860, Samuel Colt—best known for firearms, not fish—was hatching four thousand trout fry in East Hartford, Connecticut. The maestro of fish culture was undoubtedly Seth Green. Green built his first hatchery in Spring Brook, New York, in 1864. Moving beyond traditional aquaculture species like trout and salmon, Green expanded the fish culture realm to include grayling, lake herring, whitefish, and even goldfish and carp. This heyday of fish culture pioneers extended out to Mainer Charles Atkins, who was the first to spawn Atlantic salmon in the U.S., a skill he put to good use at the still-operational Craig Brook National Fish Hatchery, Maine, established in 1889.

Perhaps the most unlikely fish culture pioneer was the Reverend Livingston Stone. The Harvard-educated theologian seemed an unlikely fish culturist, but his sickly constitution combined with a prescription for more time outdoors, led him, literally, to fish. In 1866, Stone established his first hatchery, Cold Springs Trout Ponds in Charlestown, New Hampshire, one of the first commercial hatcheries in the country. He eventually became U.S. Deputy Fish Commissioner in 1872 and an invaluable asset to the fledgling U.S. Fish Commission.

America's watery kingdom was in distress throughout most of the nineteenth century. Industrialization, pollution, destruction of waterways, and overfishing had diminished formerly abundant fishery resources. Yet a cadre of conservationists and fish culturists were emerging individually in this era to chart a different course. Independently creating commissions, hatcheries, and scientific societies, they often intersected in their interests and affiliations. These early efforts at conservation were limited geographically and by the resources of state governments or private individuals. A national program could conserve fishes across the continent. A member of this milieu, Spencer Baird, would take the dreams of these visionaries and make them a reality.

THE U.S. FISH COMMISSION AND THE ORIGINS OF THE AMERICAN CONSERVATION MOVEMENT

"The U.S. should take part in the great undertaking of introducing or multiplying shad, salmon, and other food-fishes throughout the Country . . ."

—Spencer Fullerton Baird, Commissioner of Fish and Fisheries (1871–1887)

From 1871 to 1939, the U.S. Fish Commission, and its successor the U.S. Bureau of Fisheries, was the test case for conservation at a national, even continental scale. Luckily, for those of us living 150 years later, it succeeded.

The decimation by pollution and over-harvest of the nation's fisheries in the nineteenth century eventually led a minority of concerned sportsmen and early conservationists to petition Congress for a federal solution to the problem. The U.S. Fish Commission's origins were small, considering its outsized role in American conservation. On February 9, 1871, Congress established an independent U.S. Commission of Fish and Fisheries to investigate the decrease in American fish stocks and suggest possible remedies. Its modest mandate was to study the decimation of the previous seven decades, but the "Fish Commission" soon became an exemplar of what U.S. Bureau of Fisheries employee Rachel Carson would later term "conservation in action."

In that way, it reflected the character of the first U.S. Fish Commissioner, Spencer Fullerton Baird (1823–1887). One of the great nineteenth-century American naturalists, Baird was already employed full-time as assistant secretary for the growing Smithsonian Institution. When President Grant appointed Baird the first U.S. fish commissioner on February 25, 1871, he was not content to write a mere report to be considered (or not) by Congress. Baird immediately began creating a continental conservation movement. A year after its creation, the U.S. Fish Commission was stocking American shad from Vermont into Colorado waters and rearing Atlantic salmon in Maine and Chinook salmon in California. Taking full advantage of the fish culture revolution of the previous decades, Baird wasted no time in enlisting Seth Green, Charles Atkins, and Livingston Stone to supply their expertise and fisheries stocks to restore America's watery kingdom. While Green and Atkins raised fish in the longstanding private and state hatcheries of New England, Livingston Stone was sent far afield to California to open new territory

U.S. Navy sailors operate a depth-measuring device on the U.S.F.C. *Albatross* while USFC workers record data circa 1880. USFWS NFACA

for conservation. There, on the McCloud River in 1872, Stone established what would become the first national fish hatchery at Baird Station. Impressively, Stone was shipping salmon eggs back to the East Coast in his first year at the station. The Native McCloud Wintu tribe also introduced Stone and other fish culturists to the previously West Coast–limited rainbow trout, a species that would come to dominate fish hatcheries in the twentieth century. The colonization of North America by rainbow trout was emblematic of the U.S. Fish Commission's mandate to stock as many game and food fish as possible, regardless of their unknown impact on native fish species. The U.S. Fish Commission excelled at propagating and stocking lake whitefish at Alpena Fish-Cultural Station, Michigan; cutthroat trout at Yellowstone Fish-Cultural Station, Wyoming; smallmouth bass at Louisville Fish-Cultural Station, Kentucky; Chinook salmon at Battle Creek Fish-Cultural Station, California; sockeye at Afognak Fish-Cultural Station, Alaska; American shad at Gloucester City Fish-Cultural Station, New Jersey; Atlantic salmon at Grand Lakes Fish-Cultural Station, Maine; and, alas, common carp at Arsenal Carp Pond, Washington, D.C.

Baird considered the U.S. Fish Commission to be the ideal bulk retailer, providing fish eggs not only across North America, but as far afield as Germany, Colombia, and even New Zealand. As the fish-cultural stations, later known as national fish hatcheries circa 1950, onward, grew in number, so did the challenges in transporting fish and their eggs cross-country. One experiment initiated in 1880 was the U.S. Fish Commission's first floating hatchery, the U.S.F.C. *Fish Hawk*. Plying the Atlantic, the *Fish Hawk* reared American shad and cod, while also serving as a literal platform for studying a variety of marine fishes.

On land, the most efficient transport was the rails. The first transcontinental railroad was completed in 1869, just two years before the creation of the U.S. Fish Commission. In 1873, the first "aquarium car" attempted the cross-continental transport of fish with disastrous results. The water- and fish-heavy car shepherded by Stone derailed and crashed into Nebraska's Elkhorn River, sentencing at least the tautaugs, oysters, and lobsters to a freshwater grave. Clearly, a better mode of transport was required. In 1881, a modified baggage car was retrofitted as a fish transportation vehicle or "fish car." Improvements ensued and between 1881 and 1928, ten fish cars were specifically designed to transport fish across the nation—rickety wood yielded to stout steel rail cars.

Identification card of fishery expert Reginald Truitt who sailed aboard the *Albatross* under the banner of the U.S. Bureau of Fisheries. USFWS MA

This supremely efficient fish distribution method succeeded in stocking fish in practically every available waterway near a railhead. However, "near" is a relative term belied by determination. By way of example, in 1919, the U.S. Bureau of Fisheries delivered cutthroat trout to the railhead at Lake Valley, New Mexico. The small fish traveled by freight fifteen miles to Hillsboro, New Mexico, then by truck and then by panniers hanging over a mule to the remote and troutless Holden Prong, a tiny stream on the east flank of the Black Range in the Gila National Forest. This type of endeavor was carried on, almost crusade-like, in many places throughout the U.S. over a great length of time. The volume of fish migration via rail was astounding. Between 1872 and 1940, more than 200 billion fish and other aquatic species were distributed, largely by fish cars traveling 2,029,416 miles and detached messengers traveled an additional 8,104,799 miles with their fish cargo.

The final legacy of the early U.S. Fish Commission was creating a national science of fisheries conservation. From his position as museum curator and assistant secretary of the Smithsonian, Commissioner

Baird was keenly aware of the importance of good science. As such, he sought to make the U.S. Fish Commission the exemplar of national science, the Smithsonian of the seas. The U.S. Fish Commission was at the forefront of environmental sciences, identifying an ecological crisis and efforts to remediate the damage—charges still inherent, and still carried out today in our Fish and Wildlife Conservation Offices and the National Fish Hatchery System. The U.S. Fish Commission established the marine biological laboratory in Woods Hole, Massachusetts, in 1882, and it commissioned a small fleet of research vessels from 1880–1926, including the U.S.F.C. *Fish Hawk, Albatross,* and *Grampus.* The annual U.S. Fish Commission reports were profusely illustrated textbooks containing the best fisheries science of the day, and Baird, during his tenure from 1871–1887, had a scout's eye for the best scientific talent. This tradition persisted when in 1927, the agency, then the U.S. Bureau of Fisheries, hired its first permanent female scientist, Louella Cable, whose forty-three-year career as an aquatic biologist and scientific illustrator witnessed a revolution in fisheries science.

Spencer Fullerton Baird (1823–1887)

Fish came first! In the history of American conservation, the first wildlife to enjoy federal protection, propagation, and significant ongoing research were fish and the person most responsible for this was Spencer Baird.

Baird's early career is a synopsis of the origins of the American conservation movement. Born in 1823 in Reading, Pennsylvania, Baird attended Dickinson College, which awakened a longstanding interest in natural history. After graduating in 1840, he began to correspond and visit John James Audubon, who gave Baird part of his collection, taught Baird how to draw birds, and mentored him as a budding ornithologist. Other correspondents and colleagues included Ralph Waldo Emerson, Henry David Thoreau, George Perkins Marsh, and Louis Agassiz. After working as a professor of natural history at Dickinson College for a number of years, in 1850 he was appointed the first curator of the recently created Smithsonian Institution. In this role Baird supported the growth of the Smithsonian's natural history collections and coordinated the dissemination of all scientific information—a role he expanded when he became only the second secretary of the Smithsonian in 1868. Therefore, Baird was immensely qualified to take on the U.S. Fish Commission in 1871 with experience in the field, in the world of science, and in institution building.

Now for most people, helping create and fill what would become the National Museum of Natural History would have been work enough, but Baird was looking beyond the terrestrial collections, which had heretofore dominated his work. In 1870, Baird supported proposals for a commission to investigate the decline of the nation's fisheries. On February 9, 1871, Congress created the United States Commission of Fish and Fisheries, commonly called the U.S. Fish Commission, the first federal agency created exclusively for natural resource conservation. "Commission" was probably too grand a term for what was initially Baird in an unsalaried position working alone out of his home. Congress set out very modest goals for the new commission, charging it (i.e., Baird) to "determine whether a diminution of the number of food-fishes . . . has taken place . . . and, if so, to what causes the same is due." Nevertheless, Baird had a good track record in building new institutions and he set out to create a real commission focused on his interests of research, scientific

collaboration, and restoration. Baird immediately began collecting information on the history of fisheries decline in the United States and its possible remedies. These studies were dutifully published in the first Fish Commission report, which was replete with useful information thoughtfully compiled by the best scientific minds of the day.

However, Baird had grander plans to expand the Commission's role and institutional base. Congress's interest in "food-fishes" led to an appropriation of $15,000 in 1872 for fish propagation ramrodded by New York congressman Robert Roosevelt, a subject that perfectly fit Baird's research interests in the science of aquaculture and the practical field biology of replenishing the nation's streams and coasts. In keeping with Baird's vision, the first fish hatchery was no small-scale operation but a grand expedition with international repercussions. Baird sent Livingston Stone, a renowned fish culturist, to California to establish a hatchery to propagate salmon eggs. Stone established what became the Baird Hatchery

Spencer Baird on his porch with his wife and daughter. USFWS MA

U.S.F.C. *Albatross* USFWS NFACA

on the McCloud River in California, and in that first year shipped thirty thousand Chinook salmon eggs to the East Coast. This first effort was unsuccessful as only seven thousand eggs survived the journey and the two hundred to three hundred fingerling-size salmon eventually raised did not survive their transplanting into the Susquehanna River. But Baird did not give up and soon expanded the hatchery system, shipping eggs and fingerlings around the continent and, eventually, the world.

Although the nationwide system of fish hatcheries was the most visible and popular part of the commission, research was Baird's passion. He envisioned the U.S. Fish Commission becoming a Smithsonian of the seas—an institutional home for the best fisheries research. To this end, Baird began a series of research programs in 1871, which are still ongoing, to chart the changes in America's fishery stocks. He also began a series of summer research stations in 1871 along the East Coast that culminated in 1885 with the creation of the Woods Hole Marine Laboratory, only the second such lab in the world. In 1882, Baird was able to purchase a large ocean-going research vessel, the *Albatross*, to study both coasts and revolutionize American oceanography. Perhaps most importantly, Baird had succeeded in creating an institutional base for American fisheries conservation that persists 150 years later, still pursuing his vision of research, scientific collaboration, and propagation.

Baird's legacy is ongoing. His successor agency, the U.S. Fish and Wildlife Service, remains committed to the best possible research, scientific collaboration, and restoration of threatened and endangered species. Baird's visionary program persists in no small measure due to his astute scientific and political instincts. Those of us who carry on his work as federal conservationists are in a very real sense Baird's heirs.

—Mark Madison, Ph.D.

Baird was also politically astute. In 1877, Baird obtained funding to excavate fishponds on the National Mall around the Washington Monument—then under construction. Two shallow ponds were dug out and sixty-five common carp from Germany introduced into them along with a resident population of crappie, black bass, and turtles. From these humble origins, hundreds of thousands of carp were distributed around the country as far west as California. Even as carp fell out of fashion, the U.S. Fish Commission's fishponds continued to produce multitudes within literal eyesight of Congress until 1908, at which point the ponds were all filled in. Baird was well aware that for an experimental agency in need of funds for fish, proximity to power was the best fish habitat.

In 1903, the U.S. Fish Commission was renamed the U.S. Bureau of Fisheries and moved into the newly created Department of Commerce and Labor. There its trajectory increased along with its rail cars, hatcheries, and labs—both floating and anchored on solid ground. The U.S. Bureau of Fisheries quickly settled into the new department and, unsurprisingly, produced literally billions of sport and food fish for hungry and outdoorsy Americans. This was a natural extension of the U.S. Fish Commission's blueprint; the work kept with the Progressive push for efficiency that marked the early decades of the American conservation movement.

However, during the troubled 1930s there emerged a New Deal for fisheries in the wake of an ecological and economic disaster. In many ways, the 1930s were the best and worst of times for the U.S. Bureau of Fisheries. The decade began with appropriations to build twenty-five new hatcheries, three new fisheries labs, and two new fish cars over the next five years, a testament to the popularity of fisheries among both sportsmen and congressmen. In the midst of the Great Depression and Dust Bowl, the number of distributed eggs, fry, and fingerling reached a peak of 7 to 8 billion a year, a critical food source for the nearly one in four Americans out of work in this era. By 1933, fifty-two hatcheries were producing fish from Afognak, Alaska, to Welaka, Florida, with many

hatcheries enjoying the labor provided by the New Deal alphabet agencies: the Civilian Conservation Corps, Works Progress Administration, and Public Works Administration. Yet there were tradeoffs. The arid conditions of the Great Plains wreaked havoc with fisheries in drought-ridden areas. For all the CCC boys building fishponds, building contour berms, and planting trees along waterways, there were equal numbers of CCC camps building small dams, constructing roads and access to waterways, and, of course, the Tennessee Valley Authority and other large-scale New Deal projects that disrupted many natural waterways. The New Deal never met a dam project it did not like. The Fish and Wildlife Coordination Act (1934) and the Federal Power Act (1935) were responses to dam building. These laws also jump-started ecological coordination by both the Bureau of Fisheries and Bureau of Biological Survey to work with other agencies for fish and wildlife stocking, disease prevention, and fish and wildlife restoration. In spite of these early mitigation efforts, large-scale water developments from the 1930s to 1940s distressed migratory fish in West and Northeast and aquatic habitats nationwide. An ecological response to this destruction would emerge in the wake of World War II.

One of the more long-lived legacies of the "dirty thirties" was the inception of a new journal, the *Progressive Fish-Culturist*—its aspirational name a tribute to Baird's conservation vision. Started by the U.S. Bureau of Fisheries in 1934 and enduring for more than six decades through 1998, the journal chronicled and archived the evolution of American aquaculture with many of the nation's top scientists describing fish culture, nutrition, diseases, and even philosophical treatises on conservation. The journal served as a collection point where professionals learned how others performed their work in egg collection and hatching techniques and stocking innovations. Fish culturists are inventive people and that was frequently on display in journal articles crafted to inform others of progress in technology and techniques and new inventions and patents—some of which, decades later, are still in use.

American Fisheries and Fish Hooks

The history of the fish hook industry in America coincides with the rise of the U.S. Fish Commission. The hook was a part of American history long before the Columbian exchange. The Fish Commission's *Catalogue of the 1883 Berlin International Fisheries Exhibit* describes numerous native fish hooks that the American delegation displayed, made from a variety of materials including wood, reindeer horn, split quill, ivory, bone, and even a bird's claw hook made by the Ute tribe.

Iron fish hooks were a central component of European colonization. The Jamestown colony of 1607 used hooks as a significant part of maintaining their food supply, and soon they were made in America by local blacksmiths. The recent Jamestown Rediscovery Project excavation uncovered hundreds of locally made fish hooks from the seventeenth century.

While most hooks were still being imported from Britain in the eighteenth century, the literature of the day informs us that specific patterns such as the Virginia hook, a saltwater pattern still used today, was developed in America. Despite this, the British hook trade centered in Redditch, England, controlled most of the U.S. hook market well into the twentieth century.

American inventors began to chip away at this dominance. In fact, the first U.S. patent issued for a piece of fishing tackle was a fish hook invented by sixteen-year-old George Griswold in 1845 and patented on July 28, 1846 (#4670), by Theodore Engelbrecht and George Skiff. It was a spring snap hook designed to automatically hook fish. This patent was followed by hundreds of other distinctly American improvements to the fish hook.

In 1843, Job Johnson, an English immigrant from Redditch, opened the first American hook factory in Brooklyn, New York. He was followed in this trade by Thos. H. Bate, John Warrin (who developed the famed Gravitation Fish Hook), and John Court, all of New York City. These men hand-made fish hooks in the traditional labor intensive manner and were

well known to the U.S. Fish Commission, displaying their wares at most nineteenth century expositions and publishing the designs and patents in U.S. Fish Commission reports.

Dr. Chauncey O. Crosby invented the first automatic hook-making machinery in history and put the American hook industry on the map. Between 1864 and 1874 he received several patents for hook machines and founded the American Needle & Fish Hook Co. in New Haven, Connecticut. He soon began exporting American hooks around the globe.

The domestic hook industry expanded slowly over time. In 1898, the largest American tackle maker, the Enterprise Manufacturing Co. (Pflueger), bought out Crosby and moved the

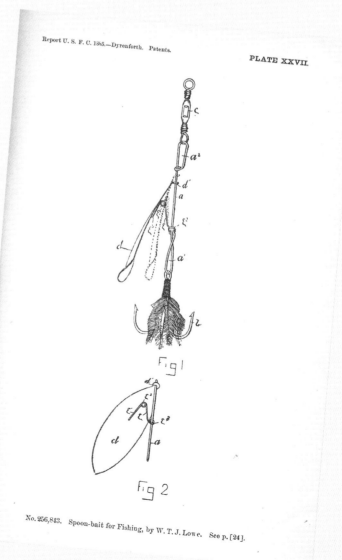

Report U. S. F. C. 1885.—Dyrenforth. Patents.

PLATE XXVII.

Fig 1

Fig 2

No. 256,843. Spoon-bait for Fishing, by W. T. J. Lowe. See p. [24].

Innovations in all sorts of fishing gear, including fishing lures such as this 1885 spinner, were reported in U.S. Fish Commission publications. USFWS

Fish hooks made a century or more ago are still with us today.
COURTESY TODD LARSON

machinery to an expanded factory in Akron, Ohio. Wright & McGill of Denver, Colorado, began making Eagle Claw hooks in the 1920s, and Bill Dewitt of the Shoe Form Co. started manufacturing hooks in Auburn, New York, in the 1930s. Dozens of other smaller companies came and went, like the Van Vleck Hook Co. in Toledo (tarpon hooks), Bing's Weedless Hook Co. of Milwaukee, and the Wm. Jamison Co. of Chicago (barbless hooks).

The height of the American hook industry occurred in the interwar period; after World War II, the influx of cheap imported fish hooks from Asia marked the demise of the domestic hook-making industry (Wright & McGill being the exception). Tackle companies that survived the 1960s and 1970s had their hooks manufactured overseas, in Norway, Japan, Taiwan, and China.

From the U.S. Fish and Wildlife Service's earliest days, hook makers, some of whom— like fish culturist Seth Green—were employees, outfitted millions of American anglers and those around the globe, and their innovations are still with us today.

—Dr. Todd E.A. Larson

Marshall McDonald (1835–1895)

Marshall McDonald was a noted fisheries scientist who served as commissioner of the U.S. Fish Commission from 1888 until his passing in 1895.

Born in Romney, Virginia, McDonald studied natural history in his youth under Spencer Baird at the Smithsonian Institution before entering Virginia Military Institute in 1855. He graduated in 1860 and briefly taught under Thomas "Stonewall" Jackson before the outbreak of war in 1861. He served in the Confederate Army throughout the Civil War as an engineering officer, was captured at Vicksburg and paroled, and ended his military career as a colonel in 1865.

After the war he taught a wide variety of classes at VMI. In the early 1870s, he took a keen interest in fish culture and oversaw the university hatchery beginning in 1872. He represented Virginia's interests at the Philadelphia Centennial in 1876 and was named state fish commissioner two years later. In 1879 he resigned this position and his professorship when Baird recommended him for a post with the U.S. Fish Commission to oversee the population census for "the Shad and Alewife Fisheries." The knowledge gained during this extensive survey was put to use in 1880 when he was named superintendent of the shad hatcheries at Fort Washington and Central Station on the Potomac River. He subsequently contributed several reports on shad propagation to the *Bulletin of the U.S. Fish Commission.*

McDonald moved quickly up the ranks, being named chief of the Division of Fish Culture before being appointed chief assistant commissioner in 1885. On August 18, 1887, when his mentor Baird died, George Brown Goode was appointed interim commissioner until President Grover Cleveland nominated McDonald to be commissioner on February 8, 1888. He was confirmed by the Senate a week later "after a long discussion in secret session," according to contemporary reports, and took his oath of office on February 18.

McDonald was a successful commissioner who spearheaded major efforts at both surveying the state of American fisheries and developing innovative methods and technologies for fish propagation. He also made major personal contributions to fish conservation through his pioneering inventions. His first was a fishway (or fish ladder) designed to allow migrating stream fish to pass over barriers while working as Virginia Fish Commissioner in the 1870s. Having studied fishways at the Philadelphia Exposition in 1876, he developed an improved version for which he received Canadian Patent CA10537A on October 13, 1879.

McDonald implemented a fishway on the Rappahannock near Fredericksburg in 1881. He oversaw further McDonald Fishways on the Potomac. The rise in the slope of the McDonald Fishway was based upon width, for which he formulated a table that was widely published at the time. He first expounded on his invention in an article entitled "A New System of Fishway Building" published in the *Bulletin of the U.S. Fish Commission.* His fishway was described in an article in the 1898 *Annual Report of the Forest, Fish & Game Commission of New York* as "entirely different from any of the others named, and in its modified form uses iron buckets."

Marshall McDonald's other major contribution to fish culture was his automatic fish-hatching jar, first utilized during his research on shad propagation. He applied for a patent and was granted U.S. Patent #263,933 on September 5, 1882. It became known as the McDonald Jar and was adapted for use with a wide variety of species ranging from whitefish and perch to cod and lobster. Modified versions can still be found in most hatcheries today.

Above: Marshall McDonald (1835–1895) was an important pisciculturist and inventor who served as U.S. fish commissioner from 1888 until his death in 1895. USFWS NFACA

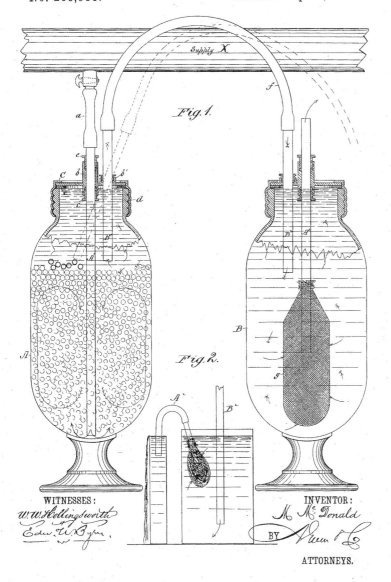

(No Model.)

M. McDONALD.

METHOD OF AND APPARATUS FOR HATCHING FISH.

No. 263,933.   Patented Sept. 5, 1882.

Fig. 1.

Fig. 2.

WITNESSES:
W. W. Hollingsworth
Edw. W. Byrn

INVENTOR:
M. McDonald
BY
ATTORNEYS.

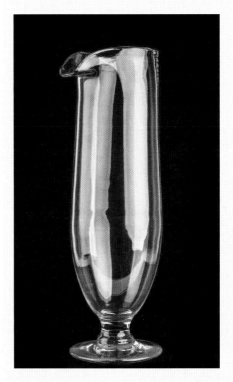

Above: Invented by Marshall McDonald, these jars keep fish eggs circulating in oxygen-bearing water while dead eggs are easily removed. McDonald Jars are still in use today.
SAM STUKEL, USFWS

Left: McDonald Hatching Jar patent.
USFWS NFACA

While McDonald is remembered for his contributions to fish culture, perhaps his greatest legacy was the reorganization the U.S. Fish Commission. McDonald drew upon his military background to remold it into a formalized government bureaucracy.

His tenure is often depicted as controversial and the militaristic manner in which he treated contemporaries, rankling. Historian Joseph E. Taylor III described his period as "convulsive and awkward and contentious." He fought against corruption and patronage and while his personality tended toward unyielding, he enjoyed warm relationships with contemporaries Dr. James Alexander Henshall and David Starr Jordan, who named the yellowfin cutthroat trout after him, *Salmo macdonaldi*.

Reflecting on his passing, Charles Hallock wrote in *Forest & Stream* that "the closing of his life is a loss to fish culture and to the public interests." McDonald was a significant figure who helped build his agency into a professional organization well prepared to meet the demands of the new century.

—Dr. Todd E.A. Larson

Meanwhile, a new agency had emerged to conserve all species non-aquatic. Its origins were similarly humble in 1885, when a Section of Economic Ornithology was established within the U.S. Department of Agriculture (USDA). This modest office of the USDA was to study both the "useful" birds (those that ate insects) and "injurious" birds (those that ate crops) in the rather narrow ecological outlook of farmers of the day. Like the early U.S. Fish Commission, this little office had a gifted leader, the naturalist C. Hart Merriam, one of the premier ornithologists and mammologists of the era. In 1886, Merriam expanded his one office and one clerk into the Division of Economic Ornithology and Mammalogy with a broader mandate to "educate" farmers about all wildlife and conduct studies on the geographic distribution of plants and animals (which a later generation would dub "ecology"). As befit this expanded mission, Merriam and his talented naturalists began to create continental studies of wildlife from Canada to Central America in what he called "Life-Zone Maps" which we would recognize today as large-scale ecosystems. As its mission grew, Merriam advocated for the more encompassing name of Division of Biological Survey in 1896. As its budget, staff, and ecological mapping continued to expand, the Division evolved into the Bureau of Biological Survey in 1905—the last name change until its absorption in 1939 with the U.S. Bureau of Fisheries. With Merriam at its helm from 1885 to 1910, the Bureau of Biological Survey flourished, carrying out important conservation studies of wildlife, even while congressional critics saw little agricultural value in far-flung surveys carried out by what they dismissed as the "Bureau of Extravagant Mammalogy." Merriam

was friends with fellow ornithologist Theodore Roosevelt and together they helped create the first bird reservation at Pelican Island, Florida, in 1903, the origin point of the National Wildlife Refuge System. Nevertheless, after Roosevelt left office, Merriam was forced out and, for the next two decades, the Biological Survey under lesser leaders increasingly focused its funding and attention on predator and rodent control.

The drastic decline in waterfowl numbers during the 1930s Dust Bowl led to a reorganization of the entire Biological Survey. Jay "Ding" Darling was an editorial cartoonist and avid sportsman who was brought in to revive the bureau in 1934. A waterfowl hunter, Darling quickly enlisted his fellow hunters to support conservation through the institution of a duck stamp in 1934 that he drew himself. As these hunters spent their buck (the original cost of the stamp) for ducks, it created a growing conservation constituency for the expanding refuge system. This sportsman-conservationists partnership was further strengthened by the 1937 Pittman–Robertson Federal Aid in Wildlife Restoration Act, which placed a small federal excise tax on firearms and ammunition to greatly expand state wildlife work on game species. At the federal level, Darling helped create a series of migratory bird refuges along corridors called "flyways" and, in so doing, created the first systematic expansion of the refuge system since Theodore Roosevelt. The nation's most successful youth in nature experiment, the Civilian Conservation Corps, helped establish forty-four wildlife refuges during the 1930s and in that decade the number of refuges expanded from fifty-one to one hundred and seventy, more than tripling in size. By 1939, the Biological Survey

U.S. Bureau of Fisheries employees paused on a cold day in 1919 for a group shot outside their Washington, D.C., headquarters. USFWS NFACA

Above: Satire magazine *Puck* found much to applaud in the U.S. Bureau of Fisheries and much to jeer in the lack of child labor laws in 1913.
COURTESY LIBRARY OF CONGRESS

Right: The U.S. Bureau of Fisheries and industry teamed up to promote eating fish during World War I. USFWS NFACA

was the premiere wildlife agency in the world and no longer a particularly good fit for the USDA, which wanted more funds funneled to eradication rather than conservation. In that year, Secretary of the Interior Harold Ickes convinced President Franklin Roosevelt and Congress to move both the Bureau of Biological Survey and the U.S. Bureau of Fisheries into the Department of the Interior in an effort to create what he hoped would be a new "Department of Conservation." That department was not established, but something nearly as important came out of this reorganization as the two bureaus were combined to form a new agency in 1940—the U.S. Fish and Wildlife Service.

EAT FISH

U. S. FOOD ADMINISTRATION
U. S. BUREAU *of* FISHERIES
U. S. DEPARTMENT *of* AGRICULTURE
and THE FISH TRADE

are helping you get

Fine Fish *at* Low Prices

SEA MULLET

THE mullet is a silvery fish, long and slender, weighing from one to three pounds. The bones are readily removed before cooking. This fish is rich in fat, which means that it can be successfully cooked by broiling. Or, it can be fried with or without a coating of corn meal or bread crumbs. It is marketed fresh, salted and smoked. The roe, too, is a delicacy and is sold salted as well as fresh. This fish is a sea mullet and should not be confused with the fresh water sucker.

Save Meat and Money
WIN THE WAR

The U.S. Bureau of Fisheries built a number of facilities throughout the U.S. during the Great Depression, including Creede Fish-Cultural Station in Colorado. WPA workers kept a fire going in the pipe to keep sand and gravel hot in sub-zero temperatures. USFWS NFACA

The Civil Works Administration put the unemployed to work constructing public buildings such as this home at Creede Fish-Cultural Station in Colorado. The CWA was short-lived, 1933–34. The station opened in 1929 and workers there raised Rio Grande cutthroat trout, Yellowstone cutthroat trout, and rainbow trout. The state of Colorado took it over in 1965. USFWS NFACA

WPA workers build a water delivery system in 1940 for present-day Creston National Fish Hatchery in Montana.
USFWS NFACA

Located at Glacier National Park, today's Creston National Fish Hatchery conserves bull trout. This image of WPA workers was taken in 1940. USFWS NFACA

Given the smiles on the faces of these WPA workers at Dexter Fish-Cultural Station in New Mexico, circa 1935, it might be payday. The laborers are bracketed on the left by Mr. Cozart and Mr. Schuler, timekeeper, on the right. The workers' names are not recorded. USFWS NFACA

WPA workers throw gravel on a new road at Dexter Fish-Cultural Station in New Mexico, circa 1935. Now called the Southwestern Native Aquatic Resource and Recovery Center, its scientists are employed conserving some of the rarest fish species found in the American Southwest. USFWS NFACA

U.S. Bureau of Fisheries workers in Blue Hole, New Mexico, 1935. WPA workers built Santa Rosa Fish-Cultural Station two years later, with the Blue Hole feeding twenty-one ponds for largemouth bass and sunfishes. The hatchery closed in 1970 and the site today is a popular summer swimming and diving destination. The spring is eighty feet wide and ninety-two feet deep and flows at three thousand gallons per minute. USFWS NFACA

Rail cars fitted with tanks, aerators, and ice storage delivered fish on rails that veined over the land, coast to coast. The U.S. Fish Commission deployed its first fish car in 1881. Ten fish cars operated under the U.S. Bureau of Fisheries from 1903 to 1939. The last car was taken out of service under the banner of the U.S. Fish and Wildlife Service in 1947. Modern roads and trucks succeeded rail cars, improving both efficiency and cost.
COURTESY LIBRARY OF CONGRESS

Above: U.S. Bureau of Fisheries employees who delivered fish were known as car messengers. These badges are preserved at the National Fish and Aquatic Conservation Archives. SAM STUCKEL, USFWS

Left: The WPA made an enduring mark. Some of their works still serve their original purpose, in this case, conveying water through the grounds of D.C. Booth Historic National Fish Hatchery in South Dakota.
CRAIG SPRINGER, USFWS

Emmeline Moore (1872–1963)

At a time when very few women were in the field of ichthyology, Emmeline Moore created a legacy that still resonates today. Not only did she earn her Ph.D. in biology, she compiled one of the most comprehensive stream surveys to this day, over sixty thousand miles of New York state waterways. Moore's impressive career and many scientific articles firmly established her in history as a reputable scientist.

Born in 1872 in Batavia, New York, Moore was raised on a nearby farm. After graduating from normal school in 1895, she attended Cornell University and Wellesley College, earning a B.A. in 1905 and M.A. in 1906. Teaching at normal schools to earn money to pay for her schooling, Moore eventually received her Ph.D. in biology from Cornell in 1916. During her time in school, Moore worked for the U.S. Bureau of Fisheries as a summer investigator, which contributed to her interest in research.

Moore worked a two-year stint for the U.S. Bureau of Fisheries from 1917 to 1919, hired to study the primary food relations of fish. In the 1919 *Report of U.S. Commissioner of Fisheries*, nine scientific articles appear, one of them by Dr. Emmeline Moore, titled "Some Plants of Importance in Pondfish Culture," and is based on work conducted in 1917 and 1918 at the U.S. Fisheries Bureau of Fisheries' Biological Station in Fairport, Iowa.

The New York State Conservation Department hired Moore in 1920. She helped conduct a watershed survey that summer that proved to be so thorough that in 1926, the surveys continued for all of the waterways in New York, and Moore directed the project. The American Fisheries Society elected Moore as its first female president in 1927. She finished out her career with the state of New York in 1944 but continued doing research and publishing papers at Yale University for several years afterward. A New York State research vessel was named after her, the *Emmeline M.* The American Fisheries Society created the Emmeline Moore Prize in 2009, which recognizes the efforts of an individual society member who demonstrated exemplary service to the cause of equal opportunity of access to higher education in fisheries or professional development in any of the disciplines of fisheries science or management.

—April Gregory

The American Fisheries Society honors the memory of early female fisheries scientist Emmeline Moore. She worked adjunct for the U.S. Bureau of Fisheries at Fairport Fish-Cultural Station in Iowa.

COURTESY AMERICAN FISHERIES SOCIETY

Above: People of all ages enjoy fishing—and for fish of any size. COURTESY LIBRARY OF CONGRESS

Left: Americans have long enjoyed fish and fishing for food and for sport. These folks caught this pair of mammoth blue catfish near Tishomingo National Fish Hatchery in 1969. USFWS NFACA

FINNED, FURRED, AND FEATHERED: THE U.S. FISH AND WILDLIFE SERVICE, 1940–1969

"Like the resources it seeks to protect, wildlife conservation must be dynamic, changing as conditions change, seeking always to become more effective."

—U.S. Fish and Wildlife Service Writer/Editor Rachel Carson, *Guarding Our Wildlife Resources* (1948)

In the middle part of the twentieth century, the American conservation movement became a scientifically based popular movement, nowhere more so than the newly created U.S. Fish and Wildlife Service. From the newly dedicated Patuxent Research Refuge to a growing series of fisheries labs at Fairport, Iowa, and Beaufort, North Carolina, and fisheries training facilities such as those at Marion, Alabama; Leetown, West Virginia; and Spearfish, South Dakota, these three decades would witness the firm linking of the new sciences of ecology to the long-practiced techniques of fish and wildlife conservation.

The first director of the newly minted U.S. Fish and Wildlife Service, Ira Noel Gabrielson, in his 1943 *Annual Report*, noted in the midst of World War II that when the soldiers returned home millions of Americans would be eager to relax and enjoy hunting and fishing opportunities. In preparation for this influx of new and returning sportsmen (many much better shots after military service), wildlife refuges expanded their access to hunters and anglers in the decades following the end of the war. The most popular post–WWII program involved the farm pond and rural fish stocking programs. By 1949, the U.S. Fish and Wildlife Service managed ninety-nine fish hatcheries in forty-three states. For the next two decades, federal hatcheries alone consistently raised around 1.5 billion fish with state hatcheries often exceeding that number. The proliferation of farm ponds sparked by the New Deal's Soil Conservation Service and new reservoirs and duck marshes coming about via the Pittman-Robertson Act on state wildlife management areas created both an insatiable appetite for sport fish and growing political support for fisheries work. The Dingell-Johnson Federal Aid in Sport Fish Restoration Act (1950) placed a small excise tax on sport fishing equipment so the U.S. Fish and Wildlife Service could provide financial assistance for state fish restoration, recreation, and management endeavors. This was a huge boon to state fish and game agencies' fishery conservation efforts, previously dependent almost exclusively on license sales. Since their

enactment, Pittman-Robertson and Dingell-Johnson have provided nearly 21 billion dollars in financial assistance for states and territories for wildlife restoration, hunter safety and education, and sport fish restoration. This is, today, the U.S. Fish and Wildlife Service's Wildlife and Sport Fish Restoration Program.

Fish culture technology grew to meet this insatiable demand for more fish. As early as 1953, plastic hatching jars were replacing glass jars at some hatcheries, not long after plastic was just becoming available for commercial use. New dissolved oxygen meters, vertical incubators, and cryopreservation techniques for preserving fish sperm were also introduced in the mid-1950s. Transport in the 1950s transitioned from rails to specially designed tanker trucks and even aerial stocking. Uniformed rail fish car attendants, called "messengers," were replaced by better aeration techniques, including electric agitators and liquid oxygen. But that is not to say that the old ways are no longer used; fish biologists still deliver fish and fish eggs to remote areas in backpacks or on top of a mule.

Fisheries science, research, and training opportunities grew to cultivate the expert personnel required to keep the fish pipeline flowing. In the 1940s, the first courses on specific aspects of aquaculture were offered at a few fisheries stations across the country—in-service training for employees. In 1946, the

Since 1937, excise taxes on firearms and ammunition, fishing gear, and boat fuel have been the bedrock of conservation funding for state fish and wildlife management agencies, administered by the Wildlife and Sport Fish Restoration Program. USFWS

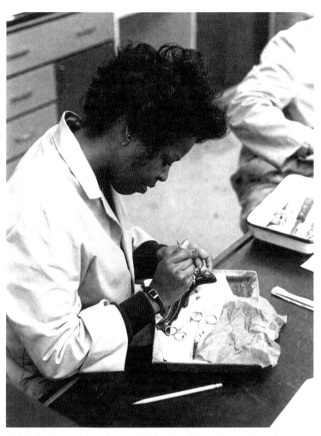

A biologist at Leetown Fish Health Laboratory in West Virginia examines a brook trout's gills for disease, circa 1980. USFWS NFACA

Cortland National Fish Hatchery in New York offered the first full course on trout propagation covering all aspects of aquaculture from nutrition to disease, water analysis, and hatchery management. In 1960, the U.S. Fish and Wildlife Service began establishing cooperative laboratories at universities; the Cooperative Fishery Research Units were brooding grounds for future fish biologists. The co-op units marshalled graduate-level fisheries research in cooperation with state fish and game agencies. The co-op units eventually spread across the country as a foundation for the dissemination and expansion of fisheries science. The professors and students at these co-op units were rigorously trained to manage and expand fisheries work to support a rapidly growing population of American anglers or answer conservation problems specified by cooperators.

In the midst of these changes, in 1945 a small Office of River Basin Studies would be the origin point for ecological services within the agency. River Basin Studies biologists began to take a more comprehensive look at major public works projects impacting fish and wildlife resources and working hard to find ecological solutions with the Army Corps of Engineers, Bureau of Reclamation, and Soil Conservation Service. The office's unofficial motto in those early years was "save the dirt!" Innovative ideas emerging from this ecological think tank included the first National Wetlands Inventory (1952–1954) and the National Survey of Hunting and Fishing Activity (1955) to take stock of wildlife habitat and those who enjoyed it.

Other scientific advances were not so amenable to fisheries. DDT was a pesticide developed during WWII that helped win the war on insect-borne diseases. By the 1950s, it had become a commercially popular pesticide used along many waterways. As early as 1946, scientists in the U.S. Fish and Wildlife Service were becoming wary of its effects on fish and birds.

One of these scientists was Rachel Carson, part of a U.S. Bureau of Fisheries tradition of hiring brilliant female scientists in an era when most federal agencies considered "female scientist" an oxymoron. Carson's indictment of DDT in *Silent Spring* would help create a new environmental movement in which the U.S. Fish and Wildlife Service played a transformative role.

Research vessel *Rachel Carson* honors the memory of the U.S. Fish and Wildlife Service fish biologist and writer. USFWS MA

FISHERIES IN THE ENVIRONMENTAL ERA, 1970–2021

"Time is but the stream I go a-fishing in. I drink at it; but while I drink I see the sandy bottom and detect how shallow it is. Its thin current slides away, but eternity remains."

—Henry David Thoreau, *Walden* (1854)

If the first one hundred years of fisheries conservation were a carrying out of Baird's legacy of sciences, stocking, and sportsmen, the last fifty years of fisheries have reflected much of Carson's ethos of ecology, imperiled species, and loss of habitat. The first Earth Day occurred in 1970, and a year later the U.S. Fish and Wildlife Service celebrated a century of fisheries conservation. Yet things were changing for fish and wildlife management as it began its second century.

For a brief halcyon three decades from 1940 to 1970, all fish and wildlife resources were under the stewardship of one agency, the U.S. Fish and Wildlife Service. However, in 1970, Congress removed marine fisheries from the U.S. Fish and Wildlife Service and moved their concern to the newly created National Marine Fisheries Service in the Department of Commerce. The timing was inopportune as this was shortly before the passage of the Marine Mammal Protection Act (1972) and the Endangered Species Act (1973), effectively dividing the authorities for protecting wildlife resources between two agencies, as it had been prior to 1940. Other changes were occurring in this era. Part of Rachel Carson's legacy was an increasing emphasis on threatened and endangered species, clean water, and habitat restoration in the late 1960s and early 1970s. The politically popular farm pond program was phased out by the mid-1980s. The primary mission of stocking fish for sportsmen, farmers, and tribes was evolving into a growing emphasis on recovery, restoration, mitigation, partnerships, and stocking federal and some tribal waters. Some former national fish hatcheries were transferred to states or tribes, while others had their missions and facilities modified to meet these new goals.

In 1972, River Basin Studies was renamed the Division of Ecological Services to better reflect a recently enlarged portfolio of protection including increasingly sophisticated analysis of water pollution, coastal habitat destruction, and environmental impacts of habitat loss. The addition of the endangered species program to Ecological Services in 1983 greatly expanded its role to protect and restore threatened and endangered wildlife.

A U.S. Fish and Wildlife Service biologist tallies a salmon as it passes through a weir on Alaska's Afognak Island, the site of the first federal refuge for wildlife, established in 1892. USFWS

President Benjamin Harrison created the Afognak Forest and Fish Culture Reserve in 1892, the first federal refuge for wildlife, primarily for sockeye salmon, at the urging of the U.S. Fish Commission.
COURTESY LIBRARY OF CONGRESS

In 1969, the first national wildlife refuge for an endangered species, the bald eagle, was created at Mason Neck, Virginia. Shortly thereafter, a number of endangered species refuges were established across the country for condors, eagles, and even endangered fish such as the narrowly endemic desert fishes protected at Ash Meadows National Wildlife Refuge in Nevada and San Bernardino National Wildlife Refuge in Arizona.

Just as the U.S. Fish Commission had worked with global partners since the 1880s, so too the U.S. Fish and Wildlife Service expanded its role in international wildlife conservation when it signed on to the 1975 Convention on International Trade in Endangered Species of Wild Fauna and Flora. This expanded conservation work beyond our own borders by joining 183 other signatories to help with international conservation of threated species such as tigers, great apes, rhinos, and elephants. Changes in the environmental sciences and a growing environmental political movement transformed the U.S. Fish and Wildlife Service into an agency that managed wildlife without borders in the most

ecologically sensitive manner possible. Ironically, some of these efforts involved removing non-native fish species, unwittingly stocked a century earlier by the U.S. Fish Commission and its successors, to revive native fishes.

As the agency entered its second century of wildlife work, its capacity grew to meet new challenges. The U.S. Fish and Wildlife Service's law enforcement role extended back to the 1900 Lacey Act providing critical protection to America's wildlife both on and off refuge lands. A new Division of Law Enforcement was created in 1972 with the addition of special agents in 1973 and wildlife inspectors in 1975 at the forefront of combatting domestic and international wildlife trafficking.

Migratory bird conservation took on an early federal role with the Migratory Bird Treaty of 1916 signed between the U.S. and Canada. Building on the earlier flyways concept of the 1930s, the U.S. Fish and Wildlife Service gradually worked toward a more comprehensive hemispheric conservation of migratory birds that included a North American Waterfowl Management Plan (1985) and Partners in Flight (1990), a public-private partnership to conserve all land birds in the Western Hemisphere. A growing realization that birds do not recognize

National Fish and Aquatic Conservation Archives curator April Gregory examines a woolen U.S. Bureau of Fisheries flag. These flags flew over research vessels and stations from 1903 to 1939 when the Bureau of Fisheries absorbed the Bureau of Biological Survey to become the U.S. Fish and Wildlife Service. CRAIG SPRINGER, USFWS

Afognak Forest and Fish Culture Reserve was established in 1892 to conserve sockeye salmon. This pair of sockeye were photographed in the Little Wenatchee River in Washington. RYAN HAGERTY, USFWS

political borders led to the creation of the first joint venture. Beginning in 1987, over 5,700 joint venture projects brought together regional partnerships of government agencies, non-profit organizations, corporations, tribes, and individuals to conserve habitat for the fish, birds, other wildlife, and people.

The origins of the U.S. Fish and Wildlife Service, the American conservation movement, and fisheries management began 150 years ago with one fish commissioner and a report outlining the causes of fisheries decline and a blueprint for recovery. Today, the U.S. Fish and Wildlife Service manages seventy national fish hatcheries, seven fish technology centers, six fish health centers, and one archives across the nation to improve, conserve, restore, and enhance fish and other aquatic resources. The U.S. Fish and Wildlife Service has also expanded its terrestrial presence managing 568 refuges and 38 wetland management districts on more than 150 million acres across the country.

President Benjamin Harrison gave a gift to Americans on Christmas Eve 1892. Upon the urging of Livingston Stone and Spencer Baird, President Harrison

created Afognak Forest and Fish Culture Reserve—the third such forest reserve and first federal refuge to conserve fish and wildlife. Sockeye salmon were the prime concern on and around Alaska's Afognak Island. Returning once more to the sea, since 2003 this modern descendent of the U.S. Fish Commission has managed aquatic resources on more than 685 million acres within five Pacific and Atlantic Marine National Monuments. An expanding landscape—matched by an evolving mission—ensures our rich American fish and wildlife resources are enjoyed by future generations.

It is worth noting that the original 1871 charge to the U.S. Fish Commission still resides in fisheries conservation work carried out today by the U.S. Fish and Wildlife Service. Then as now, the work is often performed in remote places under harsh circumstances requiring grit and perseverance, for not only the workers, but their families as well. From the depths of destruction in the nation's watery kingdom as professed by George Perkins Marsh, there arose the largest and most successful wildlife agency in the world. That is a fish tale worth recounting.

Montana Arctic Grayling

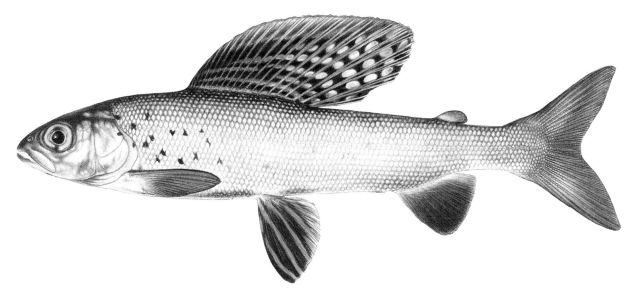

Appearing as if spawned from the Northern Lights themselves, the Montana Arctic grayling certainly have a story to tell.

Members of the trout and salmon family, Arctic grayling are travelers by their very nature, immigrating to the North American continent the same way our own ancestors later would, by crossing the Beringia land bridge that intermittently connected Alaska to eastern Siberia. The grayling's expansion continued southeastward through much of Canada until the last ice age, when vast continental glaciers formed across Canada, severing connections between populations and greatly retracting the range of this nomadic fish.

Left behind were two disconnected populations: one in Michigan and the other in Montana. Isolated at the southern extent of their historical range for at least the past twelve thousand years, the two populations adapted independently to changing environments while developing distinct genetic characteristics of their own. For the Montana grayling that meant enduring the warmer, drier climate of the West, a challenge they proved fit for, at least up until man finally caught up with them.

Montana grayling spend most of the year in mountain lakes or in the deep, cooler pool habitat of low- to medium-gradient streams fattening up on aquatic insects, zooplankton—or whatever else they can find to endure the harsh mountain winters. But each spring, life begins anew; as soon as ice leaves the lakes and stream flows and temperatures begin to rise, adults suddenly feel that inherent urge to move. Often swimming great distances—up to sixty

miles or more—they leave wintering areas in search of stony riffle habitat in tributary streams where females broadcast their plentiful supply of orange, millet-sized, adhesive eggs over clean sand and gravel. Within a few days, an otherwise barren stretch of stream can erupt with hordes of frolicking grayling, and then in the span of a few short weeks they just as quickly disappear.

Montana grayling are short lived, typically reaching maturity by their third or fourth year of life and seldom living beyond their sixth. While stream

A weir across Red Rock Creek guides migrating Arctic grayling into a trap. JIM MOGEN, USFWS

Hatcheries were, and remain, sites of civic pride. This card postmarked 1908 tells where the writer will live at Bozeman Fish-Cultural Station, marked near the flagpole. USFWS NFACA

The original Bozeman Fish-Cultural Station hatching house was designed by U.S. Fish Commission architect and inventor Hector von Bayer. The roofline is a signature element of his works. Today the site is home to the Bozeman Fish Technology Center and the Aquatic Animal Drug Approval Partnership. USFWS NFACA

Biologists from the Montana Fish and Wildlife Conservation Office trapped these Arctic grayling from Red Rock Creek on Red Rock Lakes National Wildlife Refuge during their spring migration. Biologists collect data from the fish and then send them on their way. JIM MOGEN, USFWS

residents tend to be smaller, in the most productive lake systems the larger adults often weigh more than two pounds and reach lengths greater than seventeen inches, with the largest females producing more than ten thousand eggs. Montana's record grayling was a whopping 3.6 pounds and measured 20 inches in length.

Grayling were distributed throughout the mountainous headwaters of the Missouri River, upstream from Great Falls, Montana, when Lewis and Clark and the Corps of Discovery first entered the uncharted territory in 1805. However, along with westward expansion came our thirst for water and with it our desire to control it. Beginning in the late 1800s, dams went up like dominos along the mainstem upper Missouri River and its tributaries, blocking migrations and fragmenting important grayling habitats. Countless smaller irrigation diversions dried up streams and sent grayling down farmers' ditches to desiccate in their fields. Together with habitat degradation from logging, mining, and cattle grazing, widespread introductions of non-native trout, excessive harvest by fishermen, and changing climate, these factors worked to reduce grayling to less than 5 percent of their historical range in Montana over the past century.

In Michigan, clear-cut logging devastated grayling habitats. Prime waters such at the Au Sable River near the town of Grayling warmed and filled with silt from the practice while native grayling struggled to compete with introduced fish species. By the 1930s, Michigan grayling were exterminated.

Angler Glenda Regnart caught this Arctic grayling in Alaska's Togiak River. The Arctic grayling ranged widely from Alaska through Canada. Two isolated populations existed in Montana and Michigan, with the latter now extirpated. COURTESY SCOTT RABORN

Lakes and streams on Red Rock Lakes National Wildlife Refuge harbor Arctic grayling. It was here that James Henshall established an Arctic grayling egg-collecting station for the U.S. Fish Commission in 1897.
STEVE HILDEBRAND, USFWS

Montana's native grayling, however, continued to persevere.

Not a hundred feet from the river itself, my father built our family home on the banks of the lower Yellowstone River in eastern Montana. A true Tom Sawyer, I handled just about every creepy-crawly slippery-slimy creature living in and around that monumental river, but I had never seen an Arctic grayling before—at least not until 1988.

The summer of 1988 was a hot one. National headlines focused on the plight of our beloved Yellowstone National Park as wildfire consumed massive swaths of its iconic forests. At the time, few people were aware that another natural treasure, equally as beautiful and unique but in even greater dire straits, was barely hanging on in the remaining fragments of its historical distribution in a drought-stricken Montana: Arctic grayling.

I graduated high school that spring and by autumn enrolled in the fish and wildlife program at Montana State University in Bozeman. And as luck would have it, I soon landed a part-time job working for the U.S. Fish and Wildlife Service's Bozeman Fish Technology Center. By then, serious concerns for Montana's native grayling mounted, driving scientific research, all of which centered in Bozeman at the university and federal fisheries facility. I was in the midst of it all.

Immediately upon graduation, I accepted a research assistantship with the university and embarked to learn more about the status and biology of a relic lake-dwelling grayling population that persisted in Red Rock Lakes in extreme southwest Montana. This population once numbered in the tens of thousands before isolation, changing environments, and the hands of time reduced it to a perilous few hundred fish.

The superintendent's house at Bozeman National Fish Hatchery is now the office of the Montana Fish and Wildlife Conservation Office. USFWS NFACA

A biologist checks an Arctic grayling caught through the ice. Creel surveys inform future decisions of fisheries managers. USFWS

A catch of Arctic grayling from Hoover Lake, Wasatch National Forest, Utah, planted as eyed eggs from Bozeman Fish-Cultural Station, May 1934. They were eight inches long when caught in August 1935. USFWS NFACA

Montana Fish and Wildlife Conservation Office biologists go to great lengths in all seasons to collect data on Arctic grayling at Red Rock Lakes National Wildlife Refuge. JIM MOGEN, USFWS

Red Rock Lakes, situated in the most distant headwaters of the upper Missouri-Mississippi River basin and protected within the boundaries of pristine Red Rock Lakes National Wildlife Refuge, is an amazing place. It is a place where moose, beaver, swans, and a handful of grayling still play as they always have, but a place where winter reigns supreme, often locking the valley and its shallow lakes in frozen tundra for the better part of the year and setting some animal populations back to base levels. Only eighty miles downstream from the lakes, Meriwether Lewis made the first scientific notation of this "new kind of white or silvery trout" while surveying the lower river in 1805.

It is also the place where Dr. James Henshall established the country's first successful grayling egg-taking station less than a century later, paving the way for widespread grayling introductions into numerous mountain lakes across the West.

Henshall, a medical doctor, gave up medicine for a career in conservation. He was a prolific author and foremost fishing authority who had previous experience with the then-struggling Michigan grayling. He accepted the position as the first superintendent of the U.S. Fish Commission's newly created Bozeman Fish-Cultural Station for, as he himself wrote in a 1916 *Forest & Stream* story, "the express purpose of attempting propagation of the Montana grayling, as all previous efforts in that direction with the Michigan grayling have failed."

Upon his January 1897 arrival at the Bozeman station, Henshall immediately set out in search of a reliable source of grayling eggs for his operation. Traveling by sleigh for weeks at a time, he covered hundreds of miles in several directions before finally securing a site on Elk Springs Creek, a tributary to Red Rock Lakes. While working out the kinks in captive grayling propagation, Henshall relied solely on that single egg source, which he later described as "all that could be desired during my stay at Bozeman hatchery for thirteen years." Before moving on to the U.S. Fish Commission's Tupelo Fish-Cultural Station in Mississippi, Henshall produced millions of Arctic

Dr. Molly Webb examines a mussel at Bozeman Fish Technology Center. RYAN HAGERTY, USFWS

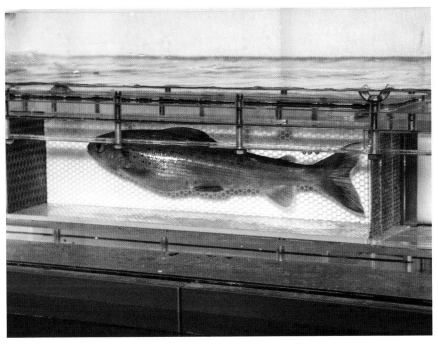

An Arctic grayling swims in a tube at Bozeman Fish Technology Center. The apparatus allows scientists to design fish passage structures for the benefit of target species. RYAN HAGERTY, USFWS

grayling eggs, fry, and fingerlings for planting into cold waters of Montana and neighboring states. He even reared a few fish to adulthood that he exhibited at world fairs in St. Louis and Seattle.

A century later, it was here at Red Rock Lakes in the first season of my graduate work where I was first introduced to native Montana grayling in their natural environment. A voyeur hidden in the streamside vegetation, I would lie for hours peering into the kaleidoscope before me as male grayling in full display danced across the shallow spawning grounds, fending off competitors and enticing the ladies with

their magnificent sail-like dorsal fins. Especially dramatic on larger males, the dark fin is fringed in fiery orange and decorated with streaks and splashes of neon blue, turquoise, and violet. It sits atop a mostly goldish-silver iridescent body tinted with all the blues, purples, and pinks of a mountain sunrise and peppered with small black freckles toward the front and onto the head and cheek. The deeply forked tail appears as if dipped in bronze while bright red and black tiger stripes adorn the pelvic fins. Along the bottom, a dark golden band separates its metallic sides from its white underbelly. When viewed underwater and illuminated in spangled sunlight, the grayling's beauty rivals that of the most spectacular freshwater fish on the continent—clearly a finished masterpiece.

Now, more than a quarter century since I first witnessed the splendor of Montana's Arctic grayling as a young graduate student, I still devote myself to conserving our native fish.

There is more symmetry to it all; my office is located in the original superintendent's house at the Bozeman station where Dr. Henshall and his wife, Hester, resided through 1908. I write these words at my desk in Henshall's former bedroom where he undoubtedly spent many a night dreaming about this magical fish. He penned the classic book *Bass, Pike, Perch, and Others* while in Bozeman, including a chapter lamenting and extoling grayling. He mused on their sporting qualities: "Experienced anglers are all aware that grayling are not so easily hooked on the rise as trout, but he offers the best compensation in his power by consenting to rise over and over again until if you do not hook him the fault is yours, not his."

Drawing on that inspiration and looking back over the past several decades, I reflect on fault and duty and the incredible work accomplished through collaboration with countless private, state, and federal partners. Although Montana's Arctic grayling persist in just a fraction of their original range, conservation keeps the few remaining natural populations intact and with promise in the refounding of another. We have created numerous populations well outside their historic range for the enjoyment of anglers and naturalists. We have developed genetically pure broodstocks, conserved water, restored habitats, and learned more about Henshall's "graceful, gliding grayling" than ever before. However, what might be the most unexpected outcome of this incredible undertaking is the friendships and alliances that formed, bringing biologists and sportsmen, ranchers and conservationists, and researchers and managers together to save a little-known, imperiled native fish.

In the daunting face of climate change and at a time when clean, cold-water habitats come at a premium, this truly unique Montana fish has unified a community of widely varying interests. While it is difficult to predict how the remaining chapters will play out for this beloved fish, one thing is for certain, the Montana grayling no longer swims alone in its plight.

—Jim Mogen

Bozeman Fish Technology Center staff research fish dietary needs. Dr. Gibson Gaylord, a physiologist, examines recently processed fish food.
RYAN HAGERTY, USFWS

Eugene W. Surber (1904–1974)

We remember Eugene W. Surber for his namesake "Surber Sampler." This elegantly compact device enabled field workers to better assess a stream's faunal prey base. Surber deemed this data essential to understanding aquatic productivity, literally, from the bottom up. His father, Dr. Thaddeus Surber, was the esteemed superintendent of fish propagation with the Minnesota Department of Conservation, and natural historian of great repute. Working with him on field surveys and collection missions gave the budding biologist an expansive view of fisheries work, beginning in his mid-teens. In 1927, Eugene became the first limnologist graduated by the University of Minnesota. By 1932, Surber was appointed superintendent of the U.S. Bureau of Fisheries' newly opened National Fish Health Research Laboratory in Leetown, West Virginia. Equally interested in fish diseases, pesticide effects, and hatchery techniques, he published groundbreaking studies on DDT and fish parasites as well as evaluations of many streams.

—Brett Billings

U.S. Bureau of Fisheries biologist Eugene Surber kneels over his namesake invention, commonly called a Surber Sampler, in a photo taken July 1936 in a Virginia stream. The apparatus allows scientists to systematically measure fish food—aquatic insects—found on stream bottoms. A. FISHER, USFWS

Yellowstone Cutthroat Trout

The route by which I became a fish biologist with an interest in Yellowstone cutthroat trout involved a bridge during a trip to Yellowstone National Park in the late 1970s. I had not yet reached the awkwardness of being a teenager, as had my older brother. We were both somewhat bored with the sights of the park—until we stopped at the infamous Fishing Bridge.

Freed from the confines of the car and after sprinting from one end to the other, dodging tourists, and never being able to outrun my older sibling, I quickly grew bored—until I happened to look over the railing. There was a moment of clarity as clear as the crystalline waters flowing below. I was transfixed and mesmerized by what lurked in the depths: Yellowstone cutthroat trout. Hundreds of them, maybe thousands—some of the biggest trout I had ever seen, and not just any trout, but a cutthroat trout named after the river I grew up along in Montana.

The moment was transcendent—it set me on a trajectory that I was compelled to follow. Those fish, so stunningly beautiful, magnificent creatures of adaption and survival, were right below me, and yet I could not grab my fly rod and try to catch one. It was frustrating and seemed so incongruous; you could not fish from the Fishing Bridge. Angling was off limits in the park due to prior overfishing. Though I could not put a name on the sentiments at the time, it was about then that I felt inspired to become a fish biologist to help conserve such a stunning native species and ensure it persisted so that others would be able to enjoy catching their own.

What I did not know then was that localized overfishing was not the only threat to Yellowstone cutthroat trout, albeit one of the easiest to address through fishing regulations. Yellowstone's native trout faced even then more menacing threats—nonnative trout and habitat degradation.

The Yellowstone cutthroat trout is one of fourteen subspecies, or strains, of cutthroat trout that range from coastal Alaskan streams southward through the

Yellowstone National Park's Fishing Bridge is visible in the distance, the site where future fish biologist George Jordan had an awakening experience in his youth. The angler in the foreground has a nice stinger of Yellowstone cutthroat trout. USFWS MA

Yellowstone cutthroat trout spawn over clean gravels in Little Arnica Creek in Yellowstone National Park. USFWS MA

Orville Fuqua with a Yellowstone cutthroat trout taken from Columbine Creek in June 1936. USFWS MA

Cascades, the Great Basin, and the Rockies to northern New Mexico. One is extinct, the Yellowfin of Colorado. Among the thirteen remaining cutthroat trout subspecies, the Yellowstone cutthroat trout is perhaps the most well known. This probably owes to the fact that the Yellowstone cutthroat originally occurred through several states with our country's first national park near the center of the trout's range.

The Yellowstone cutthroat trout has the distinction of being the first called "cutthroat." Writer Charles Hallock wrote a story in 1884 for *American Angler* magazine about an outing in Montana's Rosebud Creek, a tributary to the Yellowstone River. Hallock wrote that the trout had "a slash of intense carmine across each gill cover, as large as my little finger. It was most striking. For lack of a better description we call them cut-throat trout."

The name stuck in popular writings, though renowned U.S. Fish Commission biologists Barton

An angler shows off a nice half-dozen Yellowstone cutthroat trout. USFWS MA

Warren Evermann and David Starr Jordan vehemently opposed the appellation. They felt it was demeaning. Cutthroat trout also went by other common names: "speckled trout" and "red throat trout."

But "black-spotted trout" was by far the most commonly used name for the fish, particularly among fisheries conservationists. U.S. Fish Commission and then U.S. Bureau of Fisheries reports, as late as into

Three men working at the Mammoth rearing pools on the Wyoming-Montana state line in Yellowstone National Park where the namesake cutthroat trout were grown to a stocking size. USFWS NFACA

the 1930s, commonly referred to our present-day cutthroat trout as black-spotted trout.

Yellowstone cutthroat trout are also of greater notoriety than other subspecies because they were raised and stocked around the country.

As western expansion continued during the nineteenth and early twentieth centuries so did the desire for creating fishing opportunities, as well as fish conservation and management. Beginning in 1899, the U.S. Fish Commission established the Yellowstone Fish-Cultural Station inside our first national park. Many waters inside Yellowstone National Park served as a source of cutthroat trout eggs. Fish culture operations existed along Yellowstone Lake and at fish traps and incubation stations along multiple streams. From 1899 to 1955, the fish culture stations fertilized 818 million Yellowstone cutthroat trout eggs. The resulting fish were stocked in the national park and points well beyond.

Fish culture operations at Yellowstone were a seasonal affair. Winter lays long and heavy there. In the spring of the year, U.S. Bureau of Fisheries workers from Homer, Minnesota, got operations underway. Spring arrived at higher-elevation fish habitats as late as July. Fisheries stations in neighboring Colorado, Montana, and South Dakota figured prominently. Dewitt Clinton Booth from Spearfish Fish-Cultural Station, South Dakota, made annual forays to gather fertilized eggs to incubate at his home station and was

Frank Dufresne admires a Yellowstone cutthroat trout caught near the Fishing Bridge in 1949. Dufresne, author of numerous books including *Lure of the Open* and *Alaska's Animals and Fishes*, served as the U.S. Fish and Wildlife Service's chief of public information during and after World War II. Dufresne hired Bob Hines as staff artist in 1948. USFWS MA

The U.S. Fish Commission established Yellowstone Fish-Cultural Station in 1891, collecting "black-spotted trout" in traps throughout Yellowstone National Park. The U.S. Fish and Wildlife Service closed up shop in 1957 and turned over operations to the National Park Service. The egg crates are bound for Bozeman Fish-Cultural Station post-1903, after the Commission became the U.S Bureau of Fisheries. USFWS NFACA

Then as now, the U.S. Fish and Wildlife Service works in partnership with state agencies in conservation endeavors. Emblematic of the shared mission, the Montana Game and Fish Commission blazoned its name on top of a U.S. Bureau of Fisheries banner on this truck filled with empty milk cans used to carry cutthroat trout in Yellowstone National Park. USFWS NFACA

Secretary of Agriculture in the Hoover administration, Arthur Hyde (left), with U.S. Bureau of Fisheries administrator Fred Foster, on a Yellowstone fishing trip. Foster was in charge of all fish culture operations on the Pacific coast and in the Rocky Mountains. USFWS NFACA

C. F. Culler (left) worked seasonally at Yellowstone Fish-Cultural Station from 1909 to 1922, when he became the permanent supervisor. He's seen here with his supervisor, Fred J. Foster, director of fish cultural stations in the Rocky Mountains and Pacific coast, and a fine catch of Yellowstone cutthroat trout in 1930. USFWS NFACA

U.S. Bureau of Fisheries biologist Marc Tainter hauls camping gear in a boat on the shores of Yellowstone Lake in 1921. COURTESY FRANK H. TAINTER

TRAVEL ORDER
TO BE ISSUED BY DULY AUTHORIZED OFFICERS.

Department of Commerce and Labor
BUREAU OF FISHERIES
Washington

No. 23 – 13

SIR: By authority of order No. 23 of the Commissioner of Fisheries, dated July 1,1909, you are directed to proceed by the shortest and most direct route from Spearfish,South Dakota to Thumb of Lake,Yellowstone National Park via Gardiner,Montana.

for the purpose of carrying out the instructions hereinafter mentioned, and on completion of this duty to return to Remain at Fisheries Camp,Thumb of Lake and assist in collecting blackspotted trout eggs

On the presentation of proper accounts you will be reimbursed from the appropriation "Miscellaneous Expenses, Bureau of Fisheries, 1910," subhead "Propagation." for your actual and necessary expenses while engaged as above.

Refer to the number of this order in your account, taking up expenses incurred and upon the face and coupon of each Government request for transportation issued for travel in connection therewith.

Respectfully,

Superintendent.
(Official title.)

INSTRUCTIONS.

Mr.A.F.Fuller,
    Spearfish,South Dakota.

Sir:

You will please start to-day over the C.B & Q.R.R to Billings,Montana thence over the N.P.R.R. to Gardiner, Montana taking along and delivering to the Superintendent of Yellowstone National Park at Gardiner,25,000 brook trout

Upon the completion of this work,make out and return messenger and mileage reports and travel vouchers for your traveling expenses during May and then assist Fishculturist Seth M.Ainsworth in unloading and transporting equipment to Thumb of the Lake.

May 23,1910.

Culturing Yellowstone cutthroat trout required temporary help in season. Fish biologists converged from stations in Leadville, Colorado; Bozeman, Montana; Saratoga, Wyoming; Homer, Minnesota; and Spearfish, South Dakota, as directed in this 1910 personnel order.
COURTESY FRANK H. TAINTER

C. F. Culler sits near his boat on the Mississippi River at the Homer Fish-Cultural Station in Minnesota. Culler supervised the station where staff engaged in the grueling work of rescuing sport fish from isolated backwaters following spring floods. U.S. Bureau of Fisheries stations in upper Mississippi River received the rescued fish. Bureau boats such as this one were built at Homer. Culler and other Homer staff worked seasonally in Yellowstone. COURTESY WINONA COUNTY HISTORICAL SOCIETY

With the 1925 egg-taking season over, the Homer, Minnesota, workers head home on an REO truck. Left to right, Marc Tainter, Cleon Walker, Lester Bennett, and Roger Tanner. COURTESY FRANK H. TAINTER

charged with setting up operations at Yellowstone its first ten summers. Similarly, Leadville Fish-Cultural Station also incubated and stocked Yellowstone cutthroat trout. James Henshall from the Bozeman Fish-Cultural Station participated in gathering the cutthroat trout egg bounty, too.

The irony is palpable. Yellowstone cutthroat trout have suffered themselves, partly by the fact that non-native rainbow trout and brook trout were stocked within their native range. Rainbows and cutthroats readily hybridize with one another and non-native trout often outcompete Yellowstone cutthroat trout for food and habitat, resulting in a substantial reduction in the species' range. Their hybrid offspring are neither cutthroat nor rainbow trout.

Once widely distributed throughout south-central Montana, northwestern Wyoming, and parts of southeastern Idaho, pure Yellowstone cutthroat trout are now relegated to a fraction of their historic range where they are found mostly in remote isolated headwater reaches of streams where a waterfall or other barrier has prevented invasion by non-native fish and habitat quality remains relatively unchanged. All told, throughout their original range, they inherently possessed four distinct migratory traits, moving within or between big and small streams, and to and from lakes.

Now, some four decades after I first spotted Yellowstone cutthroat trout, my work with the U.S. Fish and Wildlife Service's Montana Fish and Wildlife Conservation Office proves most rewarding. We have restored habitats across Montana and Wyoming to benefit Yellowstone cutthroat and other species.

Perhaps most rewarding has been our work with the Crow Tribe in Montana, to conserve the native trout in native habitats in concert with the Native peoples. In the early 1990s, now-retired fish biologist Robbin Wagner and I traveled into the remote backcountry of the Crow Reservation to collect tissues from fish we suspected to be native Yellowstone cutthroat. The resulting genetic analysis revealed they were an aboriginal Yellowstone cutthroat population. Discovering this relict cutthroat population significantly expanded the known distribution of the subspecies. And since that time, the Crow Tribe designated the Yellowstone cutthroat trout as a Tribal Species of Special Concern.

Yellowstone cutthroat trout still afford wonderful angling opportunities in and around the national park in Montana and Wyoming. The fish's range is expanding one stream at a time as biologists from tribal, federal, and state governments, and other partners, build barriers to non-native fish and restock historical waters with Yellowstone cutthroats. Through these efforts, we are ensuring the subspecies is there for future generations to catch, or simply to admire while peeking over a bridge.

—George R. Jordan

Evelene Spencer (1868–1935)

The U.S. Bureau of Fisheries once employed a celebrity chef—one that people would flock to watch give live demonstrations at large department stores. Evelene Spencer worked for the U.S. Bureau of Fisheries during the Roaring Twenties, hired to promote the eating of fish. Her official title was "Fish Cookery Expert for United States Bureau of Fisheries," and she earned the nickname "Fish Evangelist."

Evelene Armstrong was born in 1868 in Toronto, Canada, and twenty years later moved to the U.S., where she married Joseph Spencer in Portland, Oregon. They had two daughters, Adrienne Spencer, born in 1890, and Evalyn Spencer, born in 1893. According to the U.S. Census records, in 1910 Evelene was forty-two years old and managed a restaurant. Her skills in the kitchen lent themselves to her hiring on as a professional chef for the U.S. Bureau of Fisheries.

Evelene created quite the name for herself; she was widely known and respected in the U.S. and Canada. In 1919, she published *Groupers, fishes you should try, with recipes for them,* the Bureau's Economic Circular No. 44. She worked for the U.S. Bureau of Fisheries from 1915 to 1922.

Her magnum opus was *Fish Cookery, Six Hundred Recipes for the Preparation of Fish, Shellfish and Other Aquatic Animals, Including Fish Soups, Salads and Entrees, with Accompanying Sauces, Seasonings, Dressings and Forcemeats.* It was coauthored with John M. Cobb, the director of the College of Fisheries at the

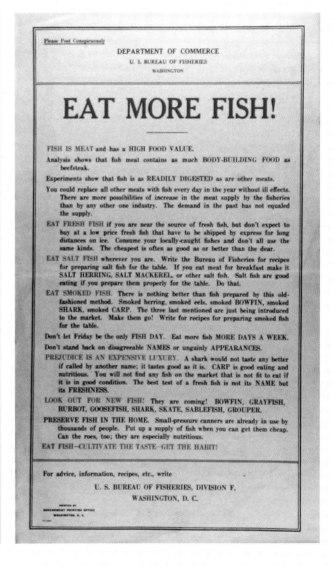

Please Post Conspicuously

DEPARTMENT OF COMMERCE
U. S. BUREAU OF FISHERIES
WASHINGTON

EAT MORE FISH!

FISH IS MEAT and has a HIGH FOOD VALUE.

Analysis shows that fish meat contains as much BODY-BUILDING FOOD as beefsteak.

Experiments show that fish is as READILY DIGESTED as are other meats.

You could replace all other meats with fish every day in the year without ill effects. There are more possibilities of increase in the meat supply by the fisheries than by any other one industry. The demand in the past has not equaled the supply.

EAT FRESH FISH if you are near the source of fresh fish, but don't expect to buy at a low price fresh fish that have to be shipped by express for long distances on ice. Consume your locally-caught fishes and don't all use the same kinds. The cheapest is often as good as or better than the dear.

EAT SALT FISH wherever you are. Write the Bureau of Fisheries for recipes for preparing salt fish for the table. If you eat meat for breakfast make it SALT HERRING, SALT MACKEREL, or other salt fish. Salt fish are good eating if you prepare them properly for the table. Do that.

EAT SMOKED FISH. There is nothing better than fish prepared by this old-fashioned method. Smoked herring, smoked eels, smoked BOWFIN, smoked SHARK, smoked CARP. The three last mentioned are just being introduced to the market. Make them go! Write for recipes for preparing smoked fish for the table.

Don't let Friday be the only FISH DAY. Eat more fish MORE DAYS A WEEK.

Don't stand back on disagreeable NAMES or ungainly APPEARANCES.

PREJUDICE IS AN EXPENSIVE LUXURY. A shark would not taste any better if called by another name; it tastes good as it is. CARP is good eating and nutritious. You will not find any fish on the market that is not fit to eat if it is in good condition. The best test of a fresh fish is not its NAME but its FRESHNESS.

LOOK OUT FOR NEW FISH! They are coming! BOWFIN, GRAYFISH, BURBOT, GOOSEFISH, SHARK, SKATE, SABLEFISH, GROUPER.

PRESERVE FISH IN THE HOME. Small-pressure canners are already in use by thousands of people. Put up a supply of fish when you can get them cheap. Can the roes, too; they are especially nutritious.

EAT FISH—CULTIVATE THE TASTE—GET THE HABIT!

For advice, information, recipes, etc., write

U. S. BUREAU OF FISHERIES, DIVISION F,
WASHINGTON, D. C.

MRS. EVELENE SPENCER

Fish Cookery Expert, U. S. Bureau of Fisheries, Author of "Fish Cookery"

Says——

Eat more Fish for your health's sake.

Get acquainted with cheaper kinds and use more of them.

Use Smoked and Salt Fish for breakfast.

Use Frozen Fish when Fresh Fish is scarce or out of season.

Use more Shell-Fish—America produces finest in the world.

Separate Fish from Friday
—Make TUESDAY a Fish Day as well
EAT MORE FISH
—A Real Health Food

ASK US FOR A RECIPE BOOK

Above: The Eat More Fish campaign sought to put more fish on plates to save beef for the U.S. military fighting in Europe during World War I. USFWS NFACA

Left: U.S. Bureau of Fisheries employee Evelene Spencer contributed to the Eat More Fish campaign during World War I with her cooking demonstrations and recipe circulars. Her habit is emblazoned with a star and U.S.B.F. USFWS NFACA

Evelene Spencer published the best-selling *Fish Cookery* in 1921. It featured recipes for fish, roe, and mussels. APRIL GREGORY, USFWS

University of Seattle, released in 1921, and can still be found in used bookstores.

More than just a listing of recipes, *Fish Cookery* includes mathematical ratios for gauging cooking times for the size and thickness of the fish and offers information on how to determine the freshness of market fish and properly fillet a fish.

The book's introduction speaks to the culture of eating across America—how one type of fish may be considered a highly prized entrée in one place while it is considered a "trash fish" in another part of the country—notions which still hold true today.

Recipes in *Fish Cookery* range from bass, shrimp, trout, and salmon to eel, shark, roe, and turtle. The authors explain that they are trying to introduce unconventional food sources that may be locally available at more economical prices.

The book features Evelene's baking method, the "Spencer Hot Oven Method." The book was a success, and Evelene traveled the country giving cooking demonstrations before moving back to Canada in 1923 to work for the National Fish Co.

Evelene died in 1935 near Toronto. Her obituary mentioned that the Bureau of Fisheries "published a cookbook prepared by Mrs. Spencer which attained a circulation to be envied by a 'best seller' in the realm of fiction."

—April Gregory

Greenback Cutthroat Trout

Cutthroat trout were unknown to Europeans until 1541, when a chronicler of the Coronado Entrada documented *truchas* swimming in a small stream, a tributary to the Pecos River near Santa Fe, New Mexico.

Another 264 years would pass before a trained scientist, Meriwether Lewis, would put ink on paper and describe the trout with a discerning eye. That was in 1805, after Private Silas Goodrich of the Lewis and Clark Expedition angled several of them at the base of the Great Falls of the Missouri River in what is now Montana. French-born naturalized American ichthyologist Charles Girard gave the fish its scientific name *Salar lewisi* the same year, 1856, that he earned his Georgetown University medical degree. Girard wrote extensively on trout and other American fishes, papers often coauthored with Spencer Baird, the first commissioner of the U.S. Fish Commission. Girard served the Confederacy in a medical capacity, and after the Civil War, returned to France where he continued to study fishes and practice medicine.

Girard's name stuck, at least partly. The classification of cutthroat trout has been revised significantly since 1856. We have come to understand that Coronado's and Goodrich's trout were but two of fourteen subspecies of cutthroat trout that range from Alaska to New Mexico in waters that vein over the Rocky Mountains, pouring east and west.

Today the cutthroat species is known as *Oncorynchus clarki*, and the fish Goodrich brought back to camp, the westslope cutthroat trout, *Oncorynchus clarki lewisi*, honoring Goodrich and the Corps of Discovery.

Among the set of fourteen cutthroat trout subspecies is the greenback cutthroat trout, found in the South Platte River drainage in Colorado. It too has a history that could be described as a roller-coaster ride. It has no epic Corps or Entrada to boast for its discovery and in comparison, might be considered plebian, but the fish's story is anything but that.

Greenback cutthroat trout were found in great abundance in the Rocky Mountains and its foothills. It is in fact, the state fish of Colorado. Native Americans and early European settlers used these colorful

A U.S. Bureau of Fisheries biologist shows off two greenback cutthroat trout caught in a live trap near present-day Leadville National Fish Hatchery.
USFWS NFACA

Greenback cutthroat trout spawning at Leadville, Colorado. USFWS NFACA

Freshly spawned cutthroat trout eggs from Colorado's Turquoise Lake are readied for shipment back to Leadville, fixed in jars and secured in marked boxes.
USFWS NFACA

Workers from Leadville ready a gill net to capture ripe greenback cutthroat trout from a Colorado lake.
USFWS NFACA

Trout were hand fed at Leadville circa 1890. USFWS NFACA

fish for food or brought them to market. Adventurers returned from the mountains with grand fish stories of huge catches. As these stories reached the newspapers, more and more anglers headed to the mountains to discover if such abundance was possible. Anglers caught hundreds of these tasty fish and preserved them, either in vinegar or by drying, in order to bring them home to share with family and friends. Early miners also sought the greenback; lore has it their fishing method frequently involved dynamite.

One settler, Horace Ferguson, greatly benefitted from this fish resource. Ferguson farmed on the Colorado plains and twice lost his crops to grasshopper infestations. The plagues ruined him financially, so he looked for a new line of work to support his family. In 1875, he headed to the mountain community of Estes Park where he met a market hunter and fisherman named Hank Farrar who supplied markets in Denver. The pair became business partners, and Ferguson immediately set out for the Horseshoe Park section

Local timber near Leadville provides a convenient source for materials needed to build weirs at fish traps.
USFWS NFACA

There are two seasons in Leadville, Colorado: winter and winter's coming. Leadville Fish-Cultural Station opened in 1889 and is among the oldest operating stations in the U.S. Fish and Wildlife Service. It also holds the distinction of being situated at the highest elevation. Hatchery grounds range from 9,500 to 12,000 feet above sea level. USFWS NFACA

Gingerbread, scallops, and fish-scaled gables typified homes of the late-Victorian era, as seen on the superintendent's home at Leadville Fish-Cultural Station. USFWS NFACA

of the Fall River, which is now part of Rocky Mountain National Park. Within three days of his arrival there, Ferguson caught 720 greenbacks. All but twelve of them came from a single beaver pond. He and his son brought them to Denver where at fifty cents a pound, the family was returned to financial solvency.

With few fish laws on the books and even fewer lawmen, greenback cutthroat trout were depleted by overharvesting. To stave that depletion, the Colorado Fish Commission built a fish hatchery in Denver in 1882. The U.S. Fish Commission followed suit in 1889 and opened Leadville Fish-Cultural Station, today known as Leadville National Fish Hatchery. That station has two distinctions: it is among the oldest operating hatcheries in the U.S. and is situated higher in elevation than any other facility. Leadville's grounds approach thirteen thousand feet above sea level. These two facilities produced millions of fish to fill the void of the depleted native fish species. During the 1920s, over twenty hatcheries operated in Colorado. Determined workers carried fish on mules or in backpacks filled with water and fish into the wilderness and stocked the streams. On one trip in Rocky Mountain National Park, they had to cut through a foot of ice in order to stock the fish.

Although fishery managers tried to raise the native cutthroat trout, difficulties arose. To keep the streams stocked and to maintain Colorado's reputation as a sportsman's paradise, trout were imported from other areas of the United States and Europe. They hoped to find the perfect species, one that could be raised easily and provide the sport that anglers desired. Unfortunately, introduction of these non-native species,

which we now know displaced and interbred with the native cutthroat, further doomed the greenback.

In 1937, the greenback cutthroat trout was declared extinct. This presumed extinction prevailed until 1969, when an inquisitive University of Colorado graduate student captured several cutthroat trout from Como Creek at the school's Mountain Research Station. The fish were different from any he had seen while growing up in Colorado. After comparing freshly caught trout from Como Creek to preserved museum specimens from the Academy of Natural Sciences in Philadelphia, where the first-ever collected greenback were stored, experts determined that the fish in Como Creek were the long-lost greenback.

Since the rediscovery, additional populations of presumed greenback were located and a massive effort undertaken to conserve the trout. Under the guidance of Dr. Robert Behnke of Colorado State University—whose preeminence in trout taxonomy was so revered that he earned the nickname "Dr. Trout"—the recovery was very successful. By the early 2000s the greenback cutthroat trout conservation was held up as one of the success stories of the Endangered Species Act to the extent that authorities considered removing the trout from the threatened and endangered species list.

But that did not happen. In the past, telling one closely related species apart from another was done by comparing physical features such as scale counts over given body parts, as well as the number of teeth and vertebrae. As techniques improved and knowledge increased, genetics became the preferred tool

Leadville hatchery had a number of substations—seasonal egg-taking sites—such as this one at Eagle Nest, New Mexico, where a worker hangs trout fillets to dry. The station operated from 1932 to 1963. Each spring, Leadville workers made a pilgrimage to catch ripe rainbow trout and fertilize their eggs from Eagle Nest Lake. The offspring were stocked in northern New Mexico and southern Colorado from Eagle Nest or sent to Leadville to incubate and stock. The truck license plate reads US FISHERIES 109. USFWS NFACA

Milk cans serve as panniers draped over horses at Eagle Nest, New Mexico, as these U.S. Bureau of Fisheries workers set out to stock rainbow trout in places not accessible by truck. USFWS NFACA

Leadville staff have a long-running association with biologists from Colorado Parks and Wildlife, who today share the common cause of conserving greenback cutthroat trout. USFWS NFACA

for taxonomists. Genetic researchers from the University of Colorado led by Jessica Metcalf compared cutthroat trout which had been collected from Colorado waters prior to 1890 and stored in museums around the country to the genetics of trout in current wild populations.

She determined that only a single unadulterated greenback cutthroat trout population existed. These fish swam in Bear Creek, a small stream pouring off the side of Pikes Peak, the promontory that inspired the song "America the Beautiful."

A homesteader named J. C. Jones stocked these fish into Bear Creek prior to 1882, where they remained until rediscovered in the 1990s. The population earned the moniker "Weird Bear Creek," because the fish appeared so different from any other previously analyzed cutthroat. Not until Metcalf's research was it known why.

As of 2020, Bear Creek remained the only naturally reproducing population of greenback cutthroat trout. The fish is getting a lift at Leadville National Fish Hatchery, where biologists conserve the genetic lineage in broodstock of what is arguably among the rarest of the cutthroat trout.

The history of the greenback cutthroat trout has been a roller coaster ride from abundance, to near extinction, to near recovery, and then back to a single population. I have been along for part of that ride in my two decades of working with them, monitoring populations, and researching their history to know how we got to where we are and to ensure the same mistakes are not made again.

—Chris Kennedy

Lahontan Cutthroat Trout

I soak in the incredible landscape. Balanced on a six-foot ladder waist deep in water—as is customary at this locale—a vast body of water stretches out before me: Pyramid Lake. Fifteen miles long, eleven miles wide. Wind is normally a factor, but not yet today. The lake is like glass reflecting the panorama's early morning moving palette, shades of crimson red, pinks, and gray. Eight-weight fly rod in hand, I present an irresistible minnow imitation almost as vibrant as the sunrise. The object of my desire, the highly coveted Lahontan cutthroat—the largest-growing trout native to North America.

This cutthroat evolved in ancient Lake Lahontan. The ice-age body of water covered approximately 8,600 square miles of Nevada and included parts of California and Oregon. As glaciers retreated, the basin dried to a few relics of its former self, such as present-day Pyramid and Walker lakes. Rain and snowmelt pour into them, but water naturally only leaves these lakes via evaporation, and with the long press of time, the sumps of the ancient Lake Lahontan basin became more alkaline, causing the Lahontan cutthroat trout to develop into a fish able to withstand environmental extremes that readily kill other fish species.

Lahontan cutthroat owe their size to their knack for preying on fish—cui-ui sucker, tui chub, and cannibalizing their own. All three fishes were culturally important and were a food source for the Northern Paiute people of the Great Basin. In 1844, while searching for the mythical Buenaventura River, John C. Fremont was the first English writer to document

the Lahontan cutthroat. At the mouth of the Truckee River members of the Pyramid Lake Paiute Tribe provided his party with specimens measuring up to four feet long. This was not an embellishment, as early settlers documented fish exceeding sixty pounds. In 1916, the largest confirmed specimen tipped the scale at sixty-two pounds. Fremont compared the Lahontan to the Chinook salmon of the Columbia River and described their flavor as "superior to that of any fish I have known."

Naturalist Henry W. Henshaw collected Lahontan specimens on the Wheeler Survey in 1876. He was venerated by U.S. Fish Commission scientist Theodore Gill and ichthyologist David Starr Jordan when they deemed the subspecies *henshawi* in 1878. The name Lahontan is derived from that of a French aristocrat. Louis-Armand de Lom d'Arce or simply Baron de Lahontan never laid eyes on the geography of the Lake Lahontan region, his namesake cutthroat, or the lands that encompass the state recreation area that bear his name. The baron, an officer with the Troupes de la Marine, explored New France with the Bourbon Regiment in the 1680s. According to his travelogue titled *New Voyages to North-America*—extremely popular and published throughout Europe—Lahontan claimed that during a four-month journey in the winter of 1688–89 he explored the "Rivière Longue." Many scholars believe this to be a fabricated tale, while others argue that Lahontan and his party of three hundred men traveled much of America's longest river—known today as the Missouri. Debates aside, his story was influential on the cartography of

Lahontan cutthroat trout closeup TYLER HERN, USFWS

Lahontan cutthroat trout TYLER HERN, USFWS

Pyramid Lake anglers get a leg up on ladders when casting to Lahontan cutthroat trout. TYLER HERN, USFWS

the Northwest. Thomas Jefferson, who commissioned Lewis and Clark to find an internal river route to the Pacific, fancied Lahontan's publication.

Fast forward to 1905, the year the very first water development project by the Bureau of Reclamation began dropping Pyramid and Walker lakes' water levels for irrigation. From 1906 to the 1970s Pyramid Lake's water level dropped by eighty feet, a reduction of one hundred thousand acres. Walker Lake lost two-thirds its volume—130 feet of elevation. All cutthroat trout, Lahontan included, must spawn in flowing water and Pyramid Lake cutthroats could no longer swim into the Truckee River to reproduce. By simple attrition from the inability to spawn, Pyramid Lake was devoid of the leviathan cutthroat trout by 1939. The fish that carried in its genes the stamp of life in harsh lake waters and the ability for tremendous growth was extinct.

Or so it was thought.

Most fish culturists know that the first artificially propagated trout in North America was the brook trout, raised on a Cleveland, Ohio, physician's property in 1853. Propagated at a private hatchery operation on the Truckee River in 1867, the Lahontan cutthroat trout could potentially be the second species cultured in captivity. Over time, various private entities and the Nevada Fish Commission obtained eggs or made great efforts to distribute the cutthroat. It found its way well beyond its native range, traveling as far away as New Zealand.

But one particular stocking has proven to be priceless. When and who moved the trout to a small fishless stream on a Utah mountainside, no one knows. One thing is for certain, museum specimens and genetic analyses reveal that the trout residing on the side of Pilot Peak are the original Truckee River-Pyramid Lake form of the Lahontan cutthroat trout—one well known to grow to massive sizes.

Working with a plethora of partners, the U.S. Fish and Wildlife Service's Lahontan Fish and Wildlife Conservation Office spearheads the resurrection of the Lahontan cutthroat trout, a fish that was among the first species listed under the Endangered Species Act. Reclassified a threatened species, fishery management and restoration efforts incorporate a vital component, the endangered cui-ui. Conservation objectives intertwine the health of the lake and riverine habitats upon which the two species depend. Two critical implements include the Lahontan National Fish Hatchery on the banks of the Carson River and the Marble Bluff Fish Passage Facility at the mouth of the Truckee.

Marble Bluff Dam, three miles upstream of Pyramid Lake, was constructed to reduce further erosion of the Truckee River caused by changes in water elevation. Touting a forty-foot-high fish elevator, the apparatus aids both Lahontan and cui-ui with their spawning migration.

The Lahontan National Fish Hatchery carefully cultivates a unique genetic strain of Lahontan broodstock from wild fish collected at Pilot Peak—representatives of the original lacustrine or lake-dwelling form of cutthroat that evolved in ancient Lake Lahontan. By design, families are kept separate, and the young are frequently graded, separating bigger fish from smaller fish to avoid cannibalism. The need to do so speaks to that inborn, innate sense for piscivory, even at the earliest ages. In due time hatchery offspring find themselves in native waters including Pyramid Lake. Once considered extinct, Lahontan cutthroat in Pyramid Lake's population is believed to be approaching one million trout where they contribute significantly to the sport fishery managed by the Paiute Indian Tribe.

Through these endeavors emanate an increased number of cutthroat that migrate up the Truckee. In 2013, a paltry number partook in the journey, not more than a few dozen. Less than ten years later,

Lahontan National Fish Hatchery biologist Amanda George transfers a female Lahontan cutthroat trout into one of the hatchery's broodstock tanks. DAN HOTTLE, USFWS

David Miller (left) and Roger Peka, Lahontan National Fish Hatchery biologists, download trout migration data from a receiver along the banks of the Truckee River. DAN HOTTLE, USFWS

David Miller, Lahontan National Fish Hatchery biologist, adjusts a telemetry receiver used to follow trout. DAN HOTTLE, USFWS

An acoustic tracking device like the one shown is implanted in Lahontan cutthroat trout to track their migration from Pyramid Lake into the Truckee River. ERIK HORGEN, USFWS

Water development projects, such as this dam on the Truckee River above Pyramid Lake, were insurmountable and caused problems for the native cutthroat trout. This photo was taken in May 1932. USFWS NFACA

record numbers were approaching two thousand. U.S. Fish and Wildlife Service biologists aspire for the fish that inhabited the area for thousands of years to once again make their ancestral pilgrimage from Pyramid to Lake Tahoe. Barriers and obstructions still exist, most notably Derby Dam—although numerous fish-friendly modifications were installed in 2020, 115 years after its construction. In the foreseeable future twenty-pound Lahontan cutthroat trout will travel through downtown Reno, past an angler or two, on their journey to spawning gravels in headwater streams.

Days prior to my Pyramid Lake venture I had the honor of assisting my U.S. Fish and Wildlife Service colleagues with the cui-ui bypass process at Marble Bluff and spawning activities at Lahontan National Fish Hatchery. The passion and the pride of the employees are apparent. They believe in their mission, and they believe in the Lahontan cutthroat

trout. Visiting field stations around the country as the agency's National Broodstock Coordinator, I have witnessed many success stories. The Lahontan cutthroat trout's comeback is my favorite.

In search of forage, the top predators make their rounds along the shores of this remnant of ancient Lake Lahontan. I drag my terminal fly within a foot of the silty bottom, a long slow pull is my preferred presentation, mimicking a fish. I ponder how many cutthroat have dismissed my offer when abruptly the line tightens. Instantaneously, I jerk backward, sharply. It is not the twenty-pounder I dreamt about, but a Lahontan cutthroat trout nonetheless. I hold in my net an artifact of nature and the consequences of conservation. Shades of crimson red, pinks, and gray adorn this beauty, all akin to the landscape around me.

—Carlos R. Martinez

Yellowfin Cutthroat Trout

In the heart of the Saguache Range of Colorado, nestled in the shadows of fourteen-thousand-foot peaks lies a pair of glacially scoured lakes near Leadville, Colorado. Aptly named Twin Lakes, these bodies of water have been embroiled in mysticism since the Utes used the area as a summer hunting ground and oasis. There are the stories of a Loch Ness-ian serpent that resided in their depths. This serpent is blamed for the sinking of the steamboat *Dauntless*, which is said to have collided with the monster during a jaunt in the fog. There are legends of fur-bearing trout, a species that evolved the trait as a result of the frigid temperatures expected at two miles above sea level. Naturally, they would shed their fur each season as the water warmed.

The yellowfin cutthroat trout is a fish of legend—yet one rooted in a kernel of truth. Since the earliest days locals talked about a gargantuan trout species that resided in Twin Lakes. The tale claims the fish was so big and abundant that it was commercially fished to feed tens of thousands of miners who became dependent on their flavorful flesh. Also seemingly far-fetched, the yellowfin is said to have lived in sympatry with the much smaller greenback cutthroat, but for some unknown reason did not feast on nor hybridize with it. There is also speculation that the *Dauntless* did not collide with a lake serpent that foggy day, but rather a large yellowfin trout cruising near the surface.

Assuredly, this fish tale is basted with exaggeration, but the yellowfin is no fable. Famed ichthyologists David Starr Jordan, the then-sitting president of Stanford University, and Barton Evermann, a U.S. Fish Commission scientist, visited Twin Lakes during

their scientific expedition to Colorado and Utah in the summer of 1889. The *Bulletin of the United States Fish Commission for 1889* provides summaries of their surveys on the upper Arkansas River headwaters. Not only did the party find the "green-back" trout in Twin Lakes, but they also acknowledged a "very distinct, yellow-finned" trout.

Jordan and Evermann provided this analysis: "This species has the lower fins bright yellow; there is a broad yellowish lateral shade, by which the species can be recognized in the water. The black spots are numerous and very small. There is little red under the throat and none at all elsewhere." Jordan and Evermann named the fish *Salmo mykiss macdonaldi* in honor of U.S. Fish Commissioner Marshall McDonald, "in recognition of his services in connection with the propagation of the American Salmonids."

The ichthyologists surmised that the populations of the two cutthroat subspecies did indeed remain isolated; the yellowfin dwelled in the dark depths and spawned on gravelly shallows while the greenback cutthroat trout roamed the shallows but spawned in Lake Creek at the inlet.

Adding credibility to the yellowfin's existence is the fortunate fact that Jordan and Evermann obtained and preserved several six- to ten-inch yellowfin specimens. Taken via fly, July was the wrong time of year for the scientists to catch a large specimen from shore via angling. Leadvillite George Fisher, presumably at the direction of Jordan, returned to Twin Lakes the following spring just as the ice receded. Fisher reported that anglers were catching large yellow-fin trout. One he verified just shy of nine pounds, stating that had the fish not already been dressed he would have sent it to Jordan. He did however obtain from another angler one that weighed more than seven pounds "fresh out of the water." Fisher noted the yellow color on the fins and throat, preserved the fish in alcohol, sealed it up in a tin box, and sent it to Jordan via "express."

Over a century later, many of Jordan's specimens were reexamined by an authority on the classification of salmonids, Colorado State University professor Dr. Robert J. Behnke. Behnke reaffirmed the earlier scientists' findings: "I have no doubt that Jordan was correct; the yellowfin trout and the greenback trout from Twin Lakes were two distinct groups of cutthroat trout."

Behnke also identified two historic photographs that he believed captured yellowfin cutthroat trout on film. The first one appeared June 16, 1891, in *Sports Afield* magazine showing three large fish caught south of Twin Lakes. The May 12, 1891, issue of the *Rocky Mountain News* mentions that these fish were presented to President Benjamin Harrison when his train made a stop in the area. The second photo, a gem found in the U.S. Fish and Wildlife Service's National Fish and Aquatic Conservation Archives, shows a freshly angled large trout caught near Leadville in 1919.

The yellowfin cutthroat trout did in fact swim the waters of Twin Lakes, making it one of fourteen cutthroat subspecies. And it holds this unfortunate distinction: it is in all probability, extinct. It is not too hard to decipher the reasons for their demise, all of which are human influenced. Prior to Jordan and Evermann's visit there had already been a number

of gold and silver booms in the immediate vicinity. With mining came the rush of people to the area, destruction and pollution of native habitat, and water diversions. There is no evidence pointing to how many yellowfin were commercially harvested, but no doubt with the lack of laws, fish were likely removed indiscriminately.

By 1870, Twin Lakes had already become a popular tourist destination. Inter-Laken Resort, serviced by the *Dauntless*, was described in 1885 as the most charming summer mountain resort in Colorado. Then of course, there was introduction of non-native trout that preyed upon and outcompeted and hybridized with the native cutthroats. Truthfully, Jordan's party was lucky to find any cutthroat trout in Twin Lakes at all.

Locals still talk about the giant cutthroat that once inhabited Twin Lakes. Pestering anglers is the Colorado state record for a native cutthroat trout—caught in Twin Lakes in 1964. The sixteen-pounder remains the state record to this day. Although no one ever documented which Colorado native cutthroat trout this record represents, one cannot help but wonder if it was a descendent of the fabled yellowfin.

Although most agree the yellowfin is probably gone forever, there is always that slight possibility that it still exists due to early egg distribution by the Leadville National Fish Hatchery. Established in 1889, partially because of the accessibility and availability of eggs from the fishery at Twin Lakes, the facility held yellowfin adults and produced yellowfin eggs on station many times throughout the turn of the century. Historic correspondence indicates that the Leadville station made several shipments of yellowfin eggs to

The only known image of a now-extinct yellowfin cutthroat trout resides at National Fish and Aquatic Conservation Archives. USFWS NFACA

Germany and France. Fish culturist Herr Siegfried Jaffe indicated in a French journal that the Prince of Bavaria received yellowfin fingerlings in 1899, and yellowfin were entered into a 1902 Fish Culture Exposition in Vienna where they won "first prize."

The yellowfin legend persists at home—and abroad. The offspring from some of Leadville's shipments were stocked in the high mountain lakes of the Alps, so the story goes, where the last surviving population of yellowfin cutthroat trout may swim today. And so goes a hopeful imagination.

—Carlos R. Martinez

What does a fish biologist do on his time off? Go fishing, of course. Tom Tighe, biologist at Mora National Fish Hatchery in New Mexico, caught this golden trout in the Wind River Range of Wyoming. Golden trout have been stocked well outside their native California range. In the 1960s, renowned test pilot Chuck Yeager on orders from General Irvin Branch illegally helicoptered golden trout out of the Sierras and transported them to New Mexico where General Branch intended to live in retirement. The golden trout apparently didn't have the right stuff for life in New Mexico and is extirpated. Yeager wrote about his clandestine deed in his 1986 autobiography. NATHAN WIESE, USFWS

David Starr Jordan (1851–1931)

Consider this: One can earn the distinguished David Starr Jordan Prize for innovative work in biology. It is conceivable to attend grade school and high school, and then earn biology or psychology degrees in buildings named after Jordan in California and Indiana.

You can drive on Jordan Avenue, wade Jordan Creek, swim Jordan Lake, climb Mount Jordan, or until recently, research ocean fisheries aboard the NOAA vessel *David Starr Jordan*. One can angle fishes in a high country stream or in the blue sea that the man described more than a century ago.

Many fish carry his name: the genera *Jordanella* and *Davidijordania*, and the species Jordan's sucker, Jordan's snapper, Jordan's sculpin, and Jordan's damsel.

David Starr Jordan's career in conservation coincided with the rise of the U.S. Fish Commission in the last quarter of the nineteenth century. While considered an academician, he worked hand-in-glove with luminaries in the golden age of ichthyology. Anyone who studied fish biology no doubt encountered his name in the scientific literature—and in the popular press.

Jordan did a great deal of work for the U.S. Fish Commission and much of it alongside William Converse Kendall and the more prominent Barton Warren Evermann. Jordan and Evermann coauthored innumerable scientific publications, many of them describing new species of fish—trout and minnows and suckers—as well as saltwater species. Their *American Food & Game Fishes*, published in 1902, was accessible to laypersons so that they may better understand the fish fauna found around farms and towns, the lowland rivers of the East, the Great Lakes, and the high mountain streams of the Rockies and Sierra Nevadas. It remains an encyclopedic milepost.

DAVID STARR JORDAN. COURTESY LIBRARY OF CONGRESS

U.S. Fish Commission reports carried Jordan's byline. Jordan came under U.S. Fish Commissioner Spencer Baird's influence around 1875; after Jordan took a teaching job at Indiana University, he made fish collection trips in the Midwest and the South with his students at the sponsorship of the Fish Commission. Jordan's prominence grew. At age thirty-four he was appointed president of Indiana University.

Jordan's work caught the attention of U.S. Senator Leland Stanford Jr., who sought someone to preside over his new university in California. Jordan headed west as founding president of Stanford. That opened up new venues for studying fishes, which he continued with Charles Gilbert who contributed a great deal to our understanding of Pacific salmon in association with the U.S. Fish Commission. Many of Jordan's students became U.S. Fish Commission or U.S. Bureau of Fisheries employees.

Jordan had other interests outside fisheries science; he was a charter member of the Sierra Club, president of the California Academy of Sciences, served on the California Fish Commission, and directed the World Peace Foundation. He was an ardent supporter of the pseudoscientific pursuit of eugenics.

Former Stanford biology professor and university president Donald Kennedy noted that Jordan's contributions to science were "significant, but not monumental." The number of fish names and place names are monuments to a prodigious fisheries scientist who was certainly a flawed individual. In the end, you can measure a man in part or overall, and by any measure Jordan's influence on the U.S. Fish Commission and conservation was profound.

—Craig Springer

Barton Warren Evermann (1853–1932)

U.S. Fish Commission scientist Barton Warren Evermann was to David Starr Jordan what Plato was to Socrates. The two met at Indiana University in the 1870s— Evermann the student and Jordan the teacher. The relationship produced a mountain of scientific papers and books on American fishes and extended well beyond the classroom and late into their lives.

Evermann enrolled in 1881 at Indiana University to study under Jordan. The two men were first acquainted in 1877, when Evermann and his wife participated in an extended fish-collecting trip with Jordan. They traveled and collected fishes throughout the Southeast under the auspices of the U.S. Fish Commission.

Evermann graduated in 1886 and published "Fishes observed in the vicinity of Brookville, Franklin County, Indiana" in the *Bulletin of the Brookville Society of Natural History*. A torrent of books, magazine stories, and scientific papers on fish, birds, and mammals would follow for the next forty-five years. Evermann earned his Ph.D. in 1891, and through Jordan, landed a job with the U.S. Fish Commission as a scientist aboard the U.S.F.C. *Albatross*.

During his career with the U.S. Fish Commission and the subsequent U.S. Bureau of Fisheries, Evermann held various titles, sometimes overlapping, while stationed in the Washington, D.C., headquarters, all of which spoke to his capabilities: chief of the Division of Statistics and Methods of Fisheries, 1902–3; chief of scientific inquiry, 1903–10; chief of Alaska fisheries, 1910–14; and ichthyologist from 1891 to 1914. All the while coauthoring books and scientific papers with Jordan.

The year 1906 is a significant benchmark. Evermann alone authored *The Golden Trout of the Southern High Sierras*, published by the U.S. Bureau of Fisheries. Stuart Edward White's book *The Mountain*

Barton Warren Evermann COURTESY LIBRARY OF CONGRESS

caught President Theodore Roosevelt's attention in 1904. White worried for the native trout in the Sierras. Roosevelt directed Evermann to investigate. In a manner seen in the capabilities of fish biologists at any of the U.S. Fish and Wildlife Service's Fish and Wildlife Conservation Offices today, Evermann mounted an expedition to learn more about these presumed rare high-country trout.

The outcome was two new species of fish: Roosevelt's trout and White's trout. Evermann's foray revealed that California's Kern River contained two rare fishes, which he named *Salmo roosevelti* and *S. whitei*, to honor the citizen-conservationist White, and the sitting U.S. president and nephew of the congressional author of the U.S. Fish Commission.

Evermann's fifty-one-page booklet, *Golden Trout*, laid out potential conservation measures for the fish. Other scientists have since revised the species designations, but Evermann's descriptions remain a testament not only to his capabilities at a desk, but in the field as well.

In 1914, Evermann said good-bye to the U.S. Bureau of Fisheries and took a job as director of the California Academy of Science, no doubt with some pull from Jordan. Evermann led the Academy until his passing in 1932. Though he traveled the world, he returned to Indiana to lie at rest.

In the span of half a century, Evermann published nearly four hundred scientific papers, nearly all having to do with fishes. Four genera honor him: *Evermanni, Evermanella, Evermanolus,* and *Evermannichthys*. Mount Evermann, the highest promontory on Isla Socorro, a Mexican possession, points to a mountain of scientific research that spanned a life.

—Craig Springer

Barton Evermann collected native trout from the high sierras at the behest of President Theodore Roosevelt and described one for the president and the other for writer Stewart White. David Starr Jordan described the third and named it after his friend and U.S. Bureau of Fisheries associate Dr. Charles Gilbert. USFWS NFACA

Gila Trout

The distinct *thump, thump, thump* of helicopter blades awoke me from a dead slumber. It took a minute to recoup my bearings and remember why I was buried under two sleeping bags. I hadn't bothered to pitch a tent the night before; a thousand stars above had been my weather forecast. But the crisp November night had the twinge of winter setting in; five thousand feet of elevation pushed the mercury below freezing but made for incredible stargazing in one of the darkest nightscapes of the continental U.S.

I grinned. As sleep finally cleared, I caught sight of the helicopter making steady progress toward my camp in southwest New Mexico. It was going to be a good morning.

I found Gila trout four years before this morning. I'd left the Clearwater River of northern Idaho to get there. It was home to some of the largest steelhead in the Columbia River basin that power through five hundred miles of river to their spawning grounds. I packed my wife and two baby daughters for the twelve-hundred-mile journey south to New Mexico—arriving as the manager of Mora National Fish Hatchery. It was at the time the only hatchery in the world rearing Gila trout.

It's hard to describe a national treasure—and Gila trout are just that. A spawning Gila trout is a sight to behold. Gold flanks are speckled with fine pepper along the dorsal. Closer examination reveals hinting of a crimson slash—a throwback from their ancestral split from rainbow trout, 1.3 million years ago. Under it all, the leading edge of white-tipped fins develop rippling akin to the edging of fine lace.

Gila trout aren't just spectacular to behold, they are a story that captivates the imagination of wild places and wild things. It's hard to decipher when Gila trout were first discovered. Early written accounts from settlers in the 1800s describe so-called mountain trout, speckled trout, and Gila chubs. Trapper James Ohio Pattie in his storied sojourn through the Southwest in 1823 wrote of catching fish in the Gila River near its forks. Pattie remarked that he tossed the fish into an adjacent thermal spring and they would cook in six minutes. Were these Gila trout? Could have been. These now rare trout wouldn't be given a scientific name until 1950.

Native only to the Southwest, Gila trout thrive in an impossible place: a desert where annual rainfall rarely reaches ten inches and rivers routinely go bone dry. It makes its home a mile above sea level in harsh canyons beneath expansive skies.

It's here that U.S. Forest Service forester Aldo Leopold first visited in 1908 and described a pristine landscape. By 1921, overgrazing and prolonged drought devastated the land. The Gila trout were gone—pushed only to the extreme headwaters of the Mogollon Rim that arc through Arizona and New Mexico. Small streams veining off the Blue Range and Black Range held the last vestiges of Gila trout.

In 1924, with Leopold's urging, the Gila Wilderness became the first designated wilderness in the world. One would have thought that designation would have protected Gila trout in perpetuity. However, an onslaught of non-native rainbow trout hybridized all but the last remaining Gila trout.

Early conservation efforts by the New Mexico Department of Game and Fish included hatchery production in the 1920s at Jenks Cabin. But the Gila trout proved difficult to raise in confined environments and the effort was abandoned. Populations continued to hang on, but by a narrow thread.

The New Mexico Department of Game and Fish banned fishing for Gila trout in the 1950s, and by 1966 the Gila trout were designated endangered under the Endangered Species Act. It took forty years of conservation work before the trout were downlisted to threatened in 2006 when the population reached an estimated 37,000 fish. The new designation opened select streams to limited Gila trout angling for the first time in fifty years.

Anglers find the Gila trout a willing participant to almost any offering presented. They inhabit mostly small streams where stealth is imperative. An errant shadow lurking over a likely hole will send these small trout scattering. You'll be hard-pressed to win a distance casting contest in Gila trout country, but creatively threading flies or bait through a tangle of streamside willows onto a glassy pool will often be rewarded.

Gila trout aren't large in the remaining habitat they occupy. Despite decades of conservation work, they remain prisoners of the highest mountain streams from five thousand to ten thousand feet in elevation. Below these highest snow-fed lifelines, rainbow trout wait to court them, washing away a million years of species differentiation by hybridization. Past that, the rivers have already succumbed to the warming climate. Snowpacks have declined precipitously, and summer temperatures push well beyond the sixty-eight degrees that Gila trout prefer. Gila trout mature at three years of age. With unlimited resources and warm overwintering habitat, that fish could reach twenty inches. However, in most cases, a mature Gila trout will be a dainty eight inches. What they lack in size, they make up for in sheer determination.

Nate Wiese, Mora National Fish Hatchery, loads Gila trout destined for Mineral Creek in Gila National Forest. CRAIG SPRINGER, USFWS

Gila trout arrive in an aerated tank at the treetops over Mineral Creek in New Mexico's Gila National Forest. CRAIG SPRINGER, USFWS

Andy Dean, New Mexico Fish and Wildlife Conservation Office biologist, received an aerated tank from a helicopter on the banks of Mineral Creek in New Mexico's Gila National Forest. CRAIG SPRINGER, USFWS

Andy Dean releases Gila trout into Mineral Creek in New Mexico's Gila National Forest. The fish were raised at Mora National Fish Hatchery.
CRAIG SPRINGER, USFWS

Jill Wick, New Mexico Department of Game and Fish biologist, holds a Gila trout delivered to Mineral Creek by helicopter. The fish was raised at Mora National Fish Hatchery. CRAIG SPRINGER, USFWS

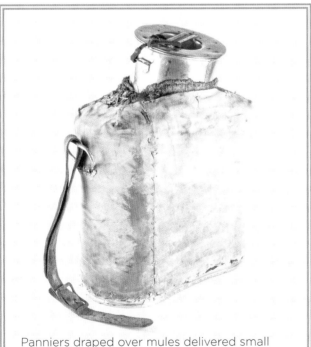

Panniers draped over mules delivered small fish to remote places—and still do—particularly in the restoration work of native trout species in the West. This pannier preserved at the National Fish and Aquatic Conservation Archives carried trout into the Sierra Nevada Mountains, circa 1930. SAM STUCKEL, USFWS

Females will carve redds from the stream beds in April and males will dart in and out for her attention. All of this occurs in water just over ankle deep.

I unzip my sleeping bag as the helicopter prepares for landing and I reflect on this journey. This past spring, I stood over an incubator tray of Gila trout eggs—forty thousand eyeballs staring back at me. Mora National Fish Hatchery experienced a record-breaking spawning season for a fish that has defied the odds.

I've brought five hundred of these fish with me this cold morning. They've grown almost an inch a month in the hatchery with unlimited food and ideal water conditions. I put the five-inch Gila trout on the truck twenty-four hours ago as we waited for everyone to get into place and this helicopter to arrive. The last leg of their journey is a twenty-minute flight into some of the roughest territory of the Gila National Forest.

Our fishery biologists spent half a day on mule and on foot to bushwhack through blow-down and burn scars to the banks of Mineral Creek, where they will receive the trout carefully lowered in a tank of cold water on a longline beneath the pulsing chop of helicopter blades.

—Nathan Wiese

Biologists Andy Dean and Jill Wick deposit Gila trout eggs into a fishless stream in the Gila National Forest. The eggs were fertilized at Mora National Fish Hatchery. ANDREW MILLER, USFWS

Gila trout in Mineral Creek, Gila National Forest. CRAIG SPRINGER, USFWS

Apache Trout

It is summertime in Arizona. Though most minds will conjure images of saguaros and sand, there is a crisp chill in the mountain air. I am at 7,500 feet above sea level—well above the Sonoran Desert where the funky cactuses grow—in the pine-studded White Mountains on the Fort Apache Indian Reservation not too far from the New Mexico state line.

The high-elevation air is thin and clean; it belies the deep, heavy breaths I take as I lug lots of fisheries field gear over downed trees and up the precipices of cascading waterfalls. We find a trail; the elk prints and bear tracks indicate it was made by wildlife, not humans.

I am here with my coworkers from the Arizona Fish and Wildlife Conservation Office, stationed in Whiteriver, Arizona. We are here to perform what may very well be a first—that is, collect and identify trout from a small and noisy silvery brook that is yet unnamed. It is our hope this small piece of water in the remote part of the world holds a pure population of Apache trout, a threatened species.

Despite the gentle beeping of the backpack electrofisher not more than twelve inches from my ears, I barely hear the signal that indicates that it is working. The roar of tumbling whitewater drowns out the high-pitched tone.

In short order, we do not need to hear that battery-powered electrofisher to know that it is working as we wade upstream. The pulsed direct-current passing from two hand-held broomstick-length probes through the water, around boulders, and into the shadow of an undercut bank stirs up fish. A few trout dart out from under a mass of streamside alder roots.

They are stunned for a brief moment, long enough to be held captive by the current that sweeps them into waiting white nylon dip nets. The mild electrical current does not harm them.

The fish recover in a five-gallon bucket of fresh stream water while the survey continues. We progress upstream, teasing more trout from beneath undercuts, from behind boulders, or from the recesses of cobbled thigh-deep pools. With twenty-five small trout ranging up to eight inches long, we pause at a streamside grassy glen. In about an hour's time, we snip off with sharp scissors a tiny piece of tail fin and note each trout's size and weight. The trout go back into the stream. Their fin sections will go to geneticists at the University of Arizona to determine their genetic purity.

All these little trout sure looked like the native Apache trout we were after: embalmed in golden hues, covered with tiny black spots, and with an anal fin tipped in a cottony white. They all sported a distinct black eye-band that gives the appearance of a mask. Nevertheless, even though these fish thrive above a waterfall that likely prevented any non-native fish from making their way upstream, we could not be sure until a laboratory analyzed their genetics. Apache trout readily hybridize with non-native rainbow and cutthroat trout turning out mongrel fishes that are neither species. This propensity to hybridize is partly the reason the rare trout is considered threatened.

Non-native trout arrived in Arizona with the European settlers that began inhabiting the area in the late 1800s. Extensive lumbering and heavy cattle grazing

Jennifer Johnson, Arizona Fish and Wildlife Conservation Office biologist, shocks Apache trout while White Mountain Apache Tribe Game and Fish staff net the fish. RUSS WOOD, USFWS

took a toll on habitats, fouling waters with sediments and destroying cooling streamside shade trees.

The Apache trout went from anonymity, to mistaken identity, to the state fish of Arizona. Fish biologist David Starr Jordan misidentified Apache trout in 1891, calling it a Colorado River cutthroat trout in a U.S. Fish Commission report. Miles of streams vein off the White Mountains into the Black and White rivers that pour eventually into the Salt River.

In 1955, the White Mountain Apache Tribe took unprecedented and prescient action to close angling to all populations of Apache trout on the Fort Apache Indian Reservation. That, in essence, saved the species well before the federal Endangered Species Act passed into law.

In the 1970s, the U.S. Fish and Wildlife Service and the Apache tribe began working in earnest on habitat restoration projects, removing non-native fishes and conducting stream-to-stream transfers of known pure Apache trout populations.

In 1972, the Apache trout was recognized as a distinct species. Its original scientific name, *Salmo apache*, honored its unique locality as well as the first conservators of this rare trout. A year later, the rare trout was placed on the federal endangered species list.

Conservation measures first employed by the White Mountain Apache had paid dividends, and the trout was downlisted to threatened status in 1975 and opened up to angling. Apache trout remains an important sport fish for the tribe, all Arizonans, and native trout aficionados from everywhere. The Apache tribe recognized the unique angling opportunities for a beautiful fish found nowhere else in the world. The tribe established trophy Apache trout fisheries in tribal lakes.

Williams Creek National Fish Hatchery raises and stocks Apache trout into those lakes, as well as into streams on the Fort Apache Indian Reservation. The Arizona Game and Fish Department relies on the federal hatchery as its source of Apache trout eggs which

Russ Wood, Williams Creek National Fish Hatchery biologist, prepares Apache trout milt for freezing and long-term storage.
JENNIFER JOHNSON, USFWS

The label on a tube holding Apache trout sperm indicates that it is to be frozen at Warm Springs Fish Technology Center in Georgia.
JENNIFER JOHNSON, USFWS

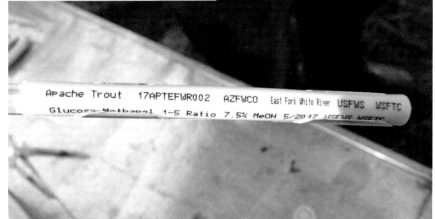

Dr. Wade Wilson, a geneticist at the Southwestern Native Aquatic Resources and Recovery Center in Dexter, New Mexico, guides broodstock management for Apache trout. MANUEL ULIBARRI, USFWS

Apache trout broodstock USFWS MA

make their way as catchable fish into waters on the Apache National Forest.

Conservation is not easy. Or fast. The Second Law of Thermodynamics paraphrased more simply by Czech novelist Ivan Klima, "to destroy is easier than to create," certainly rings true. Yet, despite centuries of a natural cycle of fires, drought, and floods, the ebb and flow of events, and a more recent history of human-caused watershed-altering threats, the Apache trout recovery proceeds apace.

Many months after my group stumbled over the downed timber and surmounted the cascades of the yet unnamed creek that chilly summer day, came a phone call. My colleague and close friend from the Arizona Game and Fish Department said two unforgettable words over the line: "They're pure," she said. Genetic analysis revealed that those trout we caught that day were unadulterated Apache trout. That discovery added one more recovery population to the number needed to achieve eventual delisting.

Though I have left behind the high mountains of eastern Arizona and my work with Apache trout, I remain confident that this yellow trout in the cold green mountains high above the Sonoran will be the first sport fish taken off the endangered species list.

—Jeremy Voeltz

Fish biologist Bradley Clarkson holds a namesake fish: an Apache trout. Clarkson is a member of the White Mountain Apache Tribe and a career biologist at Williams Creek National Fish Hatchery, overseeing Apache trout production at the facility.
CRAIG SPRINGER, USFWS

Bull Trout

To make our way through the complexity surrounding bull trout and the places they occupy is to take a fascinating and revealing journey through the mountains and rivers—and the culture of the Pacific Northwest.

Bull trout inhabit streams and lakes in the northern Rockies that in simple terms exhibit these characteristics: clean, cold, complex, and connected. Bull trout are the native aquatic predators that sit atop the food chain in most headwaters of the Columbia and Klamath River basins, as well as throughout western Canada on both slopes, east and west, of the Continental Divide. Throughout history, the bull trout has often gone by other names, such as salmon trout or Dolly Varden. For most of the twentieth century, the bull trout was underappreciated and oft maligned for its strong predatory nature. Canadian scientist George Colpitts, opining on the lamentable persecution of bull trout in western Alberta in the early 1900s, characterized the fish's perceived failings: "its image as a cowardly and lethargic sport fish, its flesh termed 'insipid,' and its character blighted by a reputation for cannibalism."

Similar persecution of bull trout occurred in much of the Pacific Northwest where bull trout were assailed as undesirables, especially in comparison to Pacific salmon and steelhead. As a result, bull trout were seldom the focus of scholarly or scientific fisheries research until the 1980s. A loosely organized group with which I affiliate calls itself the SCCS, or the "*Salvelinus confluentus* Curiosity Society," playing on the bull trout's scientific name. The one hundred or so scientist-members of SCCS log hundreds of stream miles every year, counting bull trout spawning redds, assessing the quality and quantity of habitat, and scrutinizing population trends with an eye toward recovering their generally diminishing populations.

I began my forty-two-year career as a fish biologist in 1976 in Montana's North Fork Flathead River country, bordering Glacier National Park. I retired in 2018 from my position as bull trout biologist for the U.S. Fish and Wildlife Service in Northwest Montana. As I reflect back on my four-decades-long career, bull trout swim through it all.

As a friend once remarked while we nursed a cold one after completing a long, hard day of climbing over treacherous logs and slipping across boulder gardens adorning a bull trout spawning stream, "It seems bull trout only live in beautiful places."

Perhaps that nugget of wisdom describes why the bull trout, listed as threatened under the Endangered Species Act in 1998, has become my totem animal and somewhat of a poster child for these raw and majestic landscapes of the northern Rockies. The presence of large migratory bull trout—up to the world-record size of thirty-two pounds—stacked up in a pool like churchgoers in pews, indicates that the rivers and lakes are healthy and functioning—that is, good habitats are still connected and the migratory corridors remain passable. Somewhere downstream there is a lake or large river where the bull trout is still dominant.

My favorite fishing philosopher, Dr. Paul Quinnett, in his book *Fishing Lessons* describes the intrinsic value of bull trout. He writes: "Let me note that there is nothing more thrilling than to be fishing some little Cutthroat Creek and have a five- or six- or seven-pound bull trout rush up from the dark bottom of a

Trout from Creston Fish-Cultural Station make their way to Josephine Lake in Glacier National Park. USFWS NFACA

deep pool and grab the ten-inch cutthroat that took your dry fly. A huge bull trout that comes screaming out of the depths to attack a shaker leaves your line slack, your mouth agape, and your heart pounding."

As a scientist, I have compiled a bull trout library that included nearly 1,400 citations of scholarly works and popular literature. Among that literature is Montana author Rick Bass. He lamented in *The Book of Yaak*: "The numbers are important, and yet they are not everything. We seem unable to hold the emotions aroused by numbers for nearly as long as those of images."

I have an ample number of images seared in my mind, but one of my finest days afield was the glorious September day in 2009 that I spent capturing pictures with National Geographic photographer Joel Sartore on Ram Creek in British Columbia. Bull trout gather there after migrating from far downstream in Montana—a running of the bulls, so to speak. As I had done many times before, Joel and I watched silently, enthralled as a female bull trout rolled on her side in less than two feet of clear water and dug into the stones vigorously with her tail. A cloud of milt from a shuddering attendant male enveloped her squirt of golden eggs as they settled into the spaces between clean gravels. Smaller, less dominant males darted upon the scene, trying to pass some of their genes on to the next generation. The ten- or

twelve-pound dominant male rigorously defended his mate, charging like a bull in hot pursuit. All of this Satore captured in living color hundreds of times by the camera shutter. Moving masses of fishes, the hunter-orange flanks and black pelvic fins edged bright white, all flashing in the yellow sunlight dappled by the roughness of riffled water overhead.

Ancient peoples doubtless observed these same scenes and passed what they witnessed by word of mouth, as place names and terms for bull trout live in the ethnography of Native Americans across the Pacific Northwest.

Though not as common as once before, there is good news for bull trout. They have their strongholds. And they have in their favor the law and science and people who care. In 2015, the U.S. Fish and Wildlife Service along with other conservation partners such as Native American tribes and state fish and wildlife agencies, developed plans to recover and delist the bull trout. These plans essentially guide trout biologists to promote cold, clean, complex, and connected habitats that bull trout so need. They include prescriptions for restoring fish passage, conserving and improving cold-water habitat, battling competing and predating non-native aquatic invaders, and, where needed, implementing conservation captive-rearing, which is underway at Creston National Fish Hatchery in Glacier National Park.

Today's Creston National Fish Hatchery raises bull trout for conservation purposes. USFWS NFACA

Milk cans full of trout draped over mules are on their way from Creston Fish-Cultural Station to Gunsight Lake in Glacier National Park. USFWS NFACA

A U.S. Bureau of Fisheries worker sorts trout at Creston Fish-Cultural Station, Montana. USFWS NFACA

Conservation parallels the constraints; the solutions are, by necessity, as varied and complex as the human-caused abuses that contributed to the beautiful fish's decline.

I have confidence that decades from now the largely untarnished cold and crystalline waters necessary to keep the bull trout thriving will largely remain. I see the pristine jewels in the "Crown of the Continent" where bull trout evolved will still sparkle in the eyes of our great-grandchildren. And for me, the bull trout must be there. Bull trout are truly creatures that demand the perpetuation of shimmering snow-capped landscapes—grandiose, wild— with gushing, noisy, icy mountain streams.

—Wade Fredenberg

Bull trout require cold,
clean streams to thrive.
USFWS COURTESY JOEL SATORE

Dewitt Clinton Booth (1868–1938)

A native of New York's Mohawk Valley, Dewitt Clinton Booth was born in 1868. He attended Colgate Academy, today's Colgate University, then earned a wealth of business experience in the Chicago headquarters of a prominent railway system. Booth took an appointment in the U.S. Treasury Department, where in time he was assigned to attend the World's Columbian Exposition with an expansive U.S. Fish Commission display put on by his future colleague James Henshall. It is believed the event turned him toward a career in conservation, inducing Booth to seek and obtain a position in the U.S. Fish Commission—the agency's first civil service employee.

Booth, who insisted on being called "D.C.," landed at Cape Vincent Fish-Cultural Station in New York, where he gained experience with Great Lakes fisheries. He worked for a time with marine fishes of the Atlantic coast at Woods Hole, Massachusetts. He then went from the coast to gelid trout waters ten thousand feet above sea level at the Leadville Fish-Cultural Station in Colorado. At Leadville, Booth learned the vagaries of trout biology in the Rocky Mountains—lessons that served him the rest of his career.

In 1899, D.C. Booth became the youngest superintendent in the U.S. Fish Commission when he was promoted to lead the Spearfish Fish-Cultural Station in South Dakota, nested on the northern edge of the Black Hills near the Wyoming border. Aside from a brief assignment at the Homer Fish-Cultural Station in Minnesota, where the U.S. Bureau of Fisheries built its boats, Booth firmly established his good reputation in Spearfish.

The Spearfish station was located by U.S. Fish Commission biologist Barton Warren Evermann after extensive surveys of water sources and fisheries in the Dakotas and Nebraska. The Spearfish site proved of great utility to establish sport fisheries in the Black Hills of South Dakota and Wyoming, which was largely then void of fish, aside from populations of native chubs and suckers.

Despite challenging and primitive conditions, Booth propagated a variety of species to include brook trout, brown trout, rainbow trout, cutthroat trout, steelhead, lake trout, and landlocked salmon. During his tenure, millions of eyed-eggs and fish were distributed to numerous destinations including Alaska and the British Isles. Under Booth's leadership, the reach of the Spearfish station would eventually grow to encompass a land base that was arguably the largest of any other federal hatchery. Perhaps the most notable was his work in Yellowstone National Park, four hundred miles west of Spearfish. In 1901, with the assistance of four U.S. Army soldiers, Booth investigated the fish culture possibilities at the West Thumb of Yellowstone Lake, which soon became a seasonal egg-collecting station for "black-spotted trout," or what we call today Yellowstone cutthroat trout. The fertilized eggs were incubated in Spearfish, the fry and fingerlings sent away via rail car and stocked where needed.

In a day with few roads and minimal mechanized equipment, overland expeditions to gather fish eggs in the wild were complex and arduous. The journey began in Spearfish via rail, morphing into a wagon train overflowing with specialty equipment to include boats, nets, egg crates, and troughs by the time fishery workers arrived at Yellowstone. To support the endeavor, a hatching building was eventually built on Little Thumb Creek, the first in the history of Yellowstone National Park.

In the development of this fishery, Booth made thirteen annual trips to Yellowstone National Park, spending ten summers there. During that time he harvested, shipped, and stocked millions of eggs from the Yellowstone stocks. Ultimately, Booth's

DEWITT CLINTON BOOTH. USFWS NFACA

The 1899 hatchery building at Spearfish Fish-Cultural Station is today's Hector von Bayer Museum of Fish Culture at D.C. Booth Historic National Fish Hatchery.
COURTESY LES VOORHIS

Constructed in 1905, this Neo-Colonial Revival style home was the living quarters for hatchery superintendents and their families until 1983. Known today as the Booth House, it served as Dewitt Clinton Booth's residence from 1905 to 1933. Appointed with period furnishings and accoutrements, it is a favorite of D.C. Booth visitors.
CRAIG SPRINGER, USFWS

Workers aboard fish cars and at field stations dined on American made U.S. Bureau of Fisheries china. This set is preserved in the National Fish and Aquatic Conservation Archives at D.C. Booth Historic National Fish Hatchery.
APRIL GREGORY, USFWS

Above: Fish Car #3, U.S. Bureau of Fisheries, rests on rails at D.C. Booth Historic National Fish Hatchery and replicates inside and out how the U.S. Fish Commission and later the U.S. Bureau of Fisheries transported fish long distances. USFWS NFACA

Left: Spearfish Fish-Cultural Station on a postcard. The Booth House is on the far left margin. USFWS NFACA

efforts resulted in the world's largest trout egg collecting station creating new fisheries throughout Yellowstone, the United States, and foreign countries, many of which are still enjoyed today.

Booth turned the Spearfish operation, in what originated as a subsidiary to the Leadville Fish-Cultural Station, into a prominent center for federal fisheries conservation. He was the first to experience and solve many problems in early trout cultivation related to disease and nutrition. Although considered stern, Booth was a well-respected leader.

In 1933, after forty years of public service, D.C. Booth retired in Spearfish—in a cabin adjacent to the fish hatchery—where he lived out the rest of his life. He lies at rest on a hill just up from his cabin.

His name lives on. The Spearfish National Fish Hatchery reemerged after a brief closure in the 1980s as the D.C. Booth Historic National Fish Hatchery and with a new mission. Still rearing trout for regional waters, the facility is also the official depository for U.S. Fish and Wildlife Service's fisheries program. With the climate-controlled Arden Trandahl Collection Management Facility, the National Fish and Aquatic Conservation Archives assembles, preserves, protects, interprets, and makes accessible to researchers the history of fish culture, fisheries management, the U.S. Fish Commission,

Above: Spearfish Fish-Cultural Station as it appeared shortly after its opening in 1899. The Arden Trandahl Collection Management Facility of the National Fish and Aquatic Conservation Archives now sits in place of troughs in the foreground. The archives holds 1.8 million objects associated with fisheries conservation. USFWS NFACA

Right: The National Fish and Aquatic Conservation Archives, Spearfish, South Dakota.

SAM STUKEL, USFWS

U.S. Bureau of Fisheries, and the National Fish Hatchery System.

Built in 1905, the original superintendent's home where Dewitt Clinton Booth and his family lived for almost thirty years is refurbished to its earliest years. Known as the Booth House, the residence serves as a preserved example of Neo-Colonial architecture. A popular tourist attraction, 160,000 annual visitors also enjoy the Hector von Bayer Museum of Fish Culture housed in the original 1899 hatchery building.

In 1986, the American Fisheries Society enshrined Booth into the National Fish Culture Hall of Fame. Fittingly, his induction plaque is on display in a replica icehouse on the hatchery grounds which serves as the home of the Hall of Fame and its exhibits. Booth's foresight and contributions remain a legacy in U.S. Fish and Wildlife Service history.

—Carlos R. Martinez

Pacific Salmon

If you've ever felt the tug of a shimmery salmon at the end of your line or in your net, you probably know that the act of catching is just a small piece of something much bigger.

Arguably, the most iconic fishes in the western states and Alaska, salmon have a long history with humans, as food—but so much more. Fishermen and women at sea intercept the five species of Pacific salmon when fresh red fillets underlie chrome-colored skin, and when they return to America's western rivers to spawn. Chinook, coho, sockeye, chum, pink—colloquially known as king—silver, red, dog, and humpy salmon feed our bodies and souls. They call us to our favorite waters with friends and families for the harvest and meals that follow.

Anticipating comradery or perhaps alone time, excited for the trip itself, the drive, or boat ride, the unknown—we talk about the catching, but in reality, it's only a small part of a rich overall experience.

Catching a chrome Chinook or a crimson sockeye inspires introspection and respect for the long journeys between rivers and the high seas that salmon are best known for. All salmon hatch in freshwater. Pinks and chums leave quickly for the sea, while sockeyes and cohos may spend as many as three years in freshwater before making an arduous journey to feed on an ocean buffet of nutrient-rich prey. All return to freshwater only once, putting everything they've got into their return home. Spawning is their final act before death. Their death is life affirming: their bodies bring nutrients to aquatic bugs their young will eat and they fertilize streamside trees that cool the water, and in their own obsolescence create fish habitat when they come to lay in the water. Since the

Native Americans catch migrating salmon at Celilo Falls in the Columbia River on the Washington-Oregon border. Dalles Dam inundated the falls in 1957. USFWS NFACA

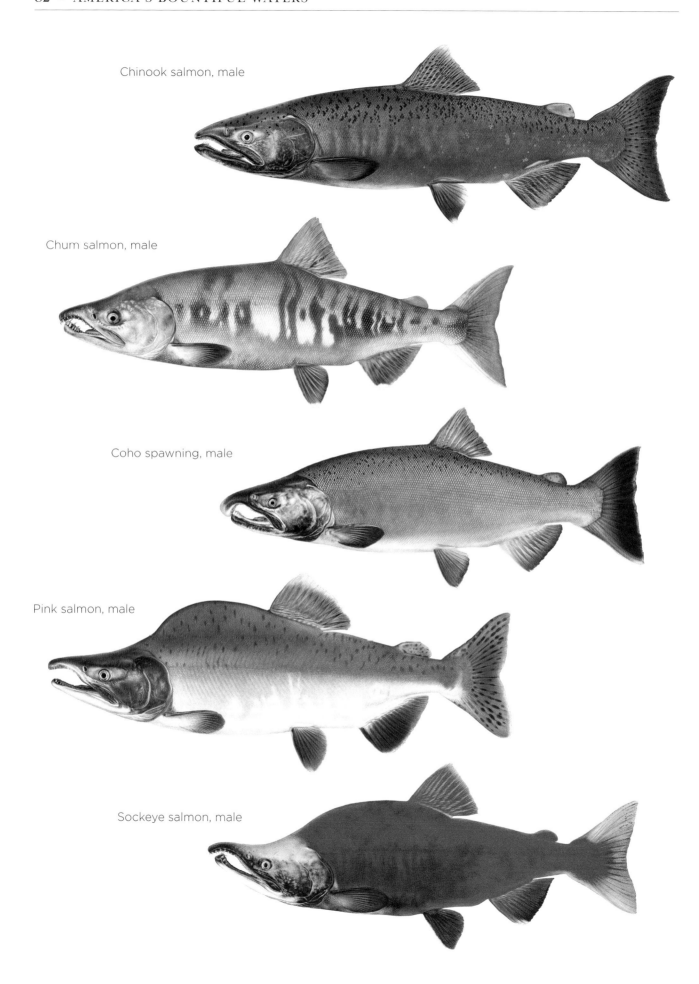

Chinook salmon, male

Chum salmon, male

Coho spawning, male

Pink salmon, male

Sockeye salmon, male

last glaciation, their migrations have marked time like clockwork.

Fishing for food is also life affirming. We may regret the quickly dulling silver sides—a life that began as an egg buried in stones in cold oxygen-rich water ended on our line. A once-living fish is reduced to a fillet on a plate—but not without some work. Filleting a fish is an art in itself that you get better at with time and practice. Chinook salmon weigh fifteen to thirty pounds, sometimes less and sometimes a lot more. The biggest Chinook landed by an angler weighed close to one hundred pounds, pulled from Alaska's Kenai River. Sockeyes are more manageable in the five to eight pound range, pink a little smaller, Coho and chum a little bigger.

Their size depends on genetics and how long they've spent at sea. A large Chinook is likely an old female that has spent four or five years feeding at sea. The bigger they get the better they position themselves to migrate hundreds—and sometimes a thousand-plus miles upstream to their freshwater spawning grounds, attract a healthy mate, and dig a deep redd that can withstand scouring river flows. The smallest species, pink salmon, spends a single year at sea and has a fixed two-year life cycle.

Meal prep and whatever that means for you—inviting friends over, sharing with family or neighbors—everyone and every place have different ways of preparing and sharing the catch. The indigenous peoples of the Pacific Northwest and Alaska have been catching and consuming salmon for thousands of years. Today, the market reach and draw of Pacific salmon are global, with fish harvested from areas such as Alaska's Copper River and Bristol Bay enjoyed by people all around the world. Fishing for wild salmon in Alaska is a bucket list item for many anglers.

Long-term geologic forces, and more recently humans, have shaped the salmon's range and habitats. A lifecycle that depends on free access between freshwater and marine habitats makes Pacific salmon particularly vulnerable to barriers along their migration routes—like dams and too-small culverts

From California to the furthest reaches of Alaska, Pacific salmon make storied migrations to their natal waters to perform a final act—to spawn and die. USFWS MA

Above: Members of the Wintu Tribe drying salmon along the McCloud River near Baird Fish-Cultural Station 1882. USFWS NFACA

Right: An Alaskan Native dries salmon for storage. USFWS MA

Entrance to Baird Fish-Cultural Station circa 1915.
COURTESY SHASTA HISTORICAL SOCIETY

U. S. Fish Hatchery near Redding, Calif.

The U.S. Fish Commission established the first national fish hatchery, Baird Fish-Cultural Station, in 1872 at the urging of Congressman Robert Roosevelt. The station lies in a watery tomb beneath Lake Shasta in northern California. USFWS NFACA

channeling streams under roads. Juveniles have to deal with high and low flows and find places to over-winter. Barriers prevent or delay adult salmon from returning home to spawn.

In the southern parts of their range, like California, Oregon, Idaho, and Washington, dams and other barriers to migration have taken their toll: a number of populations of the five species of Pacific salmon have declined so dramatically they are listed as endangered species. Others have been locally extirpated, their genetic contribution to the overall species permanently lost.

To help compensate for loss of salmon, technical solutions help reduce mortality. Hatcheries take the guesswork out of survival in the early salmon life stages. A number of national fish hatcheries operate in the Pacific Northwest to address depletions in discrete salmon stocks and Fish and Wildlife Conservation Offices address habitat concerns.

The nascent U.S. Fish Commission, a year old in 1872, set up Baird Station in northern California to culture Chinook salmon, fish that were delivered with success and failure, unknowing of potential harmful outcomes. Ahead of his time in advocating

U.S. Bureau of Fisheries posters promoting salmon consumption circa 1920. USFWS NFACA

for salmon habitat conservation, Livingston Stone made a public plea to conserve habitat. President Benjamin Harrison responded and established the Afognak Forest and Fish Culture Reserve in Alaska in 1892, principally for the conservation of sockeye salmon. This salmon refuge returned to Alaska Natives in 1980. The Afognak and Yes Bay

Hatchery workers at Baird Fish-Cultural Station on the McCloud River in northern California. This was the first fisheries facility in what would become the National Fish Hatchery System. Baird Station staff raised Chinook salmon and rainbow trout, led by Deputy Fish Commissioner Livingston Stone. USFWS NFACA

Workers at Baird Station haul in a seine filled with salmon. The apparatus behind the men is a net drying rack. USFWS NFACA

Two Native Alaskans harvest sockeye salmon. USFWS NFACA

Salmon harvested by commercial fishermen destined to market. USFWS MA

A U.S. Bureau of Fisheries flag flies over a doorway on Karluk Lake on today's Kodiak National Wildlife Refuge. Long before the refuge was established, the U.S. Fish Commission and, later, Bureau of Fisheries, conducted salmon research. The O'Malley River, so named by bureau researcher Charles Gilbert, honors U.S. Fish Commissioner Henry O'Malley. USFWS NFACA

Above: Yakama tribal member nets a salmon in the Klickitat River, Washington. RYAN HAGERTY, USFWS

Right: Baker Lake Fish-Cultural Station worker expresses milt from a sockeye salmon. The station opened under the U.S. Fish Commission in 1899. USFWS MA

Fish-Cultural Stations operated in Alaska under the banner of the U.S. Bureau of Fisheries from 1906 to 1933, shuttering as cost-saving measures during the Great Depression.

With hatcheries there are tradeoffs—the inability to replicate a healthy free-flowing river and all the natural selection pressures that keep populations diverse and resilient in the wild. In the southern part of the salmon's range, the U.S. Fish and Wildlife Service operates conservation hatcheries meant to retain wild salmon genetics and conserve habitats. The latter is challenged by costs and scope of wholesale habitat changes wrought by irrigation and hydropower.

Stone was prescient in 1892. Alaska is America's wild salmon stronghold due to large tracts of federal conservation lands, including the sixteen national wildlife refuges managed by the U.S. Fish and Wildlife Service. The Alaska National Interest Lands Conservation Act of 1980 drives salmon

Bonneville Dam on the Columbia River is a significant barrier to fish migrating upstream. This fishway, also known as a fish ladder, allows fish to proceed upstream at an acceptable slope in passible water velocities.
USFWS NFACA

management with two primary goals: safeguard Alaska's exceptional ecological and natural resources for the national public interest and for subsistence use by Alaska Natives.

While no federal fish hatcheries have operated in Alaska since 1933, three field stations dating to the 1970s focus on habitat conservation and the preservation of natural diversity of wild stocks of Pacific salmon.

Biologists at the Kenai, Fairbanks, and Anchorage Fish and Wildlife Conservation Offices inform salmon conservation work on national wildlife refuges from the Arctic to the Aleutians. They collect baseline information on salmon stocks and work with partners to identify and fix barriers that stymie fish passage in the areas of the state where roads crisscross streams. They track trends in salmon populations and timing of migrations, gather basic life history and fish distribution information, and work in the most remote and challenging locales in the U.S.

Based in Anchorage, geneticists at the Conservation Genetics Laboratory use sophisticated laboratory techniques to design and conduct research and provide expertise to address conservation and management issues in Alaska. The lab provides services in Alaska and throughout the U.S. Fish and Wildlife Service, including Fish Technology Centers and the National Fish and Wildlife Forensic Laboratory.

Salmon are more than red fillets under chrome skin. Coiled in the double helix of their DNA is a lexicon—and language of experience and survival—written by a long journey shaped by geology, humans, and many generations of salmon ancestors. For a salmon, the past is a prelude coded for the future.

—Katrina Liebich, Ph.D.

Spring Creek Fish-Cultural Station, Washington, opened in 1901 on the banks of the Columbia River, seen here in a primitive setting. USFWS NFACA

Yes Bay Fish-Cultural Station on McDonald Lake, Alaska, opened in 1906 and shuttered in 1933 as a cost-saving measure during the Great Depression. The staff of the station was steeped in raising sockeye salmon. USFWS NFACA

A U.S. Bureau of Fisheries boat tugs a raft along McDonald Lake at Yes Bay Fish-Cultural Station, Alaska, as fisheries workers pay out a net. USFWS NFACA

Water flow powers this wheel that captures migrating salmon near Spring Creek Fish-Cultural Station, Washington. USFWS NFACA

U.S. Bureau of Fisheries workers at Yes Bay Fish-Cultural Station, Alaska, haul in a seine full of salmon that were concentrated for capture by a weir seen in the distance.

USFWS NFACA

Above: A young boy looks on as biologists at Spring Creek National Fish Hatchery collect eggs from Chinook salmon in 1947. The hatchery continues to raise Chinook salmon for conservation. USFWS NFACA

Right: Salmon eggs collected and fertilized along the shores of McDonald Lake were taken to a hatching house at Yes Bay Fish-Cultural Station, Alaska, where they were incubated and shipped to other stations for eventual stocking or they were released as fry near McDonald Lake. USFWS NFACA

Left: The spouse and children of a U.S. Bureau of Fisheries worker at Yes Bay Fish-Cultural Station, Alaska, enjoy a moment of levity circa 1920. Fisheries workers and their families were often sent to remote locations where they endured privations. USFWS NFACA

Below: Fearnow pails used to haul fish served double-duty as seats during a lunch break at Yes Bay Fish-Cultural Station circa 1920. A narrow gauge tramway on the hillside delivered fish and eggs from the hatching house to be transported elsewhere. USFWS NFACA

Dr. Charles Gilbert (1859–1929)

Anointed with the power of the greatest ocean, Pacific salmon entered nineteenth century national consciousness as fish with star power. They had sustained the Northwest coast Native peoples for centuries; they attracted not only sport fishermen but industrial-strength commercial fisheries, as well. But fish populations are nothing if not dynamic, particularly when modern humans become part of the equation, as exemplified by the twentieth century decline of the same fish in their natal range and their rebirth as an exotic species in the Great Lakes. Magnificent, if meteoric, the Pacific salmon remain one of our most treasured and important families of fish, and what we know about how we might protect them today really begins with Dr. Charles Gilbert.

Born in 1859 in Rockford, Illinois, Gilbert was an ambitious, studious youth. He fell under the spell of a charismatic high school science teacher named David Starr Jordan, who was on his way to becoming the most famous ichthyologist in the country. Gilbert took the same path. He followed Jordan to Butler University, where he completed his B.A. He then followed Jordan to Indiana, where he took his Ph.D. Jordan knew talent when he saw it, and when he became president of a new university in Palo Alto, California, he asked Gilbert to join him. Gilbert chaired the Stanford University zoology department for the next thirty-five years and worked hand in glove with the U.S. Fish Commission and, later, the U.S. Bureau of Fisheries. Today Stanford has a building named in his honor.

With his Fuller-brush mustache and round wireless eyeglasses, the Gilbert in images appears more like a shopkeeper in some dusty, four-corner pharmacy than the brilliant, disciplined scientist that he became. He proved an intrepid traveler and accompanied Jordan throughout North America and Europe, where they mounted an attempt at Matterhorn and Gilbert was laid low by a falling boulder that whacked him in the head. But that only got him started on the multiple journeys in the Pacific in his search to understand Pacific salmon under the auspices of the Fish Commission. He published nearly two hundred studies (many with Jordan). Gilbert's work with salmon and steelhead institutionalized scientific methodologies and their applications to fisheries. He established the line between amateur naturalists and professional biologists. Prior to his work naturalists were the biologists, which led to plenty of data, but excesses of other sorts, not the

Dr. Charles H. Gilbert, third from left, aboard a U.S. Bureau of Fisheries steamer on its way to Alaska in 1921. Ward J. Bower on the far left was the bureau's chief of Alaska fisheries; Dr. Hugh M. Smith, the bureau's commissioner of fisheries; and bureau scientist Henry O'Malley on the right. Gilbert and O'Malley published an extensive report, *Investigation of the Salmon Fisheries of the Yukon River,* in 1921. President Harding named O'Malley U.S. Bureau of Fisheries commissioner the following year. USFWS MA

least of which were fantastic ideas on wild creatures—that crows held court with other crows, that woodcock could splint a broken wing, and so forth. As humorist Ed Zern wrote some sixty years in the future, "fishermen are born honest, but they get over it." Anglers in Gilbert's day could surely hold their own when it came to telling some "stretchers." If there was a field in need of methodology, it was fisheries science.

While at Stanford, Gilbert devoted his life to Pacific salmon. Working first for the British Columbia fisheries, Gilbert pioneered the idea of using scale size to age salmon. From 1917 until 1927 he worked with the U.S. Bureau of Fisheries and used scales to track the different species of Pacific salmon and also developed and tested tagging methods to track migratory patterns. He studied population dynamics and was one of the first to use actual data

to fight against overharvesting—particularly unrestrained commercial catch. In the end, he shaped the way fisheries biologists understood their role as a counterweight to commercial interests.

When we think of scientific heroes, it is easy to go to inventions and who discovers what when, but even more important, at least in terms of fisheries, is who set in place approaches to problems that depend on data. Gilbert is that man. He was fearless, taking on all comers, from commercial interests to flying boulders. To him, it was about the data. By the time he died in 1929, he had trained a cadre of young students who went on to become important scientists. Some call him the father of fisheries biology, because he was the first to put the biology first. Actually, he put it second. Right behind the fish.

—Will Ryan

A 1938 *Progressive Fish Culturist* published by the U.S. Bureau of Fisheries documented early endeavors to stun fish with electricity. The paper sparked interest in future research. Today the method is commonly used from small streams with backpack shockers to big jon boats rigged with booms as illustrated here. These biologists use electricity to stun and catch invasive Asian carp in the Mississippi River basin.
BRETT BILLINGS, USFWS

Hector von Bayer (1844–1926)

Hector Raimund von Bayer was an immigrant, architect, engineer, and career public servant. Born in Baden-Baden, Germany, von Bayer graduated a civil engineer from the Polytechnic School of Karlsruhe—today's Karlsruhe Institute of Technology. During his fifty-three years of federal service, his skills would prove instrumental to numerous agencies on various engineering and surveying projects, serving longest with the U.S. Fish Commission.

Von Bayer started his career in 1867 with the U.S. Lighthouse Board, followed by stints with the Department of the Navy, U.S. Hydrographic Office, and the U.S. Lifesaving Service.

In 1893, Hector von Bayer began his twenty-seven-year course as architect and engineer with the U.S. Fish Commission and subsequent U.S. Bureau of Fisheries. Von Bayer had charge of all the inspections and construction projects associated with federal fisheries stations across the country. He designed and superintended the construction of many of the most prominent fish-cultural stations including but not limited to Manchester, Iowa; San Marcos, Texas; Erwin, Tennessee; Spearfish, South Dakota; Edenton, North Carolina; White Sulphur Springs, West Virginia; Boothbay Harbor, Maine; Tupelo, Mississippi; Beaufort, North Carolina; Louisville, Kentucky, and the laboratory at Beaufort, North Carolina. They all have this in common: practicality with simple elegance emblematic of his time. Von Bayer favored mansard and shingle-style Victorian architecture with refined accouterments pleasing to the eye. Many of his buildings featured a square tower draped with wooden shingles on a gently curved roof topped with a finial.

Von Bayer was also an inventor. He devised the V-trough, a novel method of obtaining the number of eggs in a given lot of eggs—a measurement commonly used in fish culture—by measuring only a few. The device is still widely used today. Von Bayer designed the modified Cail Fishway, keeping construction costs lower than for other fish ladders of the time. He also patented a truss bridge and invented vapor pumps and ice machines. He retired from the U.S. Bureau of Fisheries at age seventy-five.

Outside of work, von Bayer served as president of the German-American Technical Society. He was a member of the Cosmos Club in Washington D.C., founded by John Wesley Powell, which honors those who have "done meritorious original work in science" and are recognized as having creative genius and intellectual distinction. Past members include U.S. presidents and vice presidents, Supreme Court justices, Nobel Prize winners, Pulitzer Prize winners, and recipients of the Presidential Medal of Freedom.

The engineer and architect earned another lasting memorial—the Hector von Bayer Museum of Fish Culture. Housed at the D.C. Booth Historic National Fish Hatchery in Spearfish, South Dakota—formerly the Spearfish National Fish Hatchery—the namesake museum is appropriately housed beneath a shingled roof, square tower, copper finial, and the garlands of the Victorian era architecture that he designed and superintended in 1899.

—Carlos R. Martinez

Architect and inventor Hector von Bayer left his imprint in many buildings that dot the American landscape, including the Manchester Fish-Cultural Station in Iowa. The U.S. Fish Commission established the station in 1897, and the U.S. Fish and Wildlife Service transferred it to the state of Iowa in 1976. USFWS MA

Above: Hector von Bayer's designs are evident in the buildings of today's Erwin National Fish Hatchery in Tennessee. The station is important in brook trout and rainbow trout production. USFWS NFACA

Left: Curtis Vincent, fish culturist at Spearfish National Fish Hatchery, uses a von Bayer V-trough to count fish eggs. USFWS NFACA

Pacific Lamprey

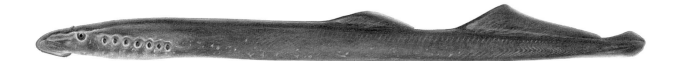

The Pacific lamprey is one among more than three dozen species. Lampreys have been on the earth for approximately 400 million years—200 million years longer than dinosaurs and even longer than trees. They have lived through several mass extinction events, each of which wiped out 80 percent of the earth's other species. Yet the lamprey's body shape has remained almost unchanged as evidenced by a 360-million-year-old lamprey fossil unearthed in South Africa.

The Pacific lamprey is one of several lamprey species native to West Coast streams. Like the salmon and steelhead with which they share habitats, the Pacific lamprey is anadromous—that is they hatch in freshwater, migrate to the Pacific Ocean to mature, and then return to freshwater to spawn and die. Female Pacific lamprey are quite fecund: they can lay up to three hundred thousand eggs in stone nests on the bottom of the stream where oxygen-rich water percolates over them. Those eggs hatch in three weeks and the newly emerged larval lampreys drift downstream on the whim of the current. They settle into slack water and burrow into the silty river bottom where they will stay, buried, for up to seven years or more.

Hidden from view during this time the lampreys are small, brown, and eyeless. They perform an essential service in the life of flowing water—they feed on dead leaves and algae—the earthworms of the underwater world. They provide the same function as earthworms, aerating and cleaning the river bottom and making it healthy for other aquatic species. In addition, larval lampreys are the perfect food for many fishes and birds that frequent Pacific Northwest streams.

As their larval stage ends, a miraculous transformation occurs in the silt. Over the course of several months, the wormlike larval lamprey grows eyeballs and a suckerlike mouth full of teeth that they will use for climbing and eating. The brown lampreys turn silver, leave the confines of the silty slack water and drift with the stream currents downstream. They become parasites and look for their first meal as they migrate to the ocean. Depending on where they were rearing in freshwater, they may travel hundreds of miles to the Pacific Ocean. Pacific lamprey juveniles attach to salmon, pollock, rockfish, sharks, and even whales for a meal.

But good parasites do not kill their host. Pacific lamprey attach for a bit, get some nourishment, and then drop off when they are full. They live in the ocean for about three years and during this time may travel across the entire Pacific Ocean. A Pacific lamprey tagged off the coast of Russia was found swimming up the Columbia River in Oregon.

Pacific lamprey return to a freshwater stream to spawn, but not necessarily to the same stream in which they hatched. They rely heavily on the pheromones, or scent, of young larval lampreys rearing in the silt to locate a suitable spawning stream. They swim upstream and wait a year or more in freshwater before spawning. And this is most remarkable: in all this time they do not eat a thing. But they themselves are eaten. Adult Pacific lamprey are a wonderful high-calorie food for sea lions, sturgeon, birds, and people. A full-grown Pacific lamprey can approach three feet long.

Native Americans have harvested Pacific lamprey for food for thousands of years and place great importance on the fish in their culture and tradition. Tribal elders recall seeing waterfalls covered in lampreys—climbing straight up watery precipices—as they make their upstream migration to their spawning grounds. Reliant as they are on Pacific lamprey for food and tradition, it was natural that Native peoples were first to note that the species seemed to be in decline.

The U.S. Fish and Wildlife Service works with the tribes and our other partners through the Pacific Lamprey Conservation Initiative; we are removing passage barriers, restoring habitat, and returning lampreys to the streams where tribal elders once saw those rocks draped with lampreys.

Pacific lamprey are an amazing fish—among one of the oldest, most enduring creatures on the earth.

—Christina Wang

Brown Trout

Like so many other success stories, the brown trout's began with being at the right place at the right time—in this case, America in the late nineteenth century. Decimated by lumbering and tanning operations and a simultaneous surge in fishing pressure, native brook trout populations were dropping like stock prices during the Panic of '73. The average size was so small that anglers took to "fishing for count," in the saying of the day. Enter *Salmo trutta*.

The brown arrived here thanks to Fred Mather, representative of the U. S. Fish Commission at the 1880 Fish Cultural Exposition in Germany. Baron Lucius von Behr took Mather trout fishing in the Black Forest of Germany, and Mather fell hard for the beautiful brown trout he caught. Mather thought he just might have discovered how to save American trout fishing.

Three years later, Mather received some brown trout eggs from von Behr, who sent him more over the next few years. Mather kept some eggs for his Cold Springs hatchery, gave others to fellow culturist Seth Green, and sent still others to the U.S. Fish Commission hatchery in Northville, Michigan. Some of the latter eggs hatched and on April 11, 1884, approximately five thousand fry found themselves swimming in the Baldwin River, a tributary to the Pere Marquette River. Eight years later, German brown trout had been stocked in thirty-eight states, competing with native brook trout in the East and cutthroats in the West. Within a generation, the newcomers changed what it meant to go trout fishing in America.

The early brown trout eggs included some each from a lake and stream form and were supplemented

Now a city park in a suburb of Detroit, Northville Fish-Cultural Station produced much of the brown trout distributed to points in and beyond Michigan. USFWS NFACA

by eggs from England and Scotland, the latter called "Loch Leven" strain. The mixture helped create the diversity that has allowed the brown trout to be so successful here. Their name "German" brown referred to the origins of von Behr's eggs, and it persisted into the twentieth century until the angling community settled on simply "brown." Three sub-groups are generally thought to be significant: those of rivers (*Salmo trutta fario*); those of lakes (*Salmo trutta lacustrine*); and those that migrate (*Salmo trutta trutta*).

The lake and migratory contributions to the brown trout blend helped the species grow to extraordinary sizes, as reflected in the current North American record of forty-one pounds, eight ounces, which bested the previous record of forty-one pounds, seven ounces. Both of these fish came from Lake Michigan, which somehow seems right, given the original stocking in the Baldwin River. Initially, the Catskill rivers provided most of the brown trout news, influenced no doubt by their proximity to New York City. A young angler named Charles Mullen made the *New York Times* in 1909 for catching the largest trout of the year in the Beaverkill (a five-pounder), with headlines: "Immense Trout Captured by Sixteen-Year-Old Boy." Anglers of the day were used to catching trout of five *inches*, so Mullen most definitely deserved his moment in the sun.

Such a size, however, also aroused suspicions. Before long, the browns came to be considered invaders that preyed on natives, a narrative that fit the larger cultural fear about immigrants, which peaked in these years. "The European variety is Piscivorous, and it preys on the American trout," as one newspaper article put it. A June 1901 article from *The New York Times* concluded that "One such freshwater shark will dominate a pool, and in turn gobble up all the other trout in it, so that when discovered, he is, in one way or another, legally or illegally, 'removed.'"

The larger takeaway was the hardiness of the brown trout. That they grew to such a size meant that they were living long lives. They eluded fishermen. They survived close to urban areas. Sometimes this capacity led to extreme initiatives. At one point brown trout were stocked in the Bronx River, as reported in the April 5, 1935, issue of the *New York Times*. Under the title of "560 trout cast to the Mercy of Bronx Anglers; Brief Tenancy in Borough Waters Predicted." "The State . . . converted the Bronx River into a trout stream yesterday," the article reported.

However temporary such a measure ended up, it did help construct our perception of browns as not only resilient, but influential as well.

The physiological features of the brown explain some of this reputation. Although they do best within the range of fifty-five to sixty degrees, brown trout can tolerate warm waters. They mature later than brook trout and at a larger size and produce more eggs. As biologist Robert Bachman notes, brown trout

Lake Michigan gave up the world-record brown trout of more than forty-one pounds. This pretty brown trout came from the Cumberland River in Kentucky, stocked from nearby Wolf Creek National Fish Hatchery.

BRETT BILLINGS, USFWS

A 1909 postcard of Northville Fish-Cultural Station's hatching house. USFWS NFACA

therefore tend to be less sensitive to spawning failure than do brook trout. They generally become piscivorous at sixteen inches, which allows them to attain great size and to flourish in ponds and lakes. They have an excess of rods in the retinas of their eyes which gives them greater night vision and explains their general preference for dim light. They also orient more to bank cover than do rainbows, for example, which allows them to live in highly pressured environments.

Because of these defining characteristics, the angling community has developed attitudes about fishing for brown trout. Early on, Montana anglers complained about being unable to catch them, and state officials concurred, noting, "The brown is a good fish, but the average angler is not skilled enough to catch it." To which European anglers would have said, "No kidding." As early as 1847, Hewitt Wheatley compared their wariness to "a miser, when his son begins to beat about the bush, introductory to some pecuniary hint." As *Field & Stream* editor Dave Hurteau has observed, "The joys of being tortured by this fish were not widely appreciated by American anglers."

As fishing resources faced growing pressure, the brown's elusiveness became a positive feature, thanks to early twentieth century writers who reframed it as "sporting," and thus worthy of pursuit. As Theodore Gordon wrote shortly before his death, "It is the constant—or inconstant change, the infinite variety in fly fishing that binds us fast. It is impossible to grow weary of a sport that is never the same on any two days of the year." Put another way, thanks to browns, angling for trout became more than packing a milk can with dead fish. "Fishing for count" belonged to the days of buggy whips and buckboards.

Today, brown trout are the most widely distributed and abundant trout in the forty-eight adjacent states. They hold over, they reproduce, and they thrive with our current catch and release in the heavily fished waters of the East; they challenge us beneath big skies of the great western rivers; and they cruise the shorelines and ascend the tributaries of our Great Lakes. Their complexity epitomizes trout (or *trutta*) fishing.

In his book *The Compleat Brown Trout*, Cecil Heacox put it well—with a nod to Winston Churchill—and called the brown "a riddle wrapped in mystery inside an enigma," which should caution against any sort of self-congratulations when we do manage to fool an adult brown trout. Modern trout fishing is about the humility that comes from matching wits with selective trout, no matter the species. If the number of brown trout fishermen wading our rivers is any indication, we have, if nothing else, learned to revel in "the joys of being tortured."

—Will Ryan

Brook Trout

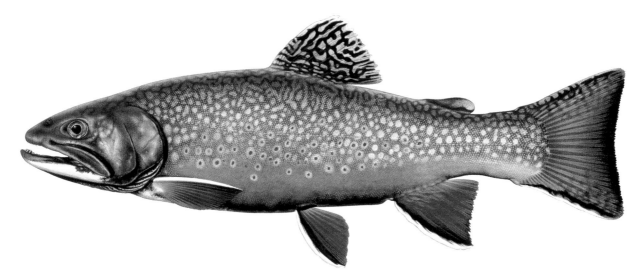

Nine fish paintings laid out in a three-by-three grid adorned my bedroom wall when I was a kid. U.S. Fish and Wildlife Service artist Bob Hines created the art for the Fisheries Centennial proclaimed by President Richard Nixon in 1971, and it was published in the book *Sport Fishing USA*. The paintings released to the public a year later as Wildlife Portrait Series No. 2. The countless times I spent in my room as a young boy, until I left home for college, those paintings transported me to the great outdoors.

Hines's art *moved* me—the smallmouth bass and rock bass lay under a log, the black and white crappies suspended above the weeds, an Arctic grayling leaped from a glassy glide, a northern pike lurked in dark water beneath lilies waiting to catch unsuspecting prey. But his brook trout painting was altogether different—it caught me—and I have had a lifelong personal and professional interest in this species.

The brook trout, large and small, is one of the most beautiful fish in the world. Its dark, olive-green back camouflaged with wormlike vermiculated markings stands in stark contrast to its bright orange belly highlighted by orange fins with bright white edges outlined in black, the sharpest color contrast on a painter's palette. The sides dotted with pale yellow spots on a dark background are sufficiently beautiful on their own, but up close, you see splendid tiny red spots surrounded by bright blue halos. It is transcendent to consider these fine details and causes one to wonder about creation and the nature of our existence.

Perhaps no other fish has so defined fishing in eastern North America and influenced our western cultural interest in angling more than the brook trout.

For more than two hundred and fifty years, the brook trout has been a favorite of anglers and was early on a baseline on which to compare other fishes. Lewis and Clark and the Corps of Discovery, as they proceeded up the Missouri River and into today's Montana, discovered new species of fish, such as bull trout and westslope cutthroat trout. Lewis contrasted them to the "speckled trout in the States." Trout angling as we know it today is rooted in techniques and equipment developed in pursuit of this fish. The pristine, often remote and forested environments in which we seek them naturally leads to a solitary, introspective, and humbling experience seldom known in today's world.

Consider what Robert Roosevelt had to say about brook trout in his 1862 book, *The Game Fish of the Northern States of Ameerica and British Provinces*. "American Trout" is his lead chapter, subtitled "The Brook Trout—the New York Charr—Salmo fontinalis." The man who would author the U.S. Fish Commission for Congress and President Grant six years later devoted a good many pages to describing and praising brook trout in his native New York and beyond. Roosevelt no doubt had an ongoing reverential regard for the fish as expressed in prosaic personification. "He is beautiful as the sunset sky, brave as bravery itself, and is our own home darling. How he flashes upon the sight as he grasps the spurious insect and turns down with a quick little slap of the tail. Who does not love the lovely trout?"

Roosevelt also lamented their diminution in select streams and that speaks to the then rising concern for fisheries conservation. He offered this advice on technique as well as a word of warning. "There is but one mode of taking them—namely, with the fly; although it is said that poachers and pot hunters capture them with worm, minnows, nets and even their own roe. These villainies are not at present punished with death or even imprisonment for life, but our legislature is looking into the matter."

Another New York legislator figures prominently into the brook story.

Dr. Samuel Latham Mitchill of New York was a consummate man of science. He was a medical doctor and the founding editor of the first medical journal in the U.S. He taught college chemistry, agriculture, and natural history at Columbia College and served in the U.S. Senate and House of Representatives. Mitchill was also an ichthyologist. Mitchill penned and self-published the 1814 book, *Report in part of Samuel L. Mitchill, M.D., Professor of Natural History, & etc, on the Fishes of New York*. The brook trout was one of twenty-four fishes from the Empire State that the medical doctor-legislator described for science. His

brook trout, the so-called type specimen, he angled from a Long Island stream.

He named the fish *Salmo fontinalis*, the latter part being most appropriate in that the trout thrives in waters born of cold springs. Long Island streams fit that description in his day. The name translates closely into "little salmon of the springs," so named for its dependence upon clean, cold water seeping through the stream bottom needed for spawning. The springs provide stable temperature and flow for eggs to develop and hatch in an otherwise harsh and variable environment. As such, the brook trout is an indicator of the health and quality of the water in which it lives. A healthy brook trout population indicates clean, cold water and an abundance of healthy shoreline habitat along the stream, pond, or lake.

Owing to their existence in cold, clear unproductive waters, brook trout are not finicky eaters. Their diet includes nearly any organism found in or along the water's edge. This propensity to eat whatever is

A young child tries her hand in the Rapidan River of Virginia. Brook trout lie in wait for bugs—or an angler's fly—to come drifting down a chute of water between boulders. USFWS MA

available is the primary reason the brook trout is a relatively easy quarry for anglers. Brook trout will rise to a dry fly or attack a sinking wooly bugger and readily hit a spinner, plug, or spoon. They have an undeniable attraction to the simplest of live baits.

Native to eastern North America, brook trout historically ranged throughout the Appalachian Mountains from Georgia northward to New England throughout the northernmost reaches of Canada, westward to the shores of Hudson Bay, and southward to the Great Lakes states. As the brook trout's native range has declined due to habitat loss and displacement by introduced species, brook trout have been introduced well outside their native range, sometimes to the detriment of the native fishes in the western U.S.

The brook trout is the only trout native to the streams that fill the Great Lakes. While they do have an affinity for flowing water, a form of brook trout, called "coasters," use the more productive, stable coastlines and embayments of the upper Great Lakes.

This life-history form grows larger and faster than the stream-bound fish, and that may have everything to do with the environment in which they thrive. "Salters" are a form of brook trout that spend a portion of their life in the brackish near-shore north of Cape Cod onward to Labrador. They take on a pronounced silvery sheen but are the same species.

The brook trout is actually no trout at all—it's a char, a close kin to lake trout of the Great Lakes, Arctic char of the North, and the bull trout and Dolly Varden of the West. The family name comes from the Celtic word "charre," meaning blood, owing to the profound hues of red, particularly in the autumn during spawning time. Chars have an inherent need for the coldest water, they spawn in the autumn, and eggs incubate over the winter. Scientists have since changed Mitchill's *Salmo* to *Salvelinus*, the genus of char species.

Lake-dwelling brook trout move up rivulets and rivers to spawn; others may move onto lake shoals.

A creel clerk checks catch information from two brook trout anglers fishing in Shenandoah National Park. Data provided by anglers yields important fishery management information. USFWS MA

Staff at the Lamar Fish-Cultural Station in Pennsylvania raised brook trout in circular ponds. It is today's Northeast Fisheries Center employing geneticists, fish culturists, and fish health biologists who work on brook trout, Atlantic sturgeon, and Atlantic salmon. USFWS MA

Right: President Herbert Hoover enjoyed fishing of all sorts—Yellowstone cutthroat trout in the national park, Lahontan cutthroat trout at Pyramid Lake, and bass and bream from ponds in his natal Midwest. But perhaps his favorite was angling for brook trout in the Rapidan River of Virginia, where this image was taken. Hoover published the book *Fishing for Fun— and to Wash Your Soul* in 1951. COURTESY PRESIDENT HERBERT HOOVER PRESIDENTIAL SITE AND LIBRARY

Females create a fish nest, known as a redd, and drop up to three thousand orange-colored eggs. The fertilized eggs are left to fend for themselves all winter as oxygen-bearing groundwater percolates over the eggs protected in their gravel lairs. The eggs are slow to hatch in the winter waters; they incubate for more than one hundred and twenty days, hatching in early spring. The young soon set about eating plankton and tiny crustaceans in the slow waters of eddies or stream margins, slowed by roots and rocks.

The brook trout has the distinction of being the first fish species spawned in captivity in the U.S. Ohio physician Theodatus Garlick spawned brook trout near his Cleveland home in late 1853. His brook trout emerged in January 1854. Some thirty-five years later and onward, several U.S. Fish Commission and later U.S. Bureau of Fisheries fish-cultural stations operating in a network supplied eggs and small brook trout to other stations and waters over much of the U.S. Fish-cultural stations at Homer, Minnesota, and Northville, Michigan, produced brook trout. Nashua National Fish Hatchery in New Hampshire kept a broodstock known as the St. Croix strain, still used in Wisconsin today.

That network still exists. Fifteen national fish hatcheries produce brook trout today. White Sulphur Springs National Fish Hatchery in West Virginia helps conserve the Appalachian brook trout. Iron River National Fish Hatchery near my home in Wisconsin raises the deep-bodied "coaster" brook trout that rim the edge of Lake Superior and run upstream in autumn when it's time to procreate—colored a palette sure to inspire any painter or poet.

The brook trout in Hines's painting that hung on the wall of my boyhood home may have been a creation of his artistic mind—but then again, the artist was known to sketch from real life. The brook trout that I observe in real life spawning in crystal-clear streams, swimming through habitats restored by the Ashland Fish and Wildlife Conservation Office where I work, lends a strong sense of fulfillment probably not unlike what Hines felt when he finished a painting.

—Henry Quinlan

Nashua National Fish Hatchery in New Hampshire maintained a broodstock of brook trout to restore populations in Wisconsin. USFWS NFACA

Brook trout were raised by staff at St. Johnsbury Fish-Cultural Station in Vermont. USFWS NFACA

Bob Hines (1912–1994)

Robert Warren Hines was the staff artist for the U.S. Fish and Wildlife Service, the only individual in the history of that organization to hold the title of National Wildlife Artist. Bob helped millions of people learn about their natural heritage.

Born and reared in Ohio, the young Bob Hines learned about the natural beauty of his home state as a boy scout. Hunting, fishing, and camping around the Sandusky River near Fremont, he loved the outdoors. After Bob graduated from high school in the shadow of the Great Depression, career options were limited. He taught himself taxidermy, which gave him insight into animal anatomy and motion, and drawing, a pastime he enjoyed. A self-taught artist, in 1939 Hines accepted an offer to join the Ohio Division of Conservation and Natural Resources in Columbus at a salary of $2,200 a year. He composed "Under Ohio Skies," a weekly feature that debuted in 1942 and appeared in some three hundred Ohio newspapers. Each column educated readers about some aspect of outdoor lore, state game laws, or natural history. In time, Hines's talent extended beyond the boundaries of Ohio.

His drawing of redhead ducks became the design for the 1946 Federal Duck Stamp. Through the Outdoor Writer's Association of America (OWAA), a chance encounter with Frank Dufresne lead to Hines's debut as an illustrator of books. Bob's pencil sketches, pen and ink drawings, and full-color plates enliven Dufresne's *Alaska's Animals and Fishes* (1946). Remarkably, Hines was able to accurately portray these subjects well before he was able to visit Alaska and observe them firsthand. That opportunity came in 1947 when he joined Dufresne and other OWAA members on an Alaskan trek. On that trip he fished for cutthroat trout from the shore of Lake Wilson in the Tongass National Forest, observed spawning salmon, and after multiple attempts, fly fished for grayling at the confluence of the Taguish River into Marsh Lake. Bob later wrote, "fishing is like living . . . you have to keep trying."

Dufresne convinced Hines to leave Ohio with an offer to join the U.S. Fish and Wildlife Service in 1948; Dufresne led the agency's information branch. At Fish and Wildlife Bob's artwork gained a platform of national circulation. Hines's first supervisor would be Rachel Carson. Dufresne couched the offer by adding, "You better come because she is something different." Bob's office relationship with

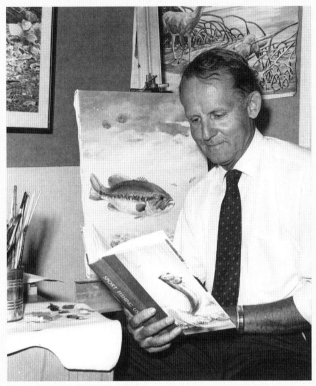

Bob Hines admires *Sport Fishing USA*, published in 1971, the centennial year of the U.S. Fish Commission and its descendant, the U.S. Fish and Wildlife Service. Hines's art appeared throughout the book, including the cover images. USFWS MA

Carson evolved into a loyal friendship and later a productive professional collaboration. His greatest commercial success came with illustrating *The Edge of the Sea*, Carson's final volume in her trilogy of sea books, published in 1955. His last major commission was illustrating a fiftieth anniversary edition of her first book, *Under the Sea-wind*, in 1991.

Already a Federal Duck Stamp artist, Bob was eager to observe and influence the selection process for the annual Duck Stamp design. He shepherded the yearly event for over thirty years, earning the moniker "Mr. Duck Stamp Contest," and introduced a more formal contest with rules, guidelines, and judges. Hines's brainchild, the only federally funded art competition in the U.S., continues to attract high-caliber artists. Revenue from the stamps, purchased by waterfowl hunters, goes with astonishing efficiency to purchase suitable wetland habitats. Most of these lands join the National Wildlife Refuge System. Collectors regularly purchase duck stamps to accompany their art prints, and in so

Brook Trout by Hines SAM STUKEL, USFWS

Golden Trout by Hines SAM STUKEL, USFWS

Arctic Grayling by Hines SAM STUKEL, USFWS

Walleye and White Bass by Hines SAM STUKEL, USFWS

Black and White Crappie by Hines SAM STUKEL, USFWS

Channel Catfish and Bullhead by Hines

SAM STUKEL, USFWS

Redfish by Hines SAM STUKEL, USFWS

Leaping Salmon by Hines SAM STUKEL, USFWS

Rainbow Trout by Hines SAM STUKEL, USFWS

Barracuda by Hines SAM STUKEL, USFWS

doing, become integral partners in the art of con-servation. To quote Hines: "The revenues from the stamp sales are all for the birds—the restoration of waterfowl. It does not matter which one of us, hunter or birdwatcher, will benefit the most. What does concern us is that wildlife artists and techni-cians are using their skills to maintain the high aims of this unique series—to keep the flocks flying. May the artists and the ducks both flourish." More importantly, however, the acquisition of these vital habitats benefits not just waterfowl, but all life that dwell in those areas.

In the mid-1950s, Bob designed the first four U.S. postage stamps that featured American wildlife. The wild turkey stamp, the first in the series, was unveiled at a well-attended event in Fond du Lac, Wisconsin, in May 1956. The pronghorn antelope stamp was released two months later in Gunnison, Colorado. Hines recalled, "At Gunnison, they put me in a rubber boat with the local game protector, and we went floating down the Gunnison River. It is clear and fast, and rocks bulged the bottom of the boat. We caught a few trout but not many." After departing for the National Elk Refuge by way of Denver, he documented "trumpeter swans and sand hill cranes, mule deer and elk, and lotsa trout. We drove to Yellowstone Lake for one day, and I got

tired of catching cutthroat trout." Hines neglected to record an emergency while fishing at Yellowstone Lake—his companions had to remove a hook that had lodged in his scalp while he was casting his fishing line. The Salmon Industry of the Northwest and the Seattle Chamber of Commerce cospon-sored the release of the king salmon stamp later that fall. The fourth stamp, a tricolor depiction of whooping cranes released in 1957, was later named one of the ten best stamps in the world by a British philatelic poll. The press run of some 500 million stamps introduced the word conservation to the general public a decade before it became part of the national lexicon.

At the dawning of a new decade in 1960, the inauguration of youthful President John F. Kennedy ushered in an era of palpable energy and promise. Kennedy and his interior secretary, Arizona Con-gressman Stewart Udall, embarked on an ambitious program of land acquisition for public use. Another emphasis of Udall's tenure was the education of the public regarding the United States' natural heritage. Hines's talents were well suited for the number of high-profile publications that the U.S. Fish and Wildlife Service would release. *Ducks at a Distance* (1963) was conceived as a pocket guide for hunters to identify waterfowl on the wing, sparing those species whose numbers were critically low. The booklet was translated into French and Spanish to aid hunters in both hemispheres of the Americas. According to Hines, *Ducks at a Distance* became "the first best seller that the Department of the Interior ever published in the last forty years." Other notable releases from Hines include *Waterfowl Tomorrow* (1965), *Birds in Our Lives* (1966), *Fifty Birds of Town and City* (1975), and *Migration of Birds* (1979).

Hines had made a splash in 1971 with the release of *Sport Fishing USA*, compiled to acknowledge the centennial of fisheries conservation in the United States. Bob's superiors approved the installation of a large aquarium in Hines's North Penthouse office in the Interior building. Members of the National Aquarium supplied the native fish—rock bass and smallmouth bass, bluegills, and yellow perch, as well as crayfish and an alligator snapping turtle. The antics of these piscine office mates inspired Bob to create illustrations for the book.

He recalled, "Now a lot of people would say drawing a fish is easy. Well, it is if you know what you are drawing. From my way of looking at it, a fish has its own set of muscles and its own way of using them. They use their fins differently each time they want to do something, aggressive or recessive or flying or whatever. You have to show these things if you want to do a good job."

At the time, modern printing techniques allowed more affordable color reproduction. The book featured twenty-two of Hines's color plates of various fish species. The illustrations are remarkable in that they convey the habits as well as the habitats of their respective subjects. The front cover depicts the energy of a leaping bass, mouth agape and gills splayed open as it loses an airborne lure. John Gottschalk, former director of the U.S. Fish and Wildlife Service, respected Bob's talent and wished to promote his artistry. Gottschalk was instrumental in having the beautifully executed fish paintings from *Sport Fishing USA* reproduced into collector's prints. The originals are preserved at the National Fish and Aquatic Conservation Archives.

Bob remained indebted to the Boy Scouts for acting as an anchor during his formative years. He illustrated three merit badge books for the Scouts, one of them *Fishing*.

In 1971, Interior Secretary Rogers C. B. Morton presented Hines the Distinguished Service Award. Included in his citation, Morton elaborated: "Through study and critical self-evaluation, he developed a characteristic style. His paintings became known for their accuracy and correctness. They also became known as works of art. Mr. Hines possesses a remarkable visual perception. He paints wildlife in the act of being alive."

An introspective Hines penned himself fishing. Unpublished.
COURTESY DR. JOHN D. JURIGA

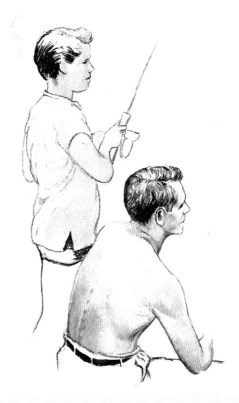

A study of catfish species found in North America drawn by Hines. BRETT BILLINGS, USFWS

APACHE TROUT

Apache trout in pen and ink, drawn by Hines and unpublished. BRETT BILLINGS, USFWS

Hines retired from the U.S. Fish and Wildlife Service in 1981 after a tenure of thirty-two years with the organization. Bob began to capitalize on his former title by signing letters as "National Wildlife Artist, retired."

With the passage of time, Hines's faltering dexterity conspired against him. With a 1989 Christmas card, Bob shared, "My own [career] is winding down—but it is not dead. Main problem is arthritis, which puts a crimp on a guy's enthusiasm." He then revealed, "No hunting—I take so many pratfalls (arthritis again) that I'd endanger everyone, even if the gun would be on safe. But fishing—Ah! I can sit on my duff and haul in bluegills and bass, and enjoy, which is what I did."

After years of failing health, Bob Hines died at eighty-two years of age in 1994. He left behind an incredible body of work, a visual legacy that allows us to connect with the natural world that Hines understood and cherished.

—John D. Juriga, M.D.

Bob Hines was most comfortable in and around water or at an easel holding a painter's palette. This photo was taken in Florida in 1957. USFWS MA

Rainbow Trout

It's June 1961, and I am a young man standing at the outlet of Lake Iliamna, in southwestern Alaska. My focus is entirely on the eight-pound test leader where it disappeared into the crystalline waters of the Kvichak River.

The line drifted with the current, then hesitated. Instinctively, I sharply lifted the rod tip and twenty-five feet away a monster rainbow trout three times broke the river surface, each time arcing like a dolphin. Its pectoral fins clearly laid back against the massive body at each breach. Its bright red two-inch-wide stripe from tail to gill cover showed clearly in the cloud-filtered sunlight as the fish headed downstream toward Bristol Bay.

The rainbow trout's heft was too great for the fly rod. The tip broke. The line tightened and snapped and went limp, as my outfit was no match for the muscular fish that moved with determination. And there I stood—dumbfounded and alone in stunned silence—more than two thousand miles from home.

While I would have enjoyed netting that fish, I can see now through the lens of sixty years that encountering that massive trout was a good omen. Rainbow trout would come to figure prominently in my long career as a fish biologist with the U.S. Fish and Wildlife Service.

Rainbow trout were described for science by a German medical doctor via an expedition through Russian waters tributary to the cold, north Pacific Ocean. Johann Julius Walbaum described the fish in 1792 from trout taken near the Kamchatka Peninsula of Siberia. Native rainbow trout rimmed the Pacific from that point, through coastal Alaska and

The U.S. Fish and Wildlife Service has produced rainbow trout from its inception as the U.S. Fish Commission 150 years ago. The fish is ideal for put-and-take seasonal fisheries or for the waters flowing from cold releases below reservoirs. It is native only to Pacific coast streams and there the agency strives to conserve its habitat and natural reproduction. USFWS MA

southward to Mexico. Rainbows have close kin in distinct species or subspecies in North American waters flowing toward the Pacific: the Kamloops of Canada; the redband in the interior western U.S.; the Mexican golden trout, Gila trout, and Apache trout in the Southwest as well as golden trout of California. All of them descend from, or are related to, rainbow trout.

Rainbow trout further exhibit their complexity by existing in two forms: one living entirely in freshwater, the other, the steelhead, which spends part of its life cycle in the Pacific Ocean or in the Great Lakes where it was introduced.

A year after my encounter with the hulking Alaskan rainbow trout, I landed at my first permanent duty station with the Fish and Wildlife Service, at Gavins Point National Fish Hatchery in South Dakota. It was one of my charges as a trainee to produce rainbow trout for stocking into suitable cold farm ponds.

I witnessed firsthand the positive results of these introductions. Planted rainbows survived for a few years and provided excellent fishing as evidenced by the stories about the sizzling runs and tail-walking antics of those crazy rainbow trout. There was no shortage of stories about "the big one that got away," which I always took as a proxy measure of success of our work. Farm ponds controlled erosion and yielded habitat not only for fish and for anglers, but songbirds and amphibians and waterfowl and a host of other wildlife.

In 1968, my work took me to Manchester National Fish Hatchery in Iowa. It was there that I waded into managing broodstocks, which I found rewarding and fulfilling. We produced more than two million rainbow trout eggs each year. We hatched, raised, and stocked rainbow trout in Iowa or in neighboring states. But a large number of fertilized eggs went to other state or federal hatcheries, the fish to be stocked in select waters.

My family and I transferred in 1973 to Ennis National Fish Hatchery in Montana, near the fabled Madison River. It was a new start for me, and a new start of the old facility, fed by reliable cold spring water quite suitable for raising trout. I remained there for nearly thirty years.

We carefully managed the rainbow trout stocks to produce fish for various management purposes. The captive rainbow trout broodstocks were managed at the genetic level at the direction of U.S. Fish and Wildlife Service fish geneticists Ray Simons and Harold Kincaid. The two were stationed at our Fish Genetics Laboratory in Beulah, Wyoming, on the state line. The research lab was an adjunct to

Staff Sergeant Roosevelt Nelson, U.S. Army, caught these rainbow trout while on leave from Ft. Benning, Georgia, in 1964. Rainbow trout from national fish hatcheries still go into military waters for the benefit of men and women in the armed services. USFWS MA

the nearby Spearfish National Fish Hatchery in South Dakota.

The six strains of rainbow trout allowed us to produce rainbow trout eggs throughout much of the year. Their attributes were so different from each other that it was hard to visualize they all came from a mixed broodstock of coastal rainbow trout and interior redband rainbows originating in California one hundred years earlier.

Through the 1990s, Ennis National Fish Hatchery produced more than 20 million trout eggs each year. The eggs made their way to points well beyond Montana. These trout eggs were incubated at many national fish hatcheries or hatcheries operated by

A nice mixed bag of rainbow and brown trout caught from the White River in Arkansas. The fish came from Greers Ferry National Fish Hatchery. USFWS MA

Rainbow trout caught on a fly rod is great sport. USFWS MA

Ennis Fish-Cultural Station is one of many federal fisheries facilities built during the Great Depression. Ennis National Fish Hatchery remains today an important rainbow trout broodstock hatchery, supplying fertilized eggs to state, tribal, and other federal hatcheries around the country. USFWS NFACA

Erwin Fish-Cultural Station, established in 1897 in Tennessee, is a rainbow trout broodstock hatchery, among the oldest in the country. USFWS NFACA

The eyes are the first visual indications that rainbow trout eggs are viable and growing.
DOUG CANFIELD, USFWS

A biologist at Norfork National Fish Hatchery in Arkansas checks a rainbow trout for maturity. The tailwater fisheries of northern Arkansas provide superb habitats for put-and-grow rainbow trout fisheries. USFWS MA

state fish and game agencies, some of which were the most unlikely of places, such as the sultry Southeast.

Rainbow trout swim in waters from the East Coast to west, over the interior, where there is at least cold water over winter. Tailwater fisheries are usually synonymous with rainbow trout in nearly every part of the country. Rainbows were the perfect fish to occupy the modified habitats made by Tennessee Valley Authority or Army Corps flood control or hydropower dams where water releases created cold-water fisheries out of what had been smallmouth bass and bream and sucker habitats. These waters provide excellent trout fishing and are a boon to local economies.

Because rainbow trout have been cultured for so long, the "how-to" is well known. Refined, even. And that refinement has lent itself to other fish species in dire need of captive culturing for conservation, such as Apache trout and Gila trout, or the leviathan Lahontan cutthroat trout. Rainbow trout culture has led to an advancement of our knowledge

Rainbow trout raised in captivity provide ample research opportunities. Fish biologist Kevin Kapperman at Bozeman Fish Technology Center collects data on a rainbow trout's response to various flow velocities. The information is essential in engineering fish passage structures. RYAN HAGERTY, USFWS

of therapeutics and pharmaceuticals for fish. The species has been the subject of research at the U.S. Fish and Wildlife Service's Aquatic Animal Drug Approval Partnership attached to Bozeman National Fish Hatchery in Montana. In the end, that has benefitted aquaculture for conservation and commerce.

Much has been learned about rainbow trout and fisheries conservation since the inception of the U.S. Fish Commission in 1871. Rainbow trout was among the first species cultured in captivity by the commission at Baird Station on the McCloud River in California. The Unitarian-minister-turned-fish-culturist Livingston Stone led the endeavor in the late 1870s. But he was not the first to try; he was preceded by an endeavor to raise rainbow trout in captivity in the basement of the San Francisco City Hall in 1870 by the California Acclimatization Society.

The U.S. Fish Commission, followed by the U.S. Bureau of Fisheries, would eventually be all in for rainbow trout. McCloud River rainbow trout eggs made their way to fish-cultural stations at Northville, Michigan; Homer, Minnesota; and Wytheville, Virginia. Others would follow over the years, eventually to include Manchester and Ennis. Rainbow trout have been stocked in forty-five countries on every continent except Antarctica. That has produced tremendous fisheries where none had occurred, and unfortunately rainbow trout has outcompeted or hybridized with native species, creating other conservation challenges.

Outwitting fish with a fly or bait or spinner in a pretty setting—be it in an urban pond in Phoenix, an emerald lake on the shortgrass prairie, a dam tailwater in Arkansas, or a pristine Alaskan river—all of them have their merits in human experience. All of them are places to make memories and can make conservationists out of anglers. A rainbow trout that I *did not* catch still swims in the rivers of memory.

—Wes Orr

U.S.F.C. *Curlew* circa 1902 USFWS NFACA

Carl Anderson died young, leaving behind his widowed mother, anguished, having already lost her two younger boys. This stone stands at Oakland Cemetery, Manchester, Iowa. Anderson died from a ten-month-long "insidious disease . . . peculiar and bafflingly." He worked at Manchester Fish Cultural-Station and on the U.S.F.C. *Curlew*, a steamer on the upper Mississippi River, where he rescued sport fish from isolated floodwaters. Anderson's obit speaks to his notable devotion to conservation. "Socially and officially he was held in the highest esteem by those with whom he associated, and by his death the Bureau of Fisheries has lost a superior man and his coworkers a never failing friend." USFWS NFACA

Livingston Stone (1836–1913)

Livingston Stone was born in Massachusetts in 1836, graduated from Harvard College in 1857, and subsequently entered Meadville Theological School where he was ordained a Unitarian minister.

Reverend Livingston Stone pastored at South Parish Church in Charleston, New Hampshire, a mere four city blocks from the banks of the Connecticut River. Perhaps the allure of flowing water was too strong. Stone resigned his clerical duties in 1866 and began a career in fisheries conservation where he became a respected authority. He helped draft the constitution of the American Fish Culturists Association, created fifty days before Congress created the U.S. Fish Commission in February 1871. Stone served the association as its first secretary. It rebranded as the American Fisheries Society in 1884 and remains the longest-serving professional society of its type.

In 1872, Stone was named U.S. Deputy Commissioner of Fisheries, a role he would hold for twenty-five years. In an attempt to mitigate for the depletion of Atlantic salmon in New England, Spencer Baird, U.S. Commissioner of Fisheries, instructed Stone to obtain a supply of Chinook salmon eggs from the Pacific coast. Despite countless hardships and difficulties that would test the mettle of any man, Stone succeeded in establishing the nation's first federal hatchery—marking the birth of the National Fish Hatchery System. Stone established Baird Station at the remote junction of the McCloud and Pit rivers in northern California. The hatchery would play an important role in fisheries history.

A year later, Baird tasked Stone to deliver fish across the continent via a retrofitted "aquarium" rail car supplied by the California Fish Commission. He shepherded a number of black bass, catfish, yellow perch, hornpouts, tautog, striped bass, eels, lobsters, oysters, and American shad, intending to stock them in West Coast waters. But that was not to be. The shipment met with disaster, derailing over the Elkhorn River in Nebraska.

Stone recounted how he cheated death: "We were, every one of us, at once wedged in by the heavy weights upon us, so that we could not move or stir. A moment after, the car began to fill rapidly with water. The heavy weights upon us began to loosen, and, in some unaccountable way, we were washed out into the river."

Three men died. The fate of the freshwater fish is unknown. Not deterred, Stone a year later delivered thirty-five thousand American shad to the Sacramento River—a fishery that now stretches along the West Coast from California to Alaska. But that's not all. Some years later, Stone delivered American shad where the Rhine River meets the North Sea.

Fish health intrigued Stone; he described at least twenty diseases and educated others on the practices to control them. He published *Domesticated Trout: How to Breed and Grow Them* in 1872, which was widely advertised in the U.S. and Europe. A second book followed, *The Artificial Propagation of Salmon on the Pacific Coast of the United States*.

In 1897, Stone relocated from California closer to home in New York where the St. Lawrence River feeds Lake Ontario. The U.S. Fish Commission planted Cape Vincent Fish-Cultural Station to raise lake trout, whitefish, brook trout, walleye, and landlocked salmon. Stone was in charge.

In 1905 alone, the station produced 28 million fish. Working at Cape Vincent for almost a decade,

Above: Livingston Stone, a fish culturist and ordained minister, evangelized for a refuge for salmon. President Harrison created the Afognak Forest and Fish Culture Reserve in 1892. Stone died twenty-one years later to the day. COURTESY SHASTA HISTORICAL SOCIETY

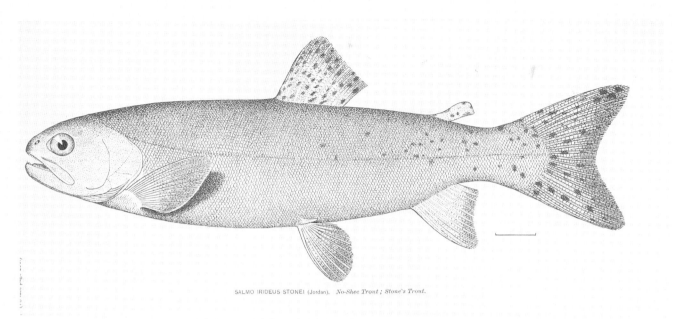

SALMO IRIDEUS STONEI (Jordan). *No-Shee Trout ; Stone's Trout.*

David Starr Jordan described a new species, Stone's trout, from the upper reaches of California's Sacramento River and named it in honor of the Deputy U.S. Fish Commissioner Livingston Stone. The scientific name translates as follows: Salmo = of the trout and salmon genus; irideus = tribute to Iris, goddess of the rainbow; and stonei, for the man. It has since been reclassified as a rainbow trout. USFWS NFACA

Livingston Stone published *Domesticated Trout* early in his tenure with the U.S. Fish Commission. This copy resides in the National Fish and Aquatic Conservation Archives. CRAIG SPRINGER, USFWS

UNITED STATES FISH HATCHERY, CAPE VINCENT, N. Y.

E-4149

Cape Vincent Fish-Cultural Station where Stone spent the last decade of his career. USFWS NFACA

his expertise and influence were felt on numerous fisheries and at fish hatcheries throughout the Northeast. The Cape Vincent station is now the Cape Vincent Fisheries Station and Aquarium, where its iconic four-story building still stands.

Stone was instrumental in creating the first federal refuge. In the August 1892 issue of *American Angler*, Stone wrote: "Let us now, at the eleventh hour, take pity on our long persecuted salmon and do him the poor and tardy justice of giving him, in our broad land that he has done so much for, one place where he can come and go unmolested and where he can rest in safety." President Benjamin Harrison took heed; he created the Afognak Forest and Fish-Culture Reserve for Pacific salmon conservation on Christmas Eve that year.

From preacher to conservationist, Livingston Stone, forever known for his pioneering and

innovative work, received several honors during his career. At the 1880 Berlin World's Fair he received a gold medal for inventions in fish culture; at the 1883 London Fishery Exhibition he was presented with a diploma from the Prince of Wales; he was awarded a bronze medal by the Society d'Acclimatization in Paris; and declined the position of the U.S. Commissioner of Fisheries. He died on the twenty-first birthday of his Afognak salmon refuge.

In 1989, the American Fisheries Society enshrined Stone in the National Fish Culture Hall of Fame. Baird Station lies entombed beneath Lake Shasta. In 1997, the U.S. Fish and Wildlife Service named Livingston Stone National Fish Hatchery in his honor, and its charge: conserve endangered winter Chinook salmon from the Sacramento River.

—Carlos R. Martinez

Steelhead

Several sport fish species have dedicated fanbases, but few are as avid as steelhead anglers. Whether trolling on the big water, casting from piers or breakwalls, river drift-boat fishing, or wetting artificial flies when the run is on, steelheaders spread the word through the countryside, in winter or summer, "The steelhead are coming."

Do an Internet search for "Steelheader Newsletters" and you will see what I mean.

Why all the fuss? Steelhead differ from their near identical twins the rainbow trout in behavior only. Rainbow trout live their entire lives in streams and lakes, while steelhead live and grow as adults in the big water, the Pacific Ocean or any one of the Great Lakes where they have been introduced, and return to their native streams to spawn.

Big and colorful, powerful swimmers, prolific jumpers, and of larger size due to a life in ocean or in a lake, steelhead can be challenging to hook and land. It is no wonder they attract a fervent following. Simply put, these fish are magnificent.

Steelhead, native to the West Coast rivers of the United States from California to Alaska, were introduced to my backyard of the Great Lakes many years ago. Early stocking records indicate steelhead were introduced in Great Lakes tributaries as early as 1876, coming from the first field station of the U.S. Fish Commission, the Baird Fish-Cultural Station on California's McCloud River. Steelhead were for a time raised at Michigan's Northville Fish-Cultural Station. Conservation and stocking efforts continue to this day on the West Coast and in the Great Lakes, and steelhead remain both an economically and culturally important species across the United States. The U.S. Fish and Wildlife Service's national fish hatcheries as well as its fish and wildlife conservation offices, intensively manage distinct stocks of steelhead, some of which are protected under the Endangered Species Act, on the West Coast. In the Great Lakes where steelhead have long acclimated, they are sought for sport.

I first encountered steelhead in Michigan in 1995 while conducting my graduate research. I spent three glorious years chasing juvenile steelhead around large rivers in the lower peninsula of Michigan trying to document the scale of natural production and the effects of habitat alteration on them. Steelhead, like Pacific salmon brought to the Great Lakes, are stocked annually by state fish and game agencies, but many have questioned their ability to successfully spawn with no access to the oceans. Several other scientists had also studied natural steelhead production in the Midwest, and all studies showed that reproduction occurred. The big questions at the time were: how much does habitat fragmentation and hydropower dam operation impact juvenile steelhead survival, and can changes in these factors positively affect steelhead?

In short, yes, more natural production than imagined occurred in some streams, and yes, subtle tweaks to habitat management can reap big dividends for steelhead. Incidentally, these same issues are being grappled with in the Pacific Northwest, homeland of steelhead.

I still remember the thousands of juvenile steelhead I encountered, the long summers in sweat-filled

Biologists at Winthrop National Fish Hatchery, Washington, caught this wild steelhead in the Methow River to bolster the station's brood stock. MICHAEL HUMLING, USFWS

waders dragging stream electrofishing units through cold, clear Michigan trout streams, the wintertime trips in gale force wind–driven blizzards, and all the fellow students, management agency colleagues, and professors who made that work possible. I was able to sneak in many mornings or evenings fly-fishing for steelhead in the Manistee and Little Manistee rivers, and in those quiet moments I connected with generations of anglers who came before me.

The one overarching lesson I still carry from this work twenty-five years later is this: if we can maintain an environment where steelhead do well in the wild, then we shall have created a better, healthier environment for the people of the United States. This lesson is an intrinsic part of the U.S. Fish and Wildlife Service mission.

The benefit to Great Lakes anglers is self-evident. When the word gets out that steelhead are on the move, in streams from New York's Niagara to Minnesota's Temperance River, anglers in waders or standing in drift boats toss flies and spinners in slackwater pools at steel-colored ten-pound trout facing into the current. Releasing a heavy-shouldered steelhead as long as your arm is an unforgettable moment—rewarding for the angler and for the conservationist.

—Aaron Woldt

An Ohio angler admires a river-run steelhead fresh from Lake Erie. CHIP GROSS

Lake Trout

It's mid-October on Lake Superior; I leave my home and take in the crisp early morning air, careful not to slip on the ice that formed on the steps overnight. I look out to the east and see an intense red sunrise behind Madeline Island. Five blocks away, a U.S. Fish and Wildlife Service research vessel, the R/V *Siscowet*, waits my arrival for another day of netting lake trout. Lake trout are fall spawners and have met to procreate on offshore reefs for more than ten thousand years. The foreboding morning sky and the swift breeze pasting the harbor flag against the gray clouds promise a rough ride as we steam to the nets twenty miles away.

In this lakeside town I now call home, lake trout has been the fortune and misfortune of many generations of Native American and later European immigrant families who fished for subsistence and profit. The once-abundant populations fell hard, ravaged by overfishing and predation by non-native sea lamprey that bypassed Niagara Falls and invaded the Great Lakes via the Welland Canal. The U.S. Bureau of Fisheries and the states rimming the Great Lakes had ardent interests in lake trout conservation dating to the 1910s. The Bureau's fish-cultural stations at Cape Vincent, New York; Put-in-Bay, Ohio; Charlevoix, Northville, and Alpena, Michigan; and Duluth, Minnesota, took on lake trout eggs numbering in the millions on a yearly basis for decades. Those federal stations have long since closed or transferred to the states.

In the 1950s an international treaty and congressional acts tasked the U.S. Fish and Wildlife Service with controlling sea lamprey and building new hatcheries across the Great Lakes to restore this fish to its

former glory. Modern national fish hatcheries at Pendills Creek, Sullivan Creek, and Jordan River in Michigan, as well as at Iron River, Wisconsin, and Allegheny, Pennsylvania, have raised millions of lake trout each year to restock all five Great Lakes. This task of native species restoration seemed simple at first, until you realize the vastness of the five Great Lakes are inland seas of cold, deep blue water. Improving the lot of lake trout is the largest fish restoration effort of its kind in the world. I hired on as a new biologist in my early thirties to help evaluate the success or failure of lake trout restoration—a simple endeavor that has become the mission of my thirty-three-year career.

Two hours have passed during which some of us nap, lulled by the sounds of the ship's engine. The aroma of strong coffee in the galley mixed with diesel fumes and cigarette smoke wafts in from the back deck. We approach the buoys that mark our gill nets set on the reef. The lake is gray, alive, churning cold by the wind blowing from the northwest—all less than welcome conditions on the largest lake in the world. The crew are well-seasoned commercial fishermen in their former days. Captain Ed Nourse yells to all, "If the sea and this boat let me grab ahold of that buoy, we are lifting these nets." We all get into position and hang on tight. The hydraulic net lifter begins to clamp onto the "float" and "lead" lines of the gill net and reels it onboard. We all wait in anticipation as the overnight catch is revealed in the light of day from the depths of the gray-green water.

In an instant, many large beautiful adult lake trout are alive; they flail and kick on the picking table, and we begin to wrestle muscular lakers, some of them up

Lake trout naturally occur in a great diversity of color and shape. This diversity was commonplace in the Great Lakes before overfishing and sea lamprey predation. CHARLES BRONTE, USFWS

to twenty-five pounds, out of the net and into waiting live-tanks. I move to the processing table, grab one fish after another shouting out information to be recorded: lengths, weights, sex, spawning condition—some of the stuff biologists need to measure progress in fisheries management. This goes on for five hours without a break.

Five nets and more than three hundred fish later we assess our catch. Lots of old, large fish—a good sign. Many fish miss fins that were clipped off in the hatchery prior to stocking to distinguish them from those fish with all their fins intact—the wild ones. Those are the ones produced in the lake—the object and goal of our work.

As the years pass, I see the numbers of these wild fish increase year by year—convincing evidence that three decades of conservation is working.

Historically the Great Lakes contained the largest lake trout populations and fisheries in the world. There were many different types of lake trout that lived in specific locations and depths of the lakes: some fat, some thin and long, some with large heads and some with small ones, some with big long fins, some very beautiful in their form, and others less attractive. They go by local names like mackinaw, redfins, paper bellies, siscowets, and humpers. Their diversity rivals that of most other fishes in the world. Some spawn in rivers and some on deep offshore

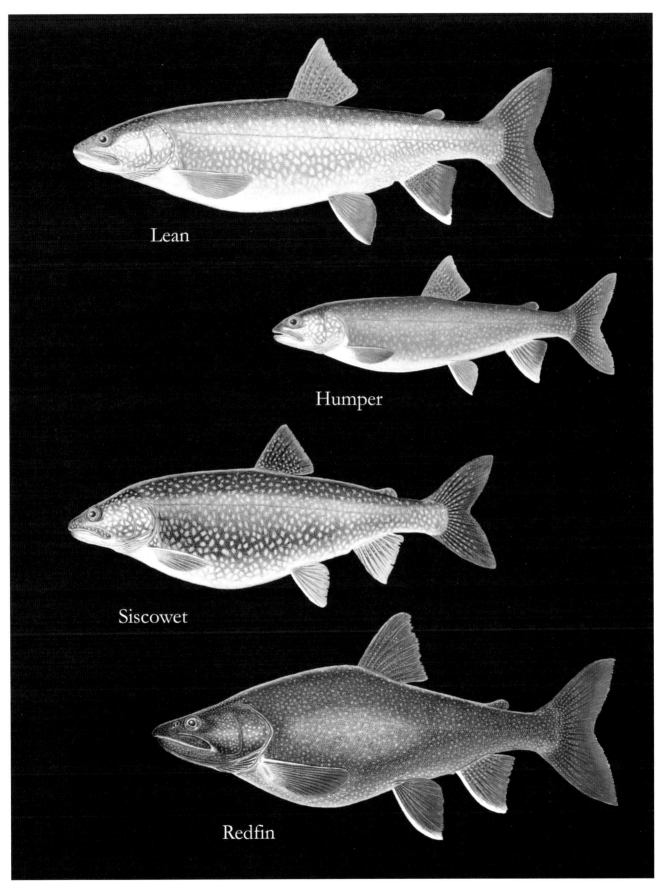

Lean

Humper

Siscowet

Redfin

Lake trout exist in Lake Superior in four subspecies. Many others existed but have been lost to overfishing and predation by sea lamprey. CHARLES BRONTE, USFWS

Fish biologist Mark Holley, Green Bay Fish and Wildlife Conservation Office, handles a recently netted lake trout aboard the R/V *Stanford H. Smith*. The fish was captured as part of a long-running assessment of lake trout in the Great Lakes. USFWS

reefs at more than two hundred and fifty feet below the surface, returning to these same sites year after year. Others like the siscowet spawn in even deeper water and we are just learning about their habitat preferences. While most lake trout spawn in October and November, I have seen others in spawning condition in April, June, and August.

Lake trout eat mostly fish, but they also consume everything from tiny plankton to insects, birds, and mice that land on the water—and even one another. They are truly a fish that is adaptable to changing food supplies. These fish can get big, commonly more than thirty pounds. When not fished too hard, they

can live well over forty years. The rare fish exceeds one hundred pounds.

Another October peels off the calendar with more forays offshore. I am fortunate to join a long list of U.S. Fish and Wildlife Service biologists reaching back to the 1920s, the likes of John Van Oosten, Ralph Hile, Paul Eschemeyer, Richard Pycha, and Louella Cable—our agency's first female scientist—but not as their peer. I'm one of many who share the passion of studying this amazing fish and helping to restore its place in the fish community of the Great Lakes.

—Charles "Chuck" Bronte

A Jordan River National Fish Hatchery biologist removes dead lake trout eggs from trays in this 1967 image when the station was only four years old. Lake trout remain a beneficiary of work at the hatchery today. The station's workers also raise cisco for stocking in Lake Huron and brook trout, grown to larger sizes and used for youth education programs—and for anglers. USFWS NFACA

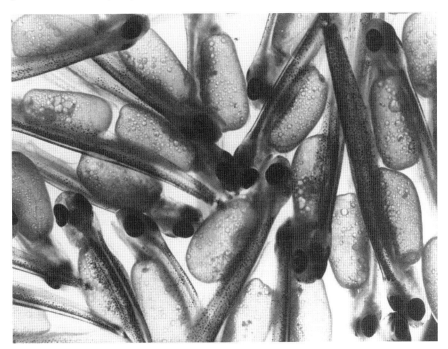

Lake trout sac fry taken at Jordan River National Fish Hatchery in 1964. USFWS NFACA

Duluth Fish-Cultural Station in Minnesota, which opened in 1889, raised lake trout and other Great Lakes species until its closure in 1947. USFWS NFACA

The M/V *Spencer F. Baird* commissioned in 2006 is a state-of-the-art stocking and assessment vessel ninety-five feet in length and carries up to 190,000 lake trout for offshore stocking over reefs. Fish population assessments conducted on the *Baird* guide Great Lakes harvest regulations for Chinook salmon, lake trout, and walleye. The vessel ports at Alpena Fish and Wildlife Conservation Office in Michigan. USFWS

Louella E. Cable (1900–1986)

Dr. Louella E. Cable was a pioneering fisheries biologist who in 1927 became the first female scientist employed by the U.S. Fish and Wildlife Service via its antecedent U.S. Bureau of Fisheries. She spent her entire career in a variety of roles and conducted significant research on a number of subjects.

Cable was born in Chamberlain, South Dakota, on July 5, 1900. She was educated in local schools and attending Dakota, Wesleyan University, where she received a teacher's certificate and subsequently taught first grade before deciding to become a zoologist. She received a B.A. (1926) and a master of arts in zoology (1927) from the University of South Dakota, where she had a summer teaching appointment in 1927 and taught botany and zoology at a salary of $2,400. In fall 1927, the U.S. Bureau of Fisheries hired Cable as a scientific illustrator to assist Dr. Samuel Hildebrand, Director of the Beaufort Laboratory in Beaufort, North Carolina. Cable thus became the first woman employed by the Bureau in a professional biologist position, narrowly beating out noted shellfish expert Dr. Vera Koehring for that distinction by a few years.

Cable contributed numerous drawings to Bureau publications and conducted a wide range of research at the Beaufort Lab. She reared several fish through their larval stages in the laboratory, which was a ground-breaking achievement for the study of early life history of fishes. Her drawings of the early life stages of these fish were widely disseminated.

Hildebrand and Cable worked together for the better part of a decade, but she also conducted her own research such as in 1931 when she went to Woods Hole to study mackerel. Cable's art was not just celebrated within her agency. An article in the Sioux Falls *Daily Argus-Leader* dated September 14, 1934, declared, "Miss Cable has become an expert in matters pertaining to fish. She paints fish, and

she does the job so well one federal official says: 'she's the best and fastest artist the Bureau ever had.'" She also made national news; a February 5, 1935, United Press wire report entitled "Woman Fish Expert Never Has Made A Catch," picked up by hundreds of newspapers, detailed Cable's career, noting that although she was regarded as "Washington's outstanding women authority on fish" she had little luck as an angler.

In 1937, Cable began studying shad on the Edisto River in South Carolina and soon became a leading expert, referenced in numerous syndicated articles over the next fifteen years. In 1941, wire reports wrote that Cable was a Junior Aquatic Biologist with the Middle Atlantic Fisheries Investigation, surveying shad spawning in the Chesapeake Bay area. By 1942, she was appointed head of this multi-state and multi-agency committee dedicated to restoring American shad fisheries. She chaired this organization from its base in College Park, Maryland, until 1949 and her work quickly caught the eye of Secretary of the Interior Harold L. Ickes. Cable's shad research culminated in a presentation made with Robert A. Nesbitt on November 17, 1943, before the Select Committee on Conservation of Wildlife Resources of the House of Representatives.

In further service of this work, she wrote a nationally syndicated article in August 1944 entitled "Delaware River Shad Fishing Has Suffered Great Reduction," reporting the committee's findings that shad catches were down 80 percent and that a 50 percent reduction in annual catch tonnage was necessary to restore it. Along with fellow U.S. Fish

Above: Louella E. Cable was the first female scientist hired by the U.S. Fish and Wildlife Service's predecessor agency, the U.S. Bureau of Fisheries. Dr. Cable was an authority on lake trout and American shad and talented artist. COURTESY UNIVERSITY OF SOUTH DAKOTA

and Wildlife Service scientist Lucille Farrier Stickel, Cable was fêted in an October 1945 wire piece entitled "Women Scientists Helped Yanks Win the War" that declared Cable "discovered a method of determining how many times a shad spawns" and "developed a unique method of tagging fish." During the war Ickes commended the pair for their stellar work in print on several occasions.

In 1950, Cable moved to Ann Arbor, Michigan, and shifted her focus to the Great Lakes, starting out concentrating on the declining lake trout fishery before researching ciscoes. Her early research culminated in a Ph.D. in Fisheries Biology from the University of Michigan in 1959. From 1957 to 1964, Cable was in charge of the agency's aquatic lab located at the venerable hatchery in Northville, Michigan, where she conducted research on ciscoes and other coregonine fish. She spent the remainder of her career in Ann Arbor, retiring in 1970 after a forty-three-year career.

Dr. Cable's research was wide ranging, encompassing everything from saltwater to freshwater species and including such varied subjects as the food eaten by bullheads, the larval stages of whiting, and plankton. A native Galapagos island fish, Cable's goby (*Eleotrica cableae*), was named after her. Her illustrations graced dozens of articles and books, and she authored or coauthored a number of research works. Both her 1928 master's thesis on

bullhead diets and her 1959 doctoral dissertation on lake trout age determination from scales were printed as stand-alone publications by the U.S. Fish and Wildlife Service. She was a member of a number of professional organizations including the American Society of Zoologists and the American Fisheries Society, where she was one of only two female members, along with Dr. Emmeline Moore.

Cable retired in 1970, but in 1972 newly hired Thomas Todd collaborated with her to finish a long-gestating research project on whitefish. This coauthored work was completed in 1976, but not published until 1981 as the final research article in her long career.

Todd recalls that Cable "became an accomplished artist with copper enameling [and] remained active in various women's professional groups in the area" and sometimes "joined staff at the [Ann Arbor] laboratory for picnics and in-house celebrations." When she died in 1986, she left her entire estate to the University of South Dakota to endow a scholarship in her name for students of zoology. The Louella E. Cable Memorial Scholarship is a fitting tribute to one of the outstanding women of science of the twentieth century and the first female professional employee of the U.S. Fish and Wildlife Service.

—Dr. Todd E.A. Larson

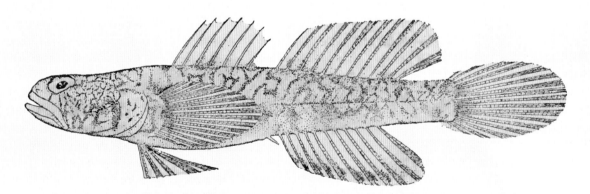

U.S. Bureau of Fisheries ichthyologist Isaac Ginsburg described a new species of fish in 1933. Louella Cable drew the fish for his publication. Ginsburg named it Cable's goby as a tribute to her help in properly assigning the new species to the correct genus.

Muskellunge

Iwas born the son of a muskie fisherman. Musky, the fish of ten thousand casts and endless obsession. I grew up listening on the edge of campfires to the stories of fifty-inchers, the legend of the Moccasin Bar, and the close encounters with the water wolves of northern Wisconsin.

It was thirty-three years ago that I cast a double-bladed white spinner bait from my Zebco 33 into the lily pad–lined bays. It was just before sunset and the lake was calm and flat as glass. My father paddled the twelve-foot aluminum boat sporadically. I'd been schooled on muskies; you only raised a fish when your lures were fishing. With a wooden Creek Chub Pikie Minnow lure the size of my forearm, my father could pull the boat down the shoreline cast after cast with rarely an oar stroke. The fish struck halfway back on my retrieve. At first, the fish felt like another twelve-inch bass. I'd caught several already. But on the first turn, we caught a glimpse of almost three feet of fish showing itself in the low light of dark water. A muskie! Every instruction of fish fighting went out of my mind and I cranked that Zebco as hard as my little fingers could manage, the ten-pound test stretching to the point of singing. As muskies do, the battle was over in minutes and dad hoisted the fish over the gunnel.

I held my breath as dad stretched the tail against the tape measure. Thirty-two inches, the minimum for a legal muskie!

The ride back was in silence. My first legal muskie. Back at the cabin, I dragged a fish almost reaching my chin up the trail to waiting aunts, uncles, and my grandfather. All had assembled in northern Wisconsin for the summer week of muskie fishing—and I had the first fish.

My younger brother and I posed for a picture with the muskie against the inside of the cabin door. It still hangs in my old room at mom and dad's house. The next night we had a feast of grilled muskie celebrating my welcome to the muskie fraternity.

That experience propelled my career into the U.S. Fish and Wildlife Service. As an agency, we have a long history with the muskellunge, *Esox masquinongy*. Robert Barnwell Roosevelt, the prodigious writer on fishing and New York congressional representative, described the Masqueallonge in 1862 as reaching six feet and seventy pounds, nine years before he wrote legislation creating the U.S. Fish Commission. Although, after Louis Spray's sixty-nine-pound 1949 world record was overturned, the current record still stands at sixty-seven pounds, just shy of Roosevelt's description.

U.S. Fish Commission biologist James Henshall, in his 1892 book, *American Game Fishes*, mused over the number of common names possessed by a fish with a somewhat limited natural distribution—from eastern Tennessee northward through the upper Mississippi and Ohio river basins and through the Great Lakes. He counted no less than twenty-eight common names all starting with the letter M and ending in a vowel. Dr. Henshall was moved by the fish's sporting qualities, writing, "it exhibits a bull-like ferocity when hooked, making furious dashes for liberty, and if not stopped in time it will eventually take to the weeds. It exhibits some great power of endurance but lacks finesse." And speaking to its predatory nature, Henshall remarked that it's lucky for the smaller fishes that muskellunge are relatively uncommon, for they are voracious fish eaters.

And later yet, William Converse Kendall, also a medical doctor turned fish biologist, did a deep dig into the life history of the muskellunge and its close kin during his long career with the U.S. Bureau of Fisheries. Dr. Kendall published a treatise in 1917 titled *The Pikes: Their Geographical Distribution, Habits, Culture, and Commercial Importance*. He too posited on the litany of spelling variations of the common name. Dr. Kendall remarked on the importance of weedy shorelines and fallen trees to large lurking muskie and their solitary nature. Anything in the shape of food is potential muskie fare.

In the wild, muskies have a diet ranging from fish to small birds and mammals. Razor teeth slash and grasp prey before it's devoured. Those same teeth mangle muskie lures and fingers during errant unhooking operations. Muskies are the "great whites" of freshwater, anything and everything is potential prey.

Anglers have pursued muskies for well over a century. In 1889, the first muskie fishing season was established in Wisconsin. By 1917, a minimum size limit was set at twenty-four inches and gradually increased statewide to forty inches by 2012. These restrictive seasons help protect these relatively long-lived fish. It takes seventeen years for a muskie to reach fifty inches.

Fishery managers collect muskie eggs each spring from wild fish and rear them in numerous fish hatcheries. Muskies are notoriously cannibalistic and must be fed constantly to avoid eating each other. An individual female can have 225,000 eggs and hybridzing female muskies with male northern pike creates tiger muskies. These tigers display hybrid vigor—a nature to grow fast and large—and a striking barred camouflage, and sterility, making them an excellent fishery management tool for reducing prey species.

In conjunction with more restrictive seasons, muskie anglers have self-imposed a catch-and-release practice to promote more and larger fish. With an average of only one adult muskie per surface acre of water in prime habitat, this catch-and-release ethic is critical to future muskie populations. In the mid-1950s anglers harvested about one hundred thousand muskies annually. Today, that number has dropped to ten thousand.

Despite lower harvest, catching a muskie is still a monumental event. The average adult muskie totals twenty-seven hours of angling per fish. Despite the long odds, a muskie fisherman always has hope. And fueled by lures that average twenty dollars apiece and boats that can run more than house payments, muskie fishing is a $425 million enterprise. Muskie fishing is a dedicated pursuit.

It was four years before I boated my second muskie. At twelve, I had graduated from a Zebco 33 to an Abu Garcia 5500 bait-casting reel, the product of delivering 3,375 newspapers by bicycle. The fish struck boatside on a swim bait and there was a short battle before it succumbed to the net.

"Is it legal?" I asked.

"Yep. 36 inches," my dad responded.

I gazed over the fish. The dorsal reflected a greenish bronze iridescence, gradually faded to olive across the lateral, and finally white on the belly. The strong fishy musk still soaked my hands as I slowly reached to touch the muskie still trapped in the web of the net. Four years . . . I could keep this fish, hoist it to the cabin to certain fanfare, and likely make the tavern brag board.

But one muskie was enough.

Dad gave me a wink with his scarred eyelid—caught by an errant Suick stickbait treble backlash on a Canadian muskie trip long ago.

"I'm proud of you son."

—Nathan Wiese

No water, no fish at a fish hatchery. Thanks to maintenance staff such as Mitchel Adams at D.C. Booth Historic National Fish Hatchery, they keep the water flowing and take care of the physical aspect of fisheries field stations. They proudly perform other duties as assigned, such as loading up a truck with trout and delivering them to the Crow Reservation in Montana.
CRAIG SPRINGER, USFWS

William Converse Kendall, M.D. (1861–1939)

Born in Freeport, Maine, William Converse Kendall attended Bowdoin College, just fifteen miles from home. After that, his choices of career and relocation became nothing less than dizzying and a little mysterious, though they do reveal a ceaseless love for science, teaching, and learning. He began his career in Minnesota, more than fifteen hundred miles from Bowdoin, where he served as principal in a public school for two years, before moving back to Maine and taking a job as a principal at the Patten Academy, near the Canadian border. He then returned to Bowdoin and studied for a master's degree, before entering medical school and receiving his M.D. from Georgetown University in 1896. When he and his wife, Ida, had a daughter in 1897, Kendall did what a sensible young man of his training and inclination might—he devoted his life to advancing our understanding of the natural world—and became a fish man.

For Kendall, it was never about the glamour; it was the work. His main professional affiliation was with the U.S. Fish Commission in Washington, D.C., where he had been an assistant (or "naturalist" in those days) and later claimed the title of ichthyologist. His talent in the laboratory and field was legendary. He worked with humility and focus. When Bowdoin College conferred to him an honorary doctorate degree, it was noted that "he can tell by the scales of a fish, as a criminal investigator could tell by fingerprints, where a fish came from, where it was caught, and who caught it."

His written work was in high demand by the widest imaginable range of audiences. He was the author of scientific papers on systematic ichthyology, geographical distribution and habits of fishes in the publications of the U.S. Fish Commission and the National Museum. He also produced countless publications on matters such as the population of pickerel in a particular Downeast Maine pond, pike in the Great Lakes, and catfishes. Every fish and every water mattered, though in truth he had a soft spot for brook trout and salmon, the satiny salmonids of home. He also wrote regular articles on angling and natural history for sportsmen's magazines and newspapers, as well as stories and articles for children. He may have left the public school rooms, but he never stopped being a teacher.

His enthusiasm for exploration was legendary. He went on countless trips for the U.S. Fish Commission, both near and far, beginning with a seven-month cruise to the tropical Pacific in the fall and winter of 1899–1900. His most notable adventure came at the end of his career when, against the better judgement of the commissioner of the U.S. Bureau of Fisheries, who worried about Kendall's health and age on such an arduous journey, he sailed on the infamous MacMillan Arctic Journey aboard *The Bowdoin* in the summer of 1929. The ship was ice-locked for days on end and was nearly crushed several times. Kendall wrote (of course) about the adventure and explained how once, thirty- to forty-foot tides combined with a "grinding flo of 300 foot ice bergs" and "pinched *The Bowdoin* and forced her hull at least 6 feet out of water." He did manage "some good fly fishing and caught some very fine fish" in one of the fiords. His obituaries called him an "explorer and naturalist."

One suspects, however, that for all his world traveling, what he really enjoyed was introducing others to the science of fish. In later life, journalist John Gould recalled his kindness:

"Another person . . . who helped make me smart was Dr. William Converse Kendall, the fish man . . . When he retired to his native Maine, he had a small laboratory in Freeport. As a boy I'd step in to see what he was doing. He was studying the biological process that allows a saltwater fish to come into fresh water to spawn. . . . He told me never to clean smelts I caught but to bring them to him and he'd clean them for me."

The boy and the scientist together examined smelt scales under the microscope, and then discussed even more mysterious matters, such as movement and migration. As Gould recalled,

"Dr. Kendall told me the American eel and the European eel are not alike, but both breed in adjacent and overlapping areas in the Sargasso Sea. Yet one comes here and one goes there, and neither ever goes to the wrong continent. How come? Very simple.

After a passive migration of three years, the American eel is ready for fresh water whereas the European eel needs seven years to reach that condition. Either will expire if he goes the wrong way."

We are most fortunate that William Converse Kendall went ours.

—Will Ryan

Northern Pike

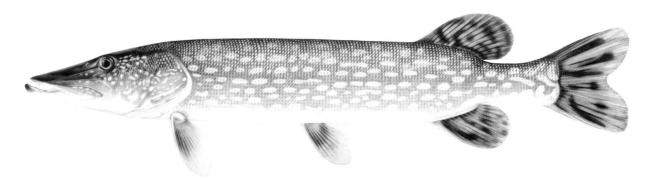

If you need a reminder who is on top of the food chain in northern waters, toss a red and white spoon, a big spinner, or a thick streamer into the shallow weedy shoreline. It is there that you will find northern pike; they are solitary by nature, and that is where they tend to lurk for food. They lie in wait in ambush and, with the stout flick of a tail, their toothy jaws envelop most anything that swims in, or lands on, the water. If that might be your offering at the end of a heavy leader line, hang on. These voracious predatory fish get big.

Anglers come in two forms: those who enjoy the pursuit of trophy northern pike and those annoyed by them while fishing for smallmouth bass, walleye, or yellow perch. I fall into the former camp—I have long enjoyed pike fishing. Moreover, I get to handle northern pike as part my daily work as a biologist at Valley City National Fish Hatchery in North Dakota.

Northern pike are meat-eaters, plain and simple. Anything with fur or fins or feathers is potential fare. Northerns forage on fish, frogs, crayfish, snakes, waterfowl, shorebirds—and hapless rodents that venture into the water. Even their own kind show up in the stomachs of the larger northern pike. This predilection for flesh lends the fish a nickname, water wolf. Their aggressive nature challenges even the most seasoned anglers.

There is a certain allure to northern pike fishing—and it's all about the size and the fight. Many state-record northern pike are greater than forty inches. A fish that long can exceed thirty-five pounds. Despite the potential monster sizes northern pike can reach, they are perhaps the most frustrating fish an angler will encounter.

Trophy-sized fish with sharp teeth in their powerful jaws can snip even the stoutest leader. And what can be more frustrating than sight-fishing with a follow-up cast to a big pike that refuses to take the bait? Then there's the hammer handles, small, skinny young pike

A U.S. Bureau of Fisheries worker Peter Olson at LaCrosse Fish-Cultural Station shows off a large northern pike. USFWS NFACA

An angler caught this twenty-five-pound northern pike in Upper Souris National Wildlife Refuge, North Dakota, in 1955. USFWS MA

foiling your fishing for other species. The dichotomy is a curious one; northern pike are either a trophy or a nuisance. No matter, the fish has an important role in nature as a top predator in keeping forage and smaller sport fish such as pumpkinseed and bluegill numbers in check.

Northern pike provide exceptional table fare. However, reducing the fish to clean fillets can further frustrate. Dealing with the Y-bones takes some extra work and removing them seems to be an art that few have mastered.

Northern pike are a prized sport fish in the United States and an important commercial fish in Canada. In the state of Alaska, they comprise an important subsistence fishery. In some places where northern pike were introduced, they can wreak havoc on native fishes.

The U.S. Fish and Wildlife Service and its ancestor, the U.S. Bureau of Fisheries, have long had interest in northern pike. Medical-doctor-turned-fisheries-scientist William Converse Kendall investigated northern pike and its close kin in 1917, publishing *The Pikes: Their Geographical Distribution, Habits, Culture, and Commercial Importance.* Kendall remarked on

the fish's habits and habitats and he had this to say about angling: "Go where pike can be found, fish for them with legitimate tackle, give them a fair chance, and they will afford as much pleasure as any royal smallmouth bass that ever swam."

Robert Barnwell Roosevelt, congressional progenitor to the U.S. Fish Commission and uncle to the future conservationist-in-chief Theodore Roosevelt, had a fair affliction for pike. Roosevelt wrote on pike fishing in his 1862 title, *The Game Fish of the Northern States of America and British Provinces*:

"Among the water-lilies the only mode is to use a long stiff rod and short line, loaded with one buck-shot about a foot from the hook, and baited either with a minnow, the belly of a yellow perch, or better than all, a slip of the skin of pork cut into something resembling a small fish. The bait is dropped into the opening among the lilly-pads sinking rapidly toward the bottom, is started up again by a twitch of the rod and goes on until the pike rendered frantic by such an absurd performance can stand it no longer and with one furious rush determines to end the gyrations of such a silly creature. By the aid of a strong rod and line, pull him out at once."

A biologist adjusts the flow of water pouring over incubating northern pike eggs at Garrison Dam National Fish Hatchery, in North Dakota. The hatchery still raises pike but also burbot, walleye, pallid sturgeon, shovelnose sturgeon, Chinook salmon, and brown, rainbow, and cutthroat trout. USFWS NFACA

Garrison Dam National Fish Hatchery and my station, Valley City, presently raise millions of northern pike for stocking in reservoirs in North Dakota and surrounding upper Midwest states. Whether by Roosevelt's high-sticking, trolling, or spin casting, our facilities supply numerous waters with pike sought after by anglers. The northern pike is in fact the state fish of North Dakota.

Biologists take advantage of the fact that northern pike are among the first fish to spawn in spring; March is winter's spring—a time of increasing light and warming water. Pike move into the shallows to procreate and are easily trapped. They may make it an interesting long-distance affair; W. F. Carbine, a U.S. Fish and Wildlife Service biologist in Michigan, reported in 1947 two pike tagged in a Lake Huron tributary, Pine River, turned up a month later twenty-five miles upstream. So strong is the instinct to reproduce.

Biologists spawn the fish along shore and fertilized eggs are shipped back to our national fish hatcheries where the eggs will roll in glass jars overflowing with oxygen-rich water until they hatch. A big female might shed a quarter-million eggs. Left to themselves, northern pike spawn over flooded vegetation where more than one male often accompanies a female. Eggs are scattered among the submerged vegetation and once fry hatch they attach themselves to the standing weeds while they absorb their yolk sac and allow their mouthparts to develop.

As soon as juvenile pike are free-swimming they are on the hunt for food and grow at a rapid pace. First on the menu is microscopic zooplankton but they quickly switch to hunting other fish—a trait they keep their entire life. All fish species that spawn later in the spring and summer have to run a gauntlet of hungry pike that have gotten a jump-start on them.

Good pike fishing can be had year-round, though there does seem to be a summer lull. Few experiences can compare to the adrenalin rush that comes with seeing an oversized bobber jogging in rippled lake water in northern Wisconsin at my uncle's cabin or that orange flag flying in an ice-fishing set up. Big fish get pulled through auger holes in winter. Such was the case for me fishing with my dad in South Dakota.

—Aaron Von Eschen

Frank N. Clark (1849–1910)

"I was very greatly pained lately to learn of the untimely death of Frank Clark. I pray you to convey to his good wife my sympathy in her afflic- tion. Mr. Clark was one of the ablest men in the field of fish culture. I do not myself know that he had any superior and it is a great pity that he should be lost so early in the great work he was doing."

—Dr. David Starr Jordan

A local fish farmer put the Detroit suburb of Northville, Michigan, on the map. Frank Clark originally of Clarkston, Michigan, came from a long line of Clarks who are historically significant in the Detroit, Michigan, area.

He was born Frank Nelson Clark on February 2, 1849. He completed his college studies at the Agricultural College of Michigan at East Lansing, Michigan. At his father's passing in 1876, Clark took over the two-year-old Northville Fish Hatchery, a privately owned business.

This fish culture enterprise in Northville was among the earliest of its kind on the American continent. Clark was considered a pioneer in the same company as Seth Green of New York and his own father, Nelson W. Clark. Though Clark encountered many challenges early on, he was regarded as a genius in the field of fish culture. His work was years in advance of the need or market for intensively reared fishes, but he was known to be a tough-out, highly motivated, smart, and always extremely resourceful. Failure for Frank Clark was not an option.

Clark, a driven man and natural leader, became widely regarded as a nationally recognized fisheries expert and innovator. And as a result, the Northville Fish Hatchery became a ground-zero of sorts in regard to fish culture techniques, hatchery operations, fish propagation, distribution, and fish transport. Frank Clark trained many young fish culturists who afterward moved on to other hatcheries in the service of both federal and state governments.

Spencer Baird, commissioner of the U.S. Fish Commission, took note. In 1880, the U.S. Fish Commission leased the hatchery with Clark at the helm. In 1890, the private hatchery became Northville Fish-Cultural Station with Clark supervis- ing rainbow trout, brook trout, lake whitefish, and smallmouth bass culture there and auxiliary stations at Alpena, Charlevoix, and Sault Ste. Marie, Michigan. The federal government constructed a new hatchery facility, complete with superinten- dents housing at Northville in 1896.

Clark continued innovating and improving the hatchery and its water supply as superintendent until his death in 1910. The station functioned as a trout and pond-fish hatchery until 1957.

—Tim Smigielski

Lake Whitefish

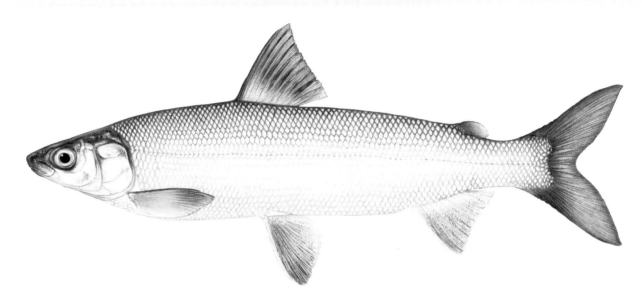

The names we pin on places tell quite a story. Take Whitefish Point, Michigan. The small town sits on Upper Peninsula on the edge of Lake Superior at the mouth of Whitefish Bay. You could confidently surmise that experience with lake whitefish might have had an influence here.

Whitefish Point is home to the Great Lakes Shipwreck Museum, and there have been a few wrecks—perhaps none more legendary than the sinking of the Great Lakes iron-ore freighter, SS *Edmund Fitzgerald*, November 10, 1975. Within the month, Gordon Lightfoot wrote the poem that memorialized twenty-nine sailors and their ship in nearly a seven-minute-long story-song: "Superior, they said, never gives up her dead/When the gales of November come early."

It is a paradox: November gales can take life, and they make life. Heavy winds are exactly what some fish species use as a cue to spawn in autumn, including lake whitefish. These strong winds mix the waters of the Great Lakes. Lake whitefish follow the frigid bottom water up to the shallow shoals to reproduce. At times, schools of these silvery fish swim along shipping docks or marinas. They begin to move into these shallow rocky areas as the weather makes a turn towards winter. Most reproductive activity occurs when the shade of cloud cover helps the fish avoid the hungry mouths of predators such as northern pike.

Lake whitefish are identifiable by their large scales, fleshy adipose fin, smaller mouth, and weak teeth velvety to the touch. The older, big fish develop a large humpback and are referred to as bowbacks and humpback whitefish. They typically inhabit lake depths of less than one hundred and eighty feet.

When freshly caught, anglers often described them as smelling like a cucumber. Lake whitefish dwell primarily near the lake bottom feeding on microscopic zooplankton, small fish, and aquatic insects.

Lake whitefish spawn every fall but only after they reach maturity around six years of age. You cannot tell the age of the fish just by looking at it, instead biologists must examine an inner ear bone called the otolith, about the size of lentil. The bone is sawed in half, examined under a microscope where a biologist counts the rings, similar to counting tree rings. Lake whitefish can live more than thirty years if conditions are right.

Each chilly November, lake whitefish return to the shoal they came from to lay their eggs. The cracks and crevices of the rocks are the perfect spots for the eggs to incubate all winter under the ice. The eggs need that protection as they are subjected to the perils of predation and wave action for five months. Once the ice melts and the water begins to warm, the eggs hatch. The larvae remain among the rock crevices for several days. After days of hiding, they emerge and swim toward the water surface and begin looking for food. At such a small size, they are at the mercy of the water currents until they are strong enough to swim and maintain their position. At this point, the key to survival is to eat, grow quickly, and avoid being eaten.

As part of my ongoing research, every spring, once the small larval lake whitefish swim up from the rocks where they hatched, I systematically tow a very small-meshed net to see how many larval lake whitefish are present. This helps determine overwinter egg

Alpena Fish-Cultural Station in Michigan produced a great number of lake whitefish. USFWS NFACA

PLEASE POST CONSPICUOUSLY

EAT FROZEN FISH

FISH HAS A HIGH FOOD VALUE

IT CONTAINS AS MUCH BODY-BUILDING MATERIAL AS BEEF-STEAK and is as readily digestible

FROZEN FISH are as WHOLESOME and NUTRITIOUS as fresh fish

BUY THEM FROZEN, THAW IN A REFRIGERATOR or other cool place, and cook promptly

ASK FOR LEAFLET GIVING FURTHER INFORMATION

DEPARTMENT OF COMMERCE
BUREAU OF FISHERIES
WASHINGTON

GOVERNMENT PRINTING OFFICE, WASHINGTON, D. C.

Lake whitefish were an important food fish and the U.S. Bureau of Fisheries encouraged fish consumption through responsible storage. USFWS NFACA

survival. Then in the late spring, I conduct a juvenile survey to see how many have survived past the larval stage. The tracking of these two life stages helps predict year-class strength and determine future management needs. Doing these surveys over time reveals important trends.

Lake whitefish are of significant economic and intrinsic importance to Great Lakes communities, and not just Whitefish Point. Former U.S. Fish Commission and U.S. Bureau of Fisheries stations had a hand in lake whitefish conservation dating to the 1880s. Former fish-cultural stations at Duluth, Minnesota; Charlevoix, Michigan; and Alpena, Michigan, sought to replenish populations from overfishing and pollution. A half-billion fertilized lake whitefish eggs came into Put-in-Bay Fish-Cultural Station on Ohio's Lake Erie in December 1917—equating to 450 bushels of eggs, noted an entry in the Bureau's *Fisheries Service Bulletin* that month. Biologist John Van Oosten was long involved in lake whitefish conservation and published a landmark study on lake whitefish age and growth research in 1923.

The species is of commercial value and cultural significance to the indigenous communities that fished for them prior to European settlement—and on into modern times. And I find this curious: Robert Roosevelt, who established the U.S. Fish Commission, argued in his 1862 book, *The Game Fish of the Northern States of America and British Provinces*, that lake whitefish deserve another name. He wrote, "The proper appellation for this fish is the Indian name, Attihawmeg, and if sportsmen would in all cases follow the names used by the aboriginals, they would show more sense than the common people of our country, who think every fish with a spiny back fin must be a bass, and every other a trout."

The average size taken by the commercial fishery in the Great Lakes today is about twenty-two inches long and three and a half pounds. This may not seem like much, but the taste and nutritional value in each fillet makes them a sought-after main dish. Roosevelt noted the fish to be bigger in 1862, citing sizes in

Freshly caught lake whitefish from Lake Erie were processed in Sandusky, Ohio. USFWS NFACA

Large, efficient nets harvested lake whitefish faster than they could reproduce or they could be augmented in U.S. Bureau of Fisheries stations. As a result, populations plummeted. USFWS MA

Put-in-Bay Fish-Cultural Station served in lake whitefish production as well as smallmouth bass. This station, situated on South Bass Island in Lake Erie, opened 1889 and was transferred to the state of Ohio in 1947.
USFWS NFACA

excess of twelve to fourteen pounds. He also had this to say about the dinner plate: "It is the finest freshwater fish of America upon the table, having no rival that approaches it in excellence except the Otsego bass. But being delicate, it should be eaten immediately on leaving the water."

Anglers know lake whitefish for their delicate mouth. They use dough balls, strips of fish flesh, grubs, and minnows on small hooks fished deep. A fingertip on the line rather than a bobber might be more sensitive in picking up the light bite of lake whitefish. Premature hook-sets miss many fish.

Despite their major significance and management efforts, lake whitefish have experienced continual challenges that have affected their population since the 1880s. The introduction of invasive species such as sea lamprey and zebra mussels, as well as habitat degradation and pollution devastated lake whitefish

numbers. The most recent decline in lake whitefish was observed in the early 2000s. Scientists have narrowed the cause to a decline in the growth and survival of early life stages. I have personally watched this species' population decline over the last decade. Yet I am always amazed by its perseverance. The Great Lakes—a giant inland sea—is always changing. This makes my work both challenging and rewarding. The U.S. Fish and Wildlife Service continually monitors trends in lake whitefish populations through fish surveys with the end goal of maintaining a healthy and sustainable fishery for anglers and commercial fishing enterprise.

When you enjoy a whitefish dinner remember those who brave the blustery elements to make sure it is an experience you can enjoy.

—Chris Olds

Dr. John Van Oosten (1891–1966)

If he could see us now, Dr. John Van Oosten would be moved by the level of sophistication of today's fisheries biologists. They manage Great Lakes fisheries using complex computer models to evaluate the status of fish stocks and predict the effects of harvest. Biologists employ satellites, GPS, and sonar technology to track fish levels, and now—the mass-marking and coded-wire tagging of every hatchery-reared trout and salmon stocked into the Great Lakes basin. Dr. Van Oosten would be pleased that modern-day fisheries scientists carry on his legacy of Great Lakes fisheries research, conservation, and management.

Dr. Van Oosten attended Calvin College near Grand Rapids, Michigan, from 1914 to 1916 and then transferred to the University of Michigan in Ann Arbor where he received three degrees, all with specializations in zoology. He received his Ph.D. in 1926.

During his forty-two-year career with the U.S. Bureau of Fisheries and U.S. Fish and Wildlife Service, Dr. Van Oosten spent more than twenty of those years serving the University of Michigan as a research associate in zoology and lecturer in the School of Natural Resources. Before receiving his doctorate degree, he was a special investigator for the U.S. Bureau of Fisheries in the early to mid-1920s. His work investigating the collapse of the lake herring fishery in Lake Erie in 1925 was the precursor to the establishment of the Bureau's Great Lakes Biological Laboratory, in Ann Arbor in 1927. Dr. Van Oosten was named its first director and served until 1949. (The laboratory is now the Great Lakes Science Center operated under the U.S. Geological Survey.)

He prodigiously continued fishery research throughout his career, having had a hand in bettering our understanding of smallmouth bass, walleye, the deep-dwelling whitefish and ciscoes, and lake trout. He published an extensive report, the *History of Red Lakes Fishery, 1917–1938*, that revealed significantly new information on the biology of walleye, brown trout, brook trout, and northern pike in Minnesota.

Known for his practical fisheries management and regulation interests, Dr. Van Oosten was sought after for his expertise. He was a trusted advisor to the commercial fishing industry and state fisheries conservation agencies. A true champion of the Great Lakes, he served as chairman of many committees including the Lake Erie Advisory Committee, Great Lakes Lake Trout Committee, and Great Lakes Sea Lamprey Committee.

Dr. Van Oosten established a worldwide reputation as an extraordinary fishery scientist, and for that reason, President Franklin Roosevelt appointed him in 1940 as the U.S. member of the International Board of Inquiry for Great Lakes Fisheries, and he served on the Great Lakes International Fact-Finding Commission for Fisheries.

A dedicated leader, Dr. Van Oosten amassed an impressive array of awards and accomplishments. In 1952, he was named a Distinguished Service Honorary member by the American Fisheries Society. A year after his retirement, Dr. Van Oosten received a Distinguished Service Citation from the U.S. Department of the Interior, with a gold medal in 1962.

—Tim Smigielski

John Van Oosten stands in front of his crew aboard the U.S.B.F. *Fulmar*, a research vessel that plied the Great Lakes. USGS

Walleye

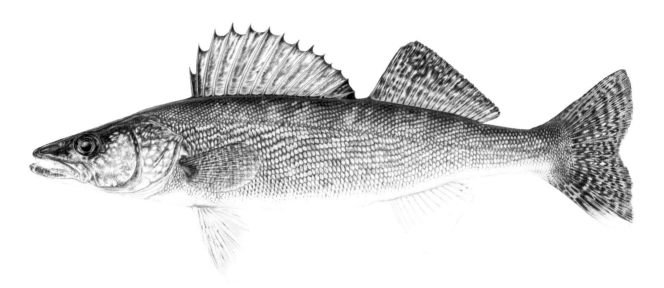

Several years back, my son, his friend, and I were fishing on the Mississippi in a fairly popular walleye spot over a mussel bed that has produced good fish in the past. My son latched into a nice fish, landed it, and yelled over to his friend in the other boat, "Hey George! Monster Walleye!" In less than five minutes, the boats close to us made a beeline for our location and we were unceremoniously dumped from the mussel bed into less than optimal fishing waters.

The walleye, a popular sport fish because of its size, fighting ability, firm texture, and mild taste, is highly prized by sportsmen and fish eaters alike. So much so, that a former governor of Wisconsin championed the Walleye Initiative, seed money for fish farms to increase walleye populations statewide so that it might boost angling opportunities.

Walleye is king in Lake Erie. It thrives there since the water quality has improved due to the Clean Water Act, the Great Lakes Water Quality Agreement, and other federal, state, and international efforts to clean up the lake. This resulted in a recovered world-class fishery that has reached record high creel returns. You can find larger-than-life statues honoring the walleye in Ohio, Wisconsin, Minnesota, and North Dakota.

The walleye is a member of the Percid family—perchlike fishes—and was for many years commonly called the pike-perch. This family of fishes is top-heavy with a great number of darter species that rarely exceed a couple of ounces. What they lack in size they make up for in a vast array of colors. These colorful walleye cousins flit around in brooks in the eastern two-thirds of the U.S.

Old U.S. Fish Commission and U.S. Bureau of Fisheries reports list exhaustive accountings of pike-perch eggs hatched and fishes planted, from stations mostly rimming the Great Lakes. Federal hatcheries such as Cape Vincent, New York; Put-in-Bay, Ohio; Alpena and Charlevoix, Michigan; LaCrosse, Wisconsin; and Duluth, Minnesota—these stations taken together accounted for immense numbers of pike-perch year after year in the mid-twentieth century.

Walleye are close kin to sauger and yellow perch found in more northern climes. A color variant of the walleye, known as the blue pike, was also once common in Great Lakes waters, with annual catch rates exceeding two to twenty-six million pounds annually in the 1950s. This blue pike was once considered a separate species, but recent genetic tests from an archived sample suggest it was simply a color variant of the walleye. The blue pike disappeared from the Great Lakes in the latter part of the previous century and was declared extinct in 1983.

U.S. Fish Commission biologists David Starr Jordan and Barton Warren Evermann were very familiar with fishes in Indiana, having both either studied or taught at Indiana University. They harshly wrote in their 1902 book, *American Food and Game Fishes*, that in "Indiana, it is known as salmon or jack salmon, names absurd and wholly without excuse." Our northern neighbors from Canada call the walleye a pickerel; it goes by yellow pike in some parts of the U.S., but now walleye is by far its most common moniker. It's named for a distinguishable layer of tissue in their eye that allows the fish to see better in low light. This gives the

Jill Smigielski, daughter of fish biologist Tim Smigielski, is happy to land this nine-pound, thirty-one-inch walleye in a Michigan lake. TIM SMIGIELSKI, USFWS

walleye an advantage for finding prey at night and in turbid, roily waters such as the Mississippi River.

Walleye are considered a cool water fish, with safe water temperature ranges between thirty-five and eighty degrees Fahrenheit. Walleye spawn in early to late spring, depending on water temperature and length of daylight, or photoperiod. For example, in Missouri you would normally look for spawning walleye over hard surface bottoms in lakes and rivers at the end of March. In the upper Mississippi River, walleye spawn generally in the month of April. In northern climes, they may not spawn until May.

Walleye keep house in all kinds of water from clear lakes to turbid rivers—and the water's clarity may dictate what time of day or night walleye anglers target their prey. Aside from interestingly set eyes, the walleye carries a distinctive white margin on the lower lobe of the tail. This, in combination with a dorsal fin with no or few undefined spots, distinguishes the walleye from its closely related, albeit slightly smaller cousin, the sauger.

The sauger has dark splotches on its sides appearing saddlelike, around the lobes of the dorsal fin. Sauger tolerate turbid waters better than walleye, though

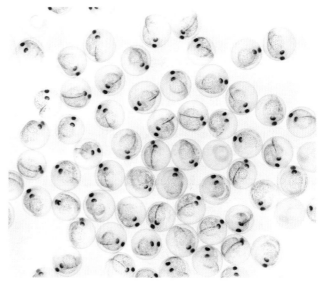

Walleye eggs incubating at Gavins Point National Fish Hatchery in South Dakota. SAM STUKEL, USFWS

they do inhabit many of the same waters and they do interbreed. It is typical to find hybrid levels of up to 5 percent of the population in waters where both species coexist. These hybrids, appropriately called saugeye, are also cultured in hatcheries for stocking reservoirs. Saugeye grow faster and are thought to be easier to catch than walleye or sauger.

Rare species of freshwater mussels rely on walleye and sauger to complete their life cycles. Larvae, also called glochidia, of the endangered Higgins Eye Pearlymussel and Black Sandshell—the size of a tip of a pencil lead—attach to the fish's gills and skin and gain nourishment from the fish for a short time. The young mussels drop off and feed on their own. So, if you like to catch walleye, find an active mussel bed and you will see where your favorite fish hang out.

Federal attempts at culturing walleye began in the early 1900s and were mainly concentrating on the harvest of eggs and the hatching of fry for stocking. Fish biologists were not able to care for captive walleye beyond the sac fry stage for lack of a food to feed the young fish. In 1906, the U.S. Bureau of Fisheries stocked more than 368 million walleye fry into the Great Lakes and tributary waters.

By the early 1950s, walleye pond culture improved as larval fish diets developed. By the 1970s, captive propagation became more intensive with greater improvements in diet allowing walleye to grow to six inches or larger before facing the rigors of the wild. The greater size ensures a somewhat greater likelihood of survival.

A U.S. Bureau of Fisheries biologist hefts a heavy walleye from a net. USFWS NFACA

Spring runs of walleye draw anglers to the water.
USFWS MA

The U.S. Fish and Wildlife Service is still at it. My station, Genoa National Fish Hatchery, is waist-deep in walleye culture, stocking tribal waters and public lakes around Wisconsin and Minnesota. Garrison Dam and Valley City National Fish Hatcheries in North Dakota and Gavins Point National Fish Hatchery, South Dakota, raise millions of walleye every spring. Add Private John Allen National Fish Hatchery in Mississippi to the mix; walleye are a northern species, but this facility is restoring a strain of walleye that has a natural tolerance for warmer waters—rivers that drain into the Gulf of Mexico.

It is easy to see why walleye is king in the hearts of many anglers: a true trophy fish, walleye reach ten pounds and thirty inches long. Frank Dufresne, the U.S. Fish and Wildlife Service's Chief of Public Information, offered this practical advice about walleye fishing in his 1949 book, *Lure of the Open*. "When the walleye are feeding, an expert fisherman can land more fish faster than he can in any other way. The explanation is simple—the fisherman never leaves the area where the fish are, while the troller is repeatedly running out of position, and has to work his way back again."

A mussel bed might be a good place to find walleye. Another good place is a hot spattering skillet—with fillets covered in bread crumbs destined for a plate.

—Doug Aloisi

Burbot

When you see your first burbot, you won't forget what they look like. You cannot mistake them for anything else, except for maybe an eel. Burbot are an unusual-looking fish for a freshwater fish biologist, let alone an unsuspecting angler. When pulled from the depths of a northern lake, the burbot takes most anglers by surprise. Depending on your location, ling, cusk, eelpout, and lake lawyer are common names used for this uncommon fish. The latter of the labels speaks to cultural perceptions as the name stems from the fish's propensity to voraciously feed on anything.

The fish is at home in the northern hemisphere, worldwide. It lives in northern Europe and Asia, and through Alaska and Canada. Here in the contiguous forty-eight, you will find it in the northernmost states, from Maine to Washington, the Dakotas, Wyoming, through the Great Lakes, the Ohio, Missouri, and upper Mississippi rivers. It is the only freshwater member of the cod family and shares the telltale goatee sported by members of that family, the single barbell dropping from its chin. The patterning of the skin with tiny embedded scales would make any camouflage manufacturer envious. Unique spotting patterns and colors enable the fish to blend into its underwater world, lying among stones on a lake or stream bottom during the day.

By day, burbot lie still. A setting sun and coming darkness enliven burbot to set about feeding. In the Great Lakes they share the great depths with whitefish and lake trout and compete for much of the same food—fish. Their broad bands of fine teeth are well suited for grasping fish. A diet study conducted in Ontario's Lake Simcoe in 1954 revealed their rapaciousness: the stomach of one large burbot held 101 yellow perch while another contained three pumpkinseed sunfish, an eight-inch smallmouth bass, and an eight-inch sucker.

Few would call themselves dedicated burbot anglers, but they are out there. Big fish are pulled through the ice on rigs baited with bacon or chunks of fish. Burbot are no delicacy but they are certainly palatable. The U.S. Bureau of Fisheries promoted burbot for the dinner table in the 1920s with promotional posters. Bureau head William Redfield published his favorite recipes for burbot hash, burbot mousse, and scalloped burbot in the March 1920 *Ladies Home Journal*. Vitamins A and D richly embalm burbot liver.

Unfortunately, camouflage is not the only trait this fish will need to protect its well-being. The same issues that have plagued several other migrational fish species have also taken their toll on the burbot, and unfortunately, it no longer haunts many of the same waters as its ancestors. A challenge lies for the fish culturist to learn the secrets of the burbot so they can be returned to lakes and rivers where they have lost hold.

Despite the marked decline in burbot numbers, information on burbot culture was not readily available at the turn of twenty-first century. There are two early studies—one from the Wyoming Game and Fish Commission on artificial propagation of the burbot and a follow-up five-page report in 1952, "to gain information usable in the wise management of this species." Our staff at Garrison Dam National Fish Hatchery learned that the suggested temperatures for egg incubation are thirty-seven to forty-three degrees Fahrenheit. Though we had mature burbot at the hatchery in 2005, the season was a bust—no spawning occurred. The following year showed some progress; we applied some techniques used in striped bass culture learned from work performed at Tishomingo National Fish Hatchery in Oklahoma twenty years prior. Eggs hatched, but the tiny sac fry did not survive.

The winter of 2007 was a turning point; we incubated burbot eggs at much colder temperatures than those the Wyoming fish culturists touted—temperatures resembling the winter months of far northern extremes—that is, near freezing.

Garrison Dam National Fish Hatchery staff work together with many state agencies in the upper Great Plains.
USFWS NFACA

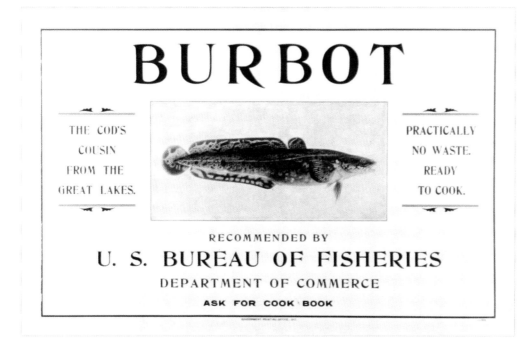

U.S. Bureau of Fisheries poster encouraged the consumption of burbot.
USFWS NFACA

It made perfect sense: burbot in nature spawn under the ice. It is unusual among fishes to spawn in such cold water. Northern pike come close, spawning at around forty degrees, but bona fide ice water—that is what made a difference in captive culture of burbot.

The yield was millions of larval burbot floating in the hatchery's tanks and jars in late winter. What do you feed a fish that is only slightly bigger than microscopic zooplankton? We allowed the larval burbot to eat from the smorgasbord of plankton provided in hatchery ponds until they were large enough to be released in the summer with some hope of surviving in the wild. Burbot grow slow; one- to three-inch fish go into Duck Lake on the Blackfeet Indian Reservation, Montana, at the guidance of the Montana Fish and Wildlife Conservation Office. We partner with the South Dakota Department of Fish, Wildlife and Parks and stock Lake Oahe on the Missouri River, June through August. We have turned out as many as two hundred thousand burbot.

It has been slow-going and the learning curve steep, but burbot were given an amazing reproductive capacity. A single female may shed a million eggs each winter that, coupled with a supportive fish hatchery crew, have ensured that the species will survive into the future.

—Rob Holm

Over the past 150 years, fish biologists used nets and seines in the same fashion as their predecessors. Hoop nets, such as this one lifted from the Missouri River by Jeff Finley (left) and Bryon Rochon from the Columbia Fish and Wildlife Conservation Office, have proved their worth for centuries. BRETT BILLINGS, USFWS

Rachel Carson (1907–1964)

Rachel Carson is best remembered for her pioneering indictment of pesticides, *Silent Spring* (1962), the book that launched the modern environmental movement. Carson's sixteen years with the U.S. Bureau of Fisheries and U.S. Fish and Wildlife Service are now largely forgotten, which is unfortunate because many of Carson's ideas and writing skills were developed while she was working for the nation's only wildlife conservation agency.

Carson had not intended to work for the government, but the Great Depression derailed her hopes of an academic career. Faced with supporting her family and armed with a master's in zoology from Johns Hopkins University, Carson sought a position with the U.S. Bureau of Fisheries, the nation's oldest conservation agency. Carson hired on to write short radio scripts on new and interesting aspects of fish biology called "Romance Under the Waters"—a much sexier title than the contents supported. She supplemented her pay of $6.50 per day by selling stories to the *Baltimore Sun* newspaper for $20 an article.

Carson's work was part of a broader New Deal attempt to use popular media to explain the growing federal role in conservation. Carson was good but not necessarily a natural at translating conservation sciences for public consumption. One of her first assignments was to create a brochure with the

U.S. Bureau of Fisheries fish biologist Rachel Carson peers into a microscope. USFWS MA

evocative title "The World of Waters." Her initial draft was far too literary for a government fish pamphlet, so her astute editor suggested she submit it to *The Atlantic*, which she did and in effect launched her professional literary career.

In 1936 Carson was able to parlay her writing skills into a full-time job as a junior aquatic biologist. Her first job as a government scientist involved studying fisheries and wildlife in the Chesapeake Bay region and then publishing reports and popular pamphlets on this work. Throughout her career, Carson was tasked with the most difficult literary chores, taking raw data and complicated scientific analysis and then translating that for public consumption.

In 1940, Carson's source material greatly expanded as the Bureau of Fisheries became the U.S. Fish and Wildlife Service, and she rose to assistant biologist in 1942. Carson remained primarily a writer, in spite of the scientific title. Despite having written the critically well-received *Under the Sea-Wind* in 1941, Carson's writing talents in the agency were underutilized. She became editor of the *Progressive Fish-Culturist* and created a series of conservation bulletins called "Food from the Sea." In 1945 she was made an "Informational Specialist," a title that reflected the nature of her work accurately over the last ten years.

Carson's ability to make fish come alive for the American public was evident in *Under the Sea-Wind*. The book was anthropomorphic, albeit engaging, in its clearheaded explanations. Her writing and editing skills allowed her to become chief editor of all publications by 1949, an important position as the U.S. Fish and Wildlife Service attempted to explain wildlife conservation for the first time to the American public. As part of this effort, Carson was put in charge of an ambitious series called *Conservation In Action*.

In addition to being the public relations arm of federal fish and wildlife conservation, editor Carson was also suddenly exposed to cutting-edge science including troubling new findings on environmental contaminants. The Fish and Wildlife Service's premiere laboratory in Patuxent, Maryland, had begun to study the effects of pesticides like DDT on certain wildlife, primarily fish and birds. This research had begun early in 1944, shortly after DDT came into widespread use as a chemical to win World War II. As chief editor, Carson oversaw all the scientific publications emanating from this new research and, as early as 1945, began considering the topic as a source of an article or book. She was already at work on her second book, *The Sea Around Us* (1951), a successful bestseller and allowed Carson to leave government service and devote herself full-time to writing. The germ of an idea had been laid, and ten years after she left the U.S. Fish and Wildlife Service in 1952 Carson wrote *Silent Spring*.

—Mark Madison, Ph.D.

Under the Sea-Wind RYAN HAGERTY, USFWS

Bering Cisco

Bering cisco are the type of fish you see and say "Yup, that's a fish" and continue with your day. They have that classic, but common fish look: silvery and fusiform. They're not impressively huge, fitting easily into two hands like a breakfast burrito. At one pound, they weigh about the same too. While they don't share the iconic status of their Pacific salmon cousins, they truly are Alaska's fish in that they're not found anywhere else. That is, except in the busy kosher markets in New York City. And this is what makes their story incredible.

Worldwide, there are only three known spawning populations of Bering cisco. All occur in Alaska, making the Bering cisco Alaska's only endemic fish. When they're not spawning in the Yukon, Kuskokwim, and Susitna rivers, they're moving between coastal marine estuaries and lagoons from the Colville Delta in the Beaufort Sea, south to the Alaska Peninsula and Cook Inlet. Their journeys can take them through hundreds and even thousands of miles of some of the wildest waters in the U.S.

Alaska Natives and rural residents look to Bering cisco and other related whitefishes as local sources of protein and a nexus for coming together to harvest and preserve wild foods, share meals, and pass on traditions. In coastal areas gill nets are used to catch Bering cisco, however, when they are migrating upstream to spawn they are most often captured with fishwheels. These large floating contraptions are held offshore in a river with two large baskets that rotate around in the current and scoop up fish. Where Bering cisco live, regional subsistence harvests of wild foods average nearly four hundred pounds per person annually, with the majority being fish.

So how did this unassuming Alaskan find itself in the Big Apple? Their high fat content has something to do with it. With the decline of deep-water cisco populations in the Great Lakes, demand for a similar product from the New York kosher market triggered the first commercial fishery for Alaska's Yukon River Bering cisco in the mid-2000s.

Alaska Native fishermen catch the ciscoes with gill nets in the lower Yukon River where it meets the Bering Sea. They take their catch to the community of Emmonak to be frozen and then shipped to Brooklyn to be smoked.

Initially, Alaska Department of Fish and Game fisheries managers were conservative, setting the annual commercial harvest quota at ten thousand fish—a nod to needing more robust information about the Yukon River population. As the commercial fishery matured and market demand intensified, harvesters annually requested increased harvest quotas. Recognizing the economic opportunity for the region, managers cautiously increased the quota through the early 2010s to twenty-five thousand fish.

As harvest pressure increased, managers became increasingly mindful of the need to understand the three stocks and their abundance. This piqued the interest of U.S. Fish and Wildlife Service fish biologist Randy Brown, stationed at the Fairbanks Fish and Wildlife Conservation Office, who came to Alaska at the age of seventeen and, for the past couple of decades, has dedicated himself to filling information gaps about anadromous fish populations that are important to subsistence users in northern and western Alaska.

Randy was among the first to recognize that Bering cisco were endemic to Alaska, that whitefish species were extremely important to subsistence users along the western and northern coasts of Alaska and the Yukon River, and that an expanding commercial fishery in the lower Yukon River could potentially affect both the species and subsistence users. Additionally, he recognized there was little known about the species and its three uniquely Alaska stocks.

Bering cisco KATRINA LIEBICH, USFWS

So he implanted individually coded radio tags into fish to locate the Yukon population's spawning destination. The results indicated the population spawned within the U.S. Fish and Wildlife Service's Yukon Flats National Wildlife Refuge.

With the spawning area identified, the next step was confirming the origin of fish captured in the commercial fishery. This would allow managers to regulate harvest more accurately as a single stock fishery or a mixed stock fishery made up of fish from more than one population. DNA and the chemistry of the inner ear bones (otoliths) of harvested fish helped answer this question. A collaborative effort between Ora Russ, a geneticist with the U.S. Fish and Wildlife Service, and Andy Padilla, a biologist with the Alaska Department of Fish and Game, concluded that more than 95 percent of the fish sampled from the commercial fishery were of Yukon River origin with few or no Kuskokwim or Susitna fish. Nearly identical results from the genetics and otolith chemistry projects provided overwhelming evidence that the Yukon stock dominated harvest in the commercial fishery and that it was likely considerably larger than the others. This greatly lessened the chance that other stocks would be intercepted. Both projects presented further support for the existence of only three populations and provided insights about ancestral relationships and geographic distribution among them.

Although management of the fishery could now proceed with the assurance of targeting only a single stock, an estimate of abundance could further improve conservation of the fishery. This led Brown to collaborate again with state fisheries biologists on a rigorous mark-recapture experiment estimating the number of spawners on the spawning grounds. The estimates found that previous and current levels of commercial harvests have not negatively affected the population, and likely will not. With the addition of the abundance estimate, managers now have a statistically sound, efficient, and repeatable method to periodically gain insights about the direct effects of the commercial fishery and, over time, develop optimum exploitation levels.

So if you ever find yourself in New York and discover a smoked gold cisco with rich, white flesh within, be sure to pause and think of the shimmery silver long-distance swimmers in Alaska and the science behind the fillet.

—Katrina Liebich, Ph.D.

Fish biologist Niccole Wandelear carefully pulls parasites from a fish's gills at the Aquatic Animal Drug Approval Partnership in Bozeman, Montana. The station's staff works to develop new aquaculture drugs for approval by the Food and Drug Administration.
RYAN HAGERTY, USFWS

Lake Sturgeon

To gaze into the eyes of a fish that is both larger and older than you gives you pause. In the Great Lakes, that can only be one species, the lake sturgeon, *Acipenser fulvescens*.

I had that experience first in 1997 as a young biologist with the U.S. Fish and Wildlife Service's Green Bay Fish and Wildlife Conservation Office. To better understand the status of this species in the Great Lakes, we began tagging these fish as they returned to spawn in a few Lake Michigan rivers, as they have done for millennia. Watching fish this large gather and splash in the shallow rapids below dams was impressive; many are over six feet long. Gently corralling them with big dip nets so we could measure, weigh, and tag each one was no small task. The work usually left us tired, very wet, occasionally bruised, but always wiser.

After a few years, I began to realize that not only were some of these fish older than me, a few of the larger ones were much older—possibly hatched in the late 1800s. Despite their advanced age, even the oldest fish were capable of outliving me, assuming my colleagues and I did our jobs well. I came to understand that making a meaningful contribution to lake sturgeon conservation would be my life's work. I felt a sense of duty to protect these fish and their kin from undue harm, to help increase their numbers, to help them persist across the Great Lakes.

No question, lake sturgeon are a unique fish—most certainly so among the Great Lakes fishes. They are among the largest and longest-living freshwater fishes on the planet. Lake sturgeon survived the events that caused the extinction of the dinosaurs. As the Pleistocene glaciers retreated, lake sturgeon lived on, coming to inhabit not only the glacier-gouged Great Lakes and St. Lawrence River but also rivers to the north draining to Hudson Bay, and to the south in the Mississippi River basin and its larger tributary rivers, as far south as Louisiana and Alabama. Appropriately, the native peoples of the Great Lakes region, the Anishinaabe, revere lake sturgeon as the King of Fishes.

Though people presume lake sturgeon are dangerous or threatening because of their size and shark-like appearance, they have no teeth, spines, or scales. They do not strike, hit, or chomp. They simply cruise their watery world and vacuum the bottom for a variety of food that now includes dreissenid mussels and round goby, two invasive species from Eurasia. U.S. Fish Commission biologists David Starr Jordan and Barton Warren Evermann cited in their 1902 book, *American Food & Game Fishes*, an 1894 lake sturgeon diet study showing crawfish, insects, gravel, and hazelnuts in the stomachs. And lake sturgeon grow and grow and grow. Particularly the females, who when mature, can produce and lay over one million eggs. Unlike most Great Lakes fish, sturgeon do not spawn every year. Females take twenty to thirty years to mature and then spawn once every three to seven years, after years of eating enough food to build up the energy to produce another one million eggs.

The largest lake sturgeon in modern records measured almost eight feet long and more than three hundred pounds. In recent years, adults seven feet long and two hundred pounds are not uncommon, and I have handled a few during my career. Before the major population declines a hundred-plus years ago, back when sturgeon numbered in the millions and were widespread across North America's large fresh water lakes and rivers, much larger fish undoubtedly existed. Early European explorers wrote of sturgeon filling rivers during their spawning migrations, congregating by the thousands in swift-flowing rapids that then existed in most large rivers.

This was before logging, dam building, and pollution, and before European settlers discovered that sturgeon, and their caviar-yielding eggs, were good to eat. Despite their geologic durability, history shows lake sturgeon are far from invincible. James Milner of

Fish biologist Eric Bruestle, Lower Great Lakes Fish and Wildlife Conservation Office, releases a lake sturgeon in the Niagara River below Niagara Falls. BRETT BILLINGS, USFWS

the U.S. Fish Commission reported in his survey of the Great Lakes fisheries in 1871–72 that some lake sturgeon were wantonly wasted after they fouled the nets of commercial fishing operations, while other operators fully used lake sturgeon. Milner reported that a business in Sandusky, Ohio, reduced lake sturgeon to smoked meats, isinglass for the glues and brewing industries, oil, and caviar exported to Germany. The company processed upwards of eighteen thousand lake sturgeon per year, caught from Lake Erie.

Jordan and Evermann noted in 1902 that, in the previous eight years, lake sturgeon harvest in the Great Lakes had suffered a serious decline. Dams that blocked migration and overfishing were taking a toll.

What had been the King of Fish in the Great Lakes for ten thousand years were nearly wiped out within a few decades in the late 1800s to early 1900s. We caught them as fast as we could, and we blocked migrations and destroyed their pristine spawning grounds. Populations all across the Great Lakes crashed. The only thing that saved the lake sturgeon from complete extinction is ironically their longevity.

In a sense, this long-lived fish could wait for us to recognize and correct our transgressions to properly conserve the fish and its habitat. Conservation in the Great Lakes began in earnest toward the end of the twentieth century. I was fortunate to be involved in this widespread conservation effort across the Great Lakes. Today, sturgeon rehabilitation is a focus of the Fish and Wildlife Service and also most tribal, state, and other federal natural resource management agencies, with important assistance from universities and many non-profit educational and recreational organizations.

Over the past twenty years, graduate students, professors, and agency professionals are all helping to answer key questions about this iconic species' habitat and critical life history needs, behavior, population status and trends, and the genetic diversity of existing populations. This has led to protection and education programs, long-term monitoring, and well-articulated management and rehabilitation plans, including novel ways to raise and stock fish designed to preserve diversity and build numbers needed for populations to thrive.

Many populations are in fact thriving well enough to support recreational fishing opportunities including catch-and-release fishing in many rivers and lakes, and in some places, a limited harvest of one fish per year for the lucky angler. In Lake Winnebago in Wisconsin and Black Lake in Michigan, a long-practiced traditional winter spear fishery is sustainably managed with assistance and support from citizen groups like Sturgeon For Tomorrow.

Today, a young child can adopt a sturgeon and begin what might be a lifelong relationship—with a fish. The child can hold the fish, feel its rough leathery skin, even gaze into its eyes, before carefully carrying it to the river's edge to let it swim free, into a river where sturgeon have been absent for a century. With luck, in twenty to thirty years this small six-inch fish might return as an adult sturgeon to repeat a seasonal rite of passage that will spawn future generations.

This fish might even cross paths with the human hands that reared and stocked it decades before. I enjoyed a similar encounter with an old acquaintance in the spring of 2019. While waist deep in a local river corralling and tagging sturgeon, I found myself looking into the eye of a fish I had captured in that same river twenty-one years before. This fish I knew better than most. Back in 1998, I surgically inserted a cigar-sized radio telemetry tag into this fish and tracked its movements around Green Bay for several years. As I examined this fish, I was pleased to see no visible scars from my earlier unskilled surgical work, only the numbered tag it carried provided proof of our earlier encounter. This sturgeon had continued to do its job perpetuating its kind for the past twenty years.

Since James Milner of the U.S. Fish Commission articulated the status of lake sturgeon in the Great Lakes nearly 150 years ago, the species has persisted precariously. The next 150 years rests squarely on us, as natural resource practitioners and as interested citizens, to continue what we have started: to provide the protection, the supporting management, and a suitable environment that ensures a lasting future for this King of Fish in the Great Lakes.

—Robert F. Elliot

Fish biologist Albert Spells, Virginia Fish and Wildlife Conservation Office, was an authority on Atlantic sturgeon. He enjoyed a forty-year career and retired in 2020. KELLY PLACE, USFWS

David Hendrix (1955–)

As a child growing up on his family's farm near Waverly, Louisiana, David Edward Hendrix didn't realize he was laying the groundwork for his future. He hunted in the woods, fished the bayou, trapped the fields, picked cotton, and tended the family livestock.

Ranking twelfth among thirteen children, David and his siblings knew the love and boundless wisdom of their parents who taught them to be kind, polite, and authentic at all times.

David was the first in his family to attend college. Seeking summer employment after his freshman year, a chance meeting with a U.S. Fish and Wildlife Service biologist steered him into the future: he landed a gig at New London National Fish Hatchery in Minnesota, raising walleye, smallmouth bass, and sunfishes. It was the furthest he had ever been from home.

David earned a B.S. in Fisheries from Southern University and later earned an M.S. at Iowa State University. After college, he hired on as a fish biologist at the Hiawatha Forest National Fish Hatchery at Pendills Creek, Michigan. There, he worked with lake trout. Early on, as David contemplated his future, he considered a career in fisheries management, fish health, and fish culture at hatcheries. He chose the latter because he preferred working with and educating the public. And fish culture was more like what he had done as a youngster on the farm.

In 1990, he became manager of the Neosho National Fish Hatchery, in Missouri. Leaving the Great Lakes fisheries around Michigan was not easy. David was joined in time by assistant hatchery manager Doug Aloisi. The two men have remained great friends ever since, even as Aloisi went on to become a manager at Genoa National Fish Hatchery, in Wisconsin. At Neosho, David and crew raised rainbow trout, imperiled pallid sturgeon, imperiled Topeka shiner, and mussels.

David declares that the move to Neosho proved to be the greatest of his life—a godsend—set on course by the circumstances of his youth. "I went to Neosho knowing I had to do my part at the hatchery, to strive for excellence. I remember my parents telling me to be myself. I have been fully accepted here—and that's why I am still here in retirement," he said.

In a professional foreign exchange program, David had the opportunity to visit China and witness fish culture operations with sturgeon. It was a revelation in that he found little differences with how sturgeon are cultured in the U.S. He was, however, shocked to see widespread impoverishment.

Neosho National Fish Hatchery is among the oldest operating hatcheries in the U.S.—and it has one of the newest, most innovative visitor centers anywhere, thanks to David's tenacity and the support of the Friends of Neosho. The new building models the classic designs commonly seen at other national fish hatcheries, crafted circa 1890 to 1910, by former U.S. Fish Commission architect Hector von Bayer. It is a wonderful attraction where the public learns about fisheries conservation and the work of the U.S. Fish and Wildlife Service. It is, in no small way, a monument to David.

David retired from the U.S. Fish and Wildlife Service in 2016, having improved the lot of fish, fisheries, and fishermen in the Midwest and Great Lakes in the span of three decades. He could serve as a model fish biologist. He is a wonderful father and grandpa, a proud American, loyal to the agency for which he worked. He knows how to lead and when to follow and has unreserved love for people. The man has the sunniest disposition. In Neosho, it was often said that if you are feeling blue just stop by the hatchery and see David.

—Kay Hively

Above: In his long conservation career, fish biologist David Hendrix worked with a variety of species from rainbow trout to pallid sturgeon. USFWS NFACA

Sea Lamprey

The past cannot be undone, but with science and technology fisheries professionals can find a fix to a particular piscatorial problem. And it starts upstream, in the smallest of rills in the uplands that pour into the Great Lakes.

The sea lamprey, as its name implies, is naturally at home in the Atlantic Ocean. The Welland Canal, built in 1829, connected the Great Lakes more directly to the eastern seaboard and there was an unintended consequence of great magnitude. The new waterway allowed sea lamprey to invade the Great Lakes. The outcome was devastating.

The sea lamprey is a fish. On the evolutionary scale, it is primitive—without scales and without bones. Its slightly cone-shaped circular mouth is loaded with rings of sharp raspy teeth. It is a parasitic pest that makes a living by grating onto its host, sucking body fluids as it clings along for the ride. The wounds it leaves cause great harm to the host fish, including death. Because of the sea lamprey, fish species native to the Great Lakes such as the lake trout have suffered tremendously.

The sea lamprey will spend twelve to twenty months in its parasitic phase in open water, killing up to forty pounds of fish through this life stage. Lake trout are not the only fish to host the invasive lamprey; landlocked salmon, steelhead, lake whitefish, lake sturgeon, walleye, and burbot are often attacked by sea lamprey.

But lake trout populations have taken a measurable toll: prior to the lamprey explosion in the 1950s, about 15 million pounds of lake trout a year were

Parasites like sea lamprey often kill host fish, like this trout. USFWS MA

An electric barrier on Michigan's Iron River keeps invasive sea lamprey at bay. USFWS NFACA

harvested from Lakes Superior and Huron. Ten years later, only three hundred thousand pounds came out of the lakes. Lake trout harvest in Lake Michigan alone went from 5.5 million pounds in 1946 to a mere 402 pounds seven years later.

With Great Lakes fisheries devastated by invasive sea lamprey, the Great Lakes Fishery Commission prompted a scientific inquiry into approximately six thousand substances to determine what might chemically control the destructive parasite.

In 1958, the compound commonly called TFM proved its worth through research conducted at the former U.S. Fish and Wildlife Service research facility in LaCrosse, Wisconsin. This selective lampricide could suppress the invasive parasite while the sea lamprey was still in its early larval stage.

Under the auspices of the Great Lakes Fishery Commission, U.S. Fish and Wildlife Service biologists now apply TFM in roughly 250 streams tributary to the Great Lakes.

It is not the adult lamprey sought by biologists applying TFM to streams. The adult lampreys swim

The sea lamprey's mouth is made for grasping fish flesh. KARLA BARTELT, USFWS

Fish biologist Jess Barber is a sea lamprey control authority stationed at Marquette Biological Station, Michigan. Barber oversees lamprey trapping, barriers, and lampricide applications in the Great Lakes. USFWS

into the tributaries in the spring of the year to spawn and then die. Their eggs hatch in gravels, and the worm-like larvae move into muck to live out the next several years before transforming into their parasitic phase and moving downstream into open lake water. The compound TFM kills sea lampreys in the larval stage in the small upland streams.

While TFM is the primary means of knocking back lampreys, it is not the only one. The Great Lakes Fishery Commission and its partners oversee an integrated pest control program, combining several control methods to target sea lamprey throughout their lifecycles. One of these methods employs barriers built or temporarily installed across several streams to block sea lamprey from moving upstream to spawn. Sea lampreys lack an ability to leap, so hundreds of small, low-head barriers on streams across the Great Lakes basin create impassable heights and prevent sea lampreys from migrating. The barriers essentially lessen the need to apply TFM above the barriers. Trapping and application of scent pheromones to either repel or attract spawning-phase adult lamprey to traps or less suitable habitat are all used to prevent sea lampreys from ascending to upstream spawning grounds.

The adage "make haste slowly" applies to the sea lamprey control. A great deal of scientific expertise and perseverance brought sea lamprey control a long way from its nadir in the 1950s. Well-trained and dedicated biologists go after sea lamprey in a measured, deliberate way.

On any application of TFM, barrier assessment or population surveys, the U.S. Fish and Wildlife Service will have deployed staff at the Lake Champlain Fish and Wildlife Conservation Office in Vermont; the Marquette Biological Station near the Lake Superior shore; or the Ludington Biological Station nested along Lake Michigan, all with impressive expertise in chemistry, limnology, hydrology, and fisheries science. That work is paying off. Desirable sport and commercial fisheries valuable to people and the Great Lakes ecosystem are on the rebound.

—Craig Springer

Pallid Sturgeon

It was beginning to feel like we were chasing a ghost. Day after day bled into week after week, searching for an apparition that never seemed to materialize in our nets. Our phantom was the pallid sturgeon, known to scientists as *Scaphirhynchus albus*. For two years I pulled gill nets from the murky depths of the Big Muddy—the Missouri River—and had yet to see this fabled fish. The listing of the pallid sturgeon under the Endangered Species Act in 1990 preceded my career commencement by less than a decade. Having seen photos of the fish, I knew to look for its pale color, unusual size, elongated snout, bald white belly, linear whiskerlike barbels, and archaic armor plates on an otherwise scaleless body. I looked forward to cradling one in my arms.

Pallid sturgeon are often touted a living fossil, or the Missouri River dinosaur, and even the ugliest fish in North America. Its scientific species name *albus* is Latin for white, pale, dull, or colorless—a most apt description. The early fossil record from earth's basement indicates its rise in existence during the Cenozoic Era, and for 60 million years it lurked uncontested in the muddy rivers of the North American continent. Although the pallid sturgeon survived the cold crush of the Pleistocene winter, the Industrial Revolution, the Gold Rush, and westward expansion to the Pacific coast, it has only recently experienced changes so extreme that they threaten its very existence.

In less than a century, overfishing, caviar trade, habitat destruction via pollution, dam construction, and changes in river flows hammered the fish. Add hybridization wrought by flow changes, and they have all forced the pallid sturgeon to stare at the face of extinction. The Pick-Sloan Flood Control Act of 1944 was part and parcel of FDR's New Deal; it dealt the final blow. The Big Muddy became a series of wide, sluggish lakes, all bravado gone. Concrete edifices stymied fish migration, blocking spawning migrations and altering flow such that larvae cannot sufficiently mature.

Fish biologist Rod May shows off a new hatchery truck sporting a pallid sturgeon image. May is an authority in sturgeon culture and manages Neosho National Fish Hatchery, in Missouri. USFWS

Form follows function: the pallid sturgeon is built for a life in big, swift rivers such as the Missouri. This image was taken Gavins Point National Fish Hatchery, South Dakota. BRETT BILLINGS, USFWS

The question looms: "Had people known these actions would jeopardize this animal, would they have proceeded?" It can never be answered. Conservation organizations and river managers try to fathom how to meet the needs of all the conflicting interests of the river and its inhabitants, including the pallid sturgeon. In order to do this, biologists must find this elusive fish to study its mysterious and complicated existence and propagate in captivity.

Our quest to find our phantom fish continued until that momentous March day in 1999. It was a misty morning where the silver fog refused to leave the confines of the Missouri River bluffs near Rocheport, Missouri. Leaves had long abandoned the trees, bone-white skeletons of bare sycamore trees glowed through the fog, listlessly rising off the river begging for the light of the sun. We could see our breath and the steam from the exhaust of the boat's motor as we launched and headed upstream.

Just off the banks of the Big Muddy National Fish and Wildlife Refuge, at the mouth of a side channel, lay our submerged net. A side channel constructed by the U.S. Army Corps of Engineers provided more natural habitat for fish, including the pallid. Our net had soaked in the depths of the river overnight. The monotony of months of pulling nets filled with shovelnose sturgeon, a close kin of the pallid, lulled the crew into mechanical routine. Lift nets. Pick fish. Move on. The rote action turned into delirium. Hopes fade, you know. But this day, halfway through picking the net, an insipidly white form appeared from the muddy depths. It was not until I had hoisted

the net over the bow rail of the boat that I realized we had finally found our phantom fish.

Early in my career, the old "river rat" biologist supervisors would often say, "a person could work their entire career and likely not see the pallid sturgeon taken off the endangered species list." Our Columbia Fish and Wildlife Conservation Office crew would from time to time over the next twenty years encounter more pallid sturgeon. The more we caught in the habitats where we found them, the more we began to understand their biology, and with that the challenges they face.

We became *de facto* experts at collecting these ghosts and soon the hatcheries were producing as many as the system could handle without swamping their genetics. Finding a genetically pure, wild fish, which had not previously spawned in the hatchery, became a near impossible challenge. The lower basin of the Missouri and Mississippi rivers has yet to see the likes of the leviathan pallid sturgeon found in the upper basin.

Eighty-pounders have lurked the depths of the Big Muddy and its large tributary rivers since before the construction of the Pick-Sloan Dams in the mid-twentieth century—well before. They are ancient beyond human reckoning. They spanned a geologic era and one can envision long whitish fish adorned with armor plates cruising waters left behind retreating glaciers ten thousand years ago. Conservation work on this fish spanning a career seems like a mere spot of time, but time well spent, the outcome of which will be determined over the horizon.

—Jeff Finley

Paddlefish

Allis-Chalmers tractors, Missouri's Osage River, and my left palm all have something in common—a connection to the oddest of American fishes, the paddlefish.

First, the tractors: the company's principal, Mr. Allis, had an affinity for finned animals and at one time offered a long-standing $1,000 reward to the person who could bring him a paddlefish less than two inches long. At the time, how the fish reproduced in the wild was still a mystery. Lore has it that the reward went unclaimed. Famed U.S. Fish Commission scientists David Starr Jordan and Barton Warren Evermann in their exhaustive 1902 text, *American Food & Game Fishes*, remarked on the paucity of information on paddlefish reproduction: "The young of the paddle-fish are scarcely, if at all, known. Indeed, we have never seen or heard of an example under 6 or 8 inches in length, and individuals so small as that are but rarely seen. Specimens under a foot in length are very greatly desired by naturalists."

It seems peculiar that so little was known to science about a creature so unusual looking that grows so large and conspicuous.

That brings me to the Osage River, April 20, 1960, following a spring freshet that washed downstream. Charles Purkett Jr., from the Missouri Department of Conservation, was himself looking into the biology of paddlefish. Purkett was the first scientist to observe paddlefish spawn; as waters receded, he watched paddlefish converge and convulse in rapids over a gravel bed at the juncture of Weaubleau Creek. Four days later, he found larval paddlefish in the gravels. A few days on, he found no paddlefish as the young had descended downstream. Purkett wrote about what he saw a year later in the scientific journal *Transactions of the American Fisheries Society*. We have since learned a great deal about paddlefish biology.

If you want to know how my hand fits in the story, read on.

Colloquial names like spoonbill, spoonbill catfish, shovelnose, oarfish, and mudshark are commonly used to refer to the paddlefish even though it is not a catfish or shark at all. The names allude to appearance and habitat. Paddlefish belong to the scientific order Acipenseriformes, a group of ray-finned fish with cartilage skeletons that included sturgeons. Two species of paddlefish exist in the world, one from the Yangtze River in China and the American paddlefish whose native range spans the entire Mississippi

After becoming a naturalized U.S. citizen, British-born Francis Rolt-Wheeler authored a number of young adult adventure books including *The Boy with the U.S. Fisheries* in 1912. BRETT BILLINGS, USFWS

Arguably the most unusual fish in North America, the paddlefish grows quite large on the smallest foods—microscopic plankton, detected by the fish's large snout. DOUG CANFIELD, USFWS

Staff at the U.S. Bureau of Fisheries' Fairport Biological Station in Iowa conducted early research on paddlefish circa 1920. USFWS NFACA

River basin from Montana to New York and from the Canadian border to the Gulf of Mexico. There is a singular record of a paddlefish from Lake Erie, which probably arrived via the Wabash and Erie Canal.

Its scientific name, *Polyodon spathula,* is Latin meaning *many toothed* and *spatula* referring to its long flat snout. Ironically, the paddlefish does not have a single tooth in its head but rather a comb-like structure called *gill rakers* used to sieve microscopic plankton—its only food source—from the water.

Its unique attribute, the paddlelike snout called a rostrum, is a mysterious and perplexing adaptation. The rostrum, webbed with specific and unique nerves, is used to locate plankton colonies in muddy water and as an antenna to navigate. The paddlefish has been around 50 million years longer than dinosaurs with fossil records indicating its emergence at around 300 to 400 million years ago. Scientists believe it to be the longest existing animal in North America. Additionally, it is one of the largest fish in American waters, frequently tipping the scales at over one hundred pounds, with the largest paddlefish on record coming from Iowa's Lake Okoboji weighing a whopping 198 pounds.

The sturgeons and paddlefish provide something to the elite classes around the globe: caviar. Their eggs are scarce and considered a delicacy.

It is also a primary reason for their global decline.

Due to their slow growth and late maturation—male paddlefish mature at age ten and females at sixteen—and since each individual will not spawn every year, they are easily overfished. Moreover, extracting caviar is lethal. Paddlefish caviar has replaced its overseas cousins as the most popular and available caviar product in the world. This is largely owed to meticulous management and monitoring in the U.S., coupled with the fact that most Americans are not very fond of this sophisticated salty snack. Paddlefish caviar is exported around the globe with the majority going to Japan.

The popularity of paddlefish caviar and its similarity to rare forms of sturgeon caviar make it a prime candidate for illicit trade and fraud. Because of this, the U.S. Fish and Wildlife Service's Missouri Fish and Wildlife Conservation Office where I work cooperated with my agency's special agents in an undercover investigation in illegal paddlefish caviar exports.

There are more conservation successes. Biologists in my shop continue to monitor paddlefish populations in the Midwest, including the outcomes of stockings. Several national fish hatcheries are nearly three decades on in raising and returning paddlefish stymied by dams in their trek to find gravel bars over which to lay their eggs. Altogether, federal hatcheries at Garrison Dam, North Dakota; Gavins Point, South Dakota; Tishomingo, Oklahoma; Private John

Fish biologist Kerry Graves handles a paddlefish at Tishomingo National Fish Hatchery in Oklahoma. The forty-year veteran biologist has led paddlefish reintroduction into waters in Kansas, Texas, and Oklahoma working with their state fishery management agencies. Restored fisheries have turned up several new state-record paddlefish.
MARY DAVIS, USFWS

Paddlefish is an important food fish, as evidenced by these workers turning a substantial catch to food staple. Date and location unknown. USFWS MA

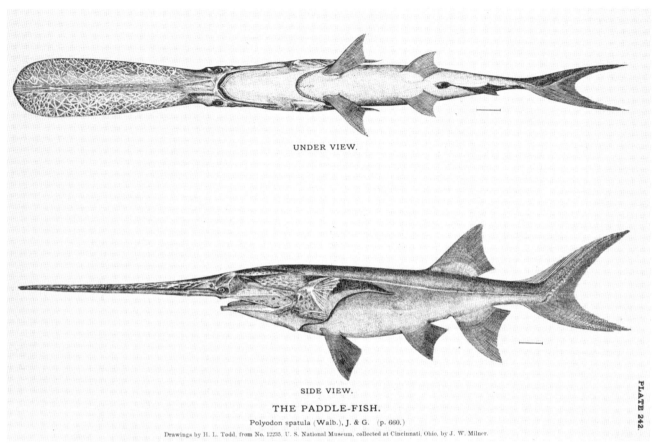

UNDER VIEW.

SIDE VIEW.

THE PADDLE-FISH.

Polyodon spatula (Walb.), J. & G. (p. 660.)

Drawings by H. L. Todd, from No. 12235, U. S. National Museum, collected at Cincinnati, Ohio, by J. W. Milner.

PLATE 242.

What's in a name: *Polydon spatula* refers to the profuse number of "teeth" on the inside of the paddlefish's gill used to rake plankton from the water that flows through its gaping mouth as it swims. *Spatula* describes its most prominent feature. J.W. Milner of the U.S. Fish Commission collected this fish during his trips to the Great Lakes states in the 1870s. USFWS NFACA

Allen, Mississippi; and Mammoth Spring, Arkansas, have released millions of young paddlefish. My counterparts at the Texas Fish and Wildlife Conservation Office recently returned paddlefish into Caddo Lake following a decades-long hiatus.

It is a good time to be a paddlefish angler. Some states have capitalized on paddlefish management by providing a free packaging and processing service to anglers in exchange for the eggs. The states market the legally caught caviar and use proceeds to reinvigorate the conservation program. Montana, North Dakota, and Oklahoma state fish and wildlife agencies use caviar earnings to pay for propagation, research, and monitoring these primitive giants. Caviar buyers love it because they know the product was not poached, and the anglers, who would otherwise most likely discard the eggs, enjoy supporting conservation and getting their fish packaged and processed free.

I have always adored the paddlefish for its unique appearance, delicious meat, and hefty fight, and I marvel still at their perseverance on this planet.

Now, about my left hand. As a student fisheries trainee I frequently assisted the Missouri Department of Conservation with tagging hatchery-reared paddlefish. Before release into the wild, these fish get a stainless steel wire tag as long as a dime is thick, each with a unique code etched into it. Tags extracted later, oftentimes years later, can tell biologists where that fish was reared or tagged in the wild, as well as valuable information regarding growth, harvest, and migration.

The tagging task is tedious; handling hundreds of thousands of hammer handle-sized paddlefish becomes a rote exercise and provides the opportunity for great conversation. Being young and eager to learn, I would team up with the hatchery manager or senior biologist to pick their brains. Once, I was so engrossed in conversation, I mistakenly tagged my palm. To this day, I carry a paddlefish tag in my left hand. And since then, I have lifted hundreds of nets, and thousands of paddlefish have passed through that hand—ever mindful that one tag was enough.

—Jeff Finley

Alligator Gar

The first time that I saw an alligator gar was quite memorable. I was about ten years old. A southwest Missouri creek had swollen after a rainstorm and subsided enough for my dad, my brothers, and me to get in a day of fishing. The fishing was slow, and we did as boys do, resorting to skipping rocks over the flat glassy pools. That is when we encountered the carcass of a massive fish on the bank—an alligator gar.

This dead fish was as long as I was tall—torpedo-shaped, big, tough scales, olive-green, with a massive fan-shaped tailfin and a broad, triangular, spatula-shaped snout full of teeth. The formidable hulking body mesmerized me. I drifted into thoughts of catching the monster fish with my Zebco 202 reel and secondhand rod.

I was curious why the dead gar lay so far up on the bank. Dad offered that gator gar were not good for anything; anglers killed them purposely thinking that throwing them up on the bank saved the game fish. I was immediately infatuated.

Fast forward a few decades and a few hundred miles from southwest Missouri. I am a Fish Biologist at the Tishomingo National Fish Hatchery, Oklahoma, where I have waded chest-deep into alligator gar conservation.

The big fish are the beneficiary of leading-edge conservation work performed at my station—and it has been badly needed. The alligator gar suffered a bad reputation as a marauder that has probably contributed to decades of overharvest. To stave off the decline in gator gar numbers, the U.S. Fish and Wildlife Service supplements alligator gar populations by rearing them in national fish hatcheries, the offspring stocked into the species' native waters. State fish and game agencies have imposed reduced creel limits and educated anglers about the plight of the big gar and its importance in river ecosystems.

In our efforts to spawn alligator gar at Tishomingo National Fish Hatchery, we aim to breed at least three

females with three males each spring. Sounds simple enough, but the females must exceed one hundred pounds each, as fish that large are likely to carry more than three hundred thousand eggs. Because the females live about twice as long as males, they also grow about twice as large. Bigger fish require bigger nets and tanks.

That is how I found myself several years ago bundled up against the cold March weather, standing on the bow of a small boat wafting down the Red River on the Texas-Oklahoma state line, fishing for big broodstock.

There was a method and purpose to this. By overwintering captive gar at the hatchery, I had learned that they grow very quickly in the first year but go dormant in water colder than sixty-eight degrees Fahrenheit, refusing to eat until temperatures rise again in the spring.

Local anglers know this; they take big alligator gar in the deepest river holes when the water is its coldest. That March day, I had already snagged woody debris on the river bottom a couple of times with my 4/0 treble hook on 100-pound test braided line. I had done it again when the log at the other end began to move.

The giant fish awakened from its slumber to put up a powerful fight. After what seemed like hours of reeling and stripping, the fish finally came to the surface beside the boat. It was half the length of my fourteen-foot jon boat. We safely secured the live fish and transported it to the hatchery, hoping for a female.

My alligator gar turned out to be a ninety-pound male, and we used him for spawning before returning him to his native Red River. Releasing him later that fall was as memorable as catching him. I stood on the end of the tank trailer to watch his sinuous form swim past the flooded picnic tables next to the river. The high water seemed a good omen.

Alligator gar need flooded plains at the right time of year with the right water temperatures to spawn in the wild. Vegetated flooded plains serve as an incubator for the sticky fertilized eggs and nursery for the hatchlings until they can swim off into the river channel. This flooding needs to last for about ten days to give the young gar a good chance of survival.

In southern Oklahoma, the young gar grow over twenty-four inches in their first six months of life before laying off feed for the next five months in the cold weather. Dams and flood control channels in the Mississippi River basin where alligator gar naturally occurred have decimated alligator gar spawning habitats.

A marvel of the fish's life history is also a confounding factor in their conservation. Alligator gar live a long time, more than sixty years. They are slow to mature and females may not reproduce until fifteen years old. Natural cues such as flow and water temperature must line up at the right time with fish the right age. Taking out too many big females could crash a population quickly.

Popular opinion of alligator gar seems to be shifting. Anglers recognize its potential as a sport fish; the world-record fish checked in at 327 pounds and nearly nine feet long. Alligator gar is the second-largest freshwater fish in North America behind white sturgeon.

The alligator gar is an apex predator and stands atop of the food chain in big rivers in the South and much of the Midwest. Unlike other fish, it waits in ambush for prey nearly one-third its own body length. It shoots forward with explosive speed to catch food in its toothy jaws. Alligator gar have an extra row of teeth in their upper jaws to hold larger prey until they can swallow them whole. Research in stomach content analysis revealed that alligator gar eat a wide variety of fish and small mammals, but carp, drum, and buffalo fish species dominate its diet—rough species of fish that can overpopulate rivers when left unchecked.

Imagine a 250-pound alligator gar ambushing an angler's offering with explosive speed. The fish leaps, breaking the water surface in a silver spray, surely to leave an indelible mark in the mind.

That gator gar carcass I encountered as a ten-year-old kid remains seared in mine. Time has not dulled the memory; the experience shifted my way of looking at the big fish. I like to think that the dead fish had already spawned ahead of the receding flood plain, and its offspring still swims that creek. That is entirely possible these decades later.

—Ralph Simmons

Fish biologist Kayla Kimmel, Baton Rouge Fish and Wildlife Conservation Office, raises an alligator gar netted during a population survey onto her boat. RYAN HAGERTY, USFWS

These two men show off a large alligator gar that probably weighed in the one-hundred-pound range. The two appear to be commercial fishermen given the substantial gill nets and hoop nets behind them. Date and location unknown. USFWS MA

Gar species, the alligator gar especially, has long suffered from the misconception that they are destructive and dangerous. Alligator gar are impressive reaching three hundred pounds and thirteen feet long. COURTESY LIBRARY OF CONGRESS

Commercial fishermen bring in a haul, a small alligator gar and two buffalo fish. Date and location unknown. USFWS MA

Alligator Snapping Turtle

Growing up in northwest Ohio the largest turtle I was aware of was the common snapping turtle. I would occasionally catch one while catfishing and really thought I had a monster. Little did I realize back then that common snapping turtles pale in comparison to the size of alligator snapping turtles that roam the southern wetlands and drainages of the Mississippi River.

As a young biologist at Tishomingo National Fish Hatchery, Oklahoma, I was asked to lead the alligator snapping turtle "head start" program. I remember that day vividly in 2005 when Hatchery Manager Kerry Graves asked me what I knew about turtles. My response was honest—and underwhelming. I admitted that I knew they were aquatic and had a shell.

The national fish hatchery waded into alligator snapping turtle conservation in 2000, following research by Dr. J. Daren Riedle that revealed turtle populations in Oklahoma were on the decline. The fish hatchery got into the turtle business, collecting adult turtles from a healthy population in eastern Oklahoma.

Under the leadership of veteran biologist Graves, I spent the next twelve years absorbed in developing techniques for adult turtle care, experimenting with housing tanks and pond designs, and locating and excavating nests. I learned by full immersion all about egg incubation, juvenile husbandry, disease prevention, tagging, transport, and reintroducing turtles to the wild.

This leading-edge work was not performed alone. We collaborated with Missouri State University professor Dr. Day Ligon and his team of graduate students: Denise Thompson, Mitch East, Jessica Miller,

Randon Peoples (left) and Brian Fillmore measure the shell of an alligator snapping turtle at Tishomingo National Fish Hatchery. MARY DAVIS, USFWS

Biologists Kristen Sardina (left) and Sarah Spangler, Tishomingo National Fish Hatchery, about to release captive-reared alligator snapping turtles into Oklahoma's Verdigris River. BRIAN FILLMORE, USFWS

Sarah Spangler, and Kristen Sardina. Their research provided evidence-based management strategies for the hatchery to benefit turtles. Kay Backues, DVM, of the Tulsa Zoo provided a great deal of veterinary care and assisted with multiple influential studies, one of which allowed for the sexing of juvenile turtles, a technique then unknown.

Over the years, I have been asked why we raise turtles at a fish hatchery. Foremost, our work responds to the decline of the turtle—and in doing so we have learned a great deal about the animal. Alligator snapping turtles possess intrinsic value in nature as an apex predator. Due to their secretive and aquatic lifestyle, alligator snapping turtle populations are extremely difficult to monitor in the wild. We spend much time setting and checking baited hoop nets set out overnight in bogs and oxbows and river slack waters to determine more about where and how they live.

We have learned something curious about their nature: male alligator snapping turtles rarely leave the water; females will come onto land under the cover of darkness in May and June, but only to dig a nest. A hole ten inches deep in loamy soil holds about thirty eggs that closely resemble ping-pong balls. The eggs incubate ninety days when hatchlings emerge from the earth seeking the closest water source.

Fewer than 1 percent of eggs naturally laid in the wild survive to adulthood with most never hatching due to predation from raccoons, feral hogs, otters, and bobcats. Both sexes reach maturity at approximately fifteen years old, with males reaching sizes of up to 250 pounds and females rarely exceeding 60 pounds. A full-grown turtle reaches five feet from snout to tail. Both males and females have the potential to live beyond seventy-five years. Humans are the only true predators of large alligator snapping turtles.

Perhaps because alligator snapping turtles are so secretive—and, well, interesting to look at—they are the subject of wives' tales. These legacies in particular seem to persist: they are of a vicious nature; they eat all the sport fish; and once they snap their jaws on something, they will not let up until they hear thunder.

That's fanciful lore, but here is the truth. Alligator snapping turtles serve an important function in nature as a predator and in removing carrion—dead animals—an all-important custodial role. It is true that the turtles eat fish—they draw unsuspecting fishes toward their mouth with a "lingual lure," a piece of skin on their tongue that wiggles like a worm at the bottom of an open mouth. Some fish find it irresistible and they become turtle food. Their temperament has been completely misrepresented. These creatures are gentle giants unless provoked. If someone places a stick in your face or tries to pick you up by your shirt collar and belt, you are going to have something to say about it. If an alligator snapping turtle clamps on your finger, you'll most likely lose it.

Alligator snapping turtles are modern day dinosaurs, and we have much more to learn about these fascinating creatures.

—Brian Fillmore

Fish passage engineer Heather Hanson, Anchorage Fish and Wildlife Conservation Office. She works to design replacement road culverts in Alaska to emulate a natural stream channel and easily allow fish to pass upstream and move between various habitats they need through the seasons and through their lives.
KATRINA LIEBICH, USFWS

James Spinymussel

Harrison Lake National Fish Hatchery is woven into the American story. The young men of the Civilian Conservation Corp built the hatchery in 1934 on land formerly part of the Berkeley Hundred, established in 1619. The Berkeley Plantation of the mid-eighteenth century was an important producer of grain and flour. The bucolic Charles City County, Virginia, belies the turbulent Civil War defensive earthworks built by Federal troops on what is now a national fish hatchery. Union soldiers bivouacked here in the hot summer of 1862, after Confederates pushed them from Richmond at the culmination of the Peninsula Campaign.

Hardwoods and longleaf pines tower over the hatchery grounds today, adorned with a scattering of flowering redbud and dogwood trees. In the beginning, the hatchery raised channel catfish, bluegill, crappie, and largemouth bass to stock public, military, and private waters.

In the 1980s, the hatchery and its staff answered the call to help restore important migratory fishes such as striped bass, American shad, and river herring to Virginia and Maryland rivers.

Over the past fourteen years, the hatchery's conservation efforts have broadened to include freshwater mussels. The hatchery is home to the Virginia Fisheries and Aquatic Wildlife Center—a collaboration with the U.S. Fish and Wildlife Service and the Virginia Department of Game and Inland Fisheries and local universities. Its mission is to conserve declining or imperiled mussels native to Atlantic Slope rivers.

This was not the first venture into mussel culture. Near the turn of the twentieth century, the U.S. Bureau of Fisheries developed mussel culture methods to stave declines in the Mississippi River associated with pollution and overharvest from the button industry. With the advent of plastics, however, the demand for shell material declined and by 1929, the Great Depression had brought the shell-button industry to a halt. Interest in culturing mussels also halted, but those early methods developed by the Bureau of Fisheries provided the seeds for growing the technology used today to recover endangered species and restore ecological function of mussels in rivers.

In 2008, work at Harrison Lake National Fish Hatchery commenced with common species, and

James spinymussel is no more than inches in length, but en masse, large mussel beds filter massive amounts of river water. USFWS

Clam dredges hang on racks of a clam boat on the Mississippi River at Homer Fish-Cultural Station, Minnesota.
COURTESY WINONA COUNTY HISTORICAL SOCIETY

Freshwater
mussel dredge
used to harvest
mussels
from river
bottoms. USFWS MA

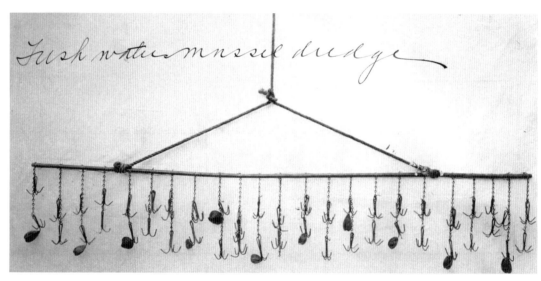

This image from
the U.S. Bureau of
Fisheries Fairport
Biological Station
shows how one
mussel could
be parsed into
many mother-of-
pearl products.
USFWS NFACA

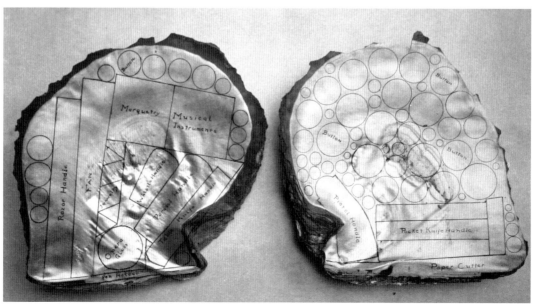

Mussel biologist Rachel Mair with floating baskets of mussels grown out in ponds at the Harrison Lake National Fish Hatchery. MATTHEW PATTERSON, USFWS

Tangerine darters, a close kin to walleye, swim about a bed of James spinymussels that look more like rocks than living organisms. RACHEL MAIR, USFWS

as the interagency team improved its capabilities, it expanded to rarer mussel species including the federally endangered James spinymussel.

Remnant populations of the James spinymussel persist in the upper reaches of the James and Dan rivers in Virginia, West Virginia, and North Carolina. They are part of an ancient group of mussels—the spinymussels—found only in eastern North America, whose origin dates back 150 million years. In 1988, the James spinymussel was listed as endangered due to habitat loss from poor water quality. Remaining populations were isolated from one another. Captive rearing and restocking once habitats improved would allow the mussel beds to rebuild.

Rachel Mair, lead mussel biologist at Harrison Lake, pioneered culture methods for the James spinymussel. Her careful techniques for infesting small host fish, such as the rosyside dace, with larval mussels was a mark of progress; the outcome was measurable. The interagency team has stocked more than 1,450 spinymussels since 2017 into three tributaries to the James River and one Dan River tributary.

The collaborative conservation work performed at the Virginia Fisheries and Aquatic Wildlife Center has raised thirteen different mussel species and released over 320,000 individual mussels into rivers of the Atlantic Slope: the James, Rappahannock, Appomattox, Mattaponi, Pamunkey, Meherrin, Dan, and Nottoway.

Freshwater mussels are intrinsicly and ecologically valuable. Mussels lie en masse on river bottoms and estuaries, continuously feeding themselves by filtering water. With the vast quantities of water that pass through mussel beds, they remove immense amounts of algae, bacteria, and nitrogen from the river. What the mussels do not use for food they excrete, the remains of which are consumed by aquatic insects and fungi and is further decomposed—all important to the life of water.

What is old is new. The work of the former U.S. Bureau of Fisheries is in a way reconstituted here—but with tools and technology far more advanced. The exigence is still essentially the same—to stave off a decline. In the past twenty years, we have learned much more about freshwater mussel biology; we better understand the mussel's role in nature. Restoring beds of freshwater mussels—and the services they provide—will help reverse the decline in a rare species, while protecting economically valuable fisheries that rely on good water.

—Catherine Gatenby, Ph.D.

Biologist Carlos Echevarria, Warm Springs National Fish Hatchery, Georgia, holds a purple bankclimber, a threatened mussel species. Carlos and hatchery colleagues study the animal's biology and potential host fish species. BRETT BILLINGS, USFWS

Texas Blind Salamander

Specimens of Texas blind salamander welled up into the light of day and into the luminosity of science in 1896, from 190 feet below, via a well casing sunk by the U.S. Fish Commission. The well serviced the Fish-Cultural Station at San Marcos, Texas, then located on the campus of Texas State University.

Otherworldly, pallid, and spindly, the Texas blind salamander makes its living in the watery labyrinth of the Edwards Aquifer of central Texas. They live out their entire lives in the dark limestone caves beneath the I-35 corridor. They have no skin pigment and a tiny vestige of eyes—small black dots, eye stems—that soon disappear with age. It was by chance that they were discovered and by happenstance, the discoverer is now its key conservator.

Unique habitat and good water made a home for an unusual animal. Competition for good water is its bane—water that influenced settlement dating to an 1831 Mexican land grant. The water brought renowned U.S. Fish Commission scientist Barton Warren Evermann there to locate a hatchery. He wrote in an 1892 U.S. Fish Commission report: "The river has its rise in a number of springs at the foot of a limestone ledge or hill just above town. All these springs together form a large deep stream from the bottom of which, near the upper end, wells up the principal spring. Many water-plants were found in the river and such species of fish as largemouth bass, sunfish, and various species of cyprinoids are abundant."

The necessary elements for a hatchery were present: water for fish, a railroad for distribution, and an enthusiastic newspaper editor. The *Hays County Times* flattered the construction engineer, William Benton, in November 1894: "The work is in the hands of a skilled and competent man whose artistic taste is displayed in both the plans and their execution and the people of San Marcos have good reason to congratulate themselves on being lucky enough to get the fish culture station."

The same article summed up the new hatchery's charge. "This station consists entirely of an outdoor pond hatchery, and the kind of fish that will be kept and hatched therein will be black bass and rock bass."

Two years later, Evermann facilitated the collection and scientific description of the eyeless amphibian. Now 115 years later, the facility Evermann located

A Texas blind salamander held in captivity at the San Marcos Aquatic Resources Center. They hatch with a vestige of an eye, the root of an optic nerve, but it disappears with age. DOUG CANFIELD, USFWS

Biologist Josh Abel, San Marcos Aquatic Resources Center, on the hunt for Texas blind salamanders. U.S. Fish and Wildlife Service scuba teams around the country collect rare species, assess habitats, and monitor aquatic invasive species. DOUG CANFIELD, USFWS

proves pivotal in conserving this most unusual of animals.

Largemouth bass and sunfishes were long the mainstay. In fact, the station closed for a time in the early 1920s, refusing to raise largemouth bass until the state legislature gave the fish the protection of the law. Today, largemouth bass fishing holds immense intrinsic and economic value in Texas and well beyond. The fish cultural station is now called the San Marcos Aquatic Resources Center. It has since moved off the college campus to a few miles away, still reliant on the same water. Scientists there are fully immersed in imperiled species conservation, chief among them, the Texas blind salamander, an endangered species.

The San Marcos Aquatic Resources Center maintains in captivity a backup population of Texas blind salamander in concert with the Edwards Aquafer Authority. The federal fisheries facility keeps a target of 250 wild-caught Texas blind salamanders on station in the unfortunate event that the wild population suffers catastrophic loss. The facility stands ready to return healthy salamanders back into the wild.

Station scientists research ways to better maintain the colorless salamanders in the wild. They also research tagging methods, aiming to learn how to mark them, a technique useful in learning more about the animal's habits and habitats.

San Marcos combined with its substation, Uvalde National Fish Hatchery, is only one of a few places where the animal exists in captivity. University of Massachusetts researchers have studied the captive animals in how they regenerate lost limbs.

San Marcos has regenerated itself, from raising and stocking sport fish to standing on the leading edge of imperiled species conservation. The "water-plant" Evermann noted in his 1892 U.S. Fish Commission report was undoubtedly Texas wild-rice, another imperiled organism, also found exclusively at San Marcos.

—Craig Springer

Texas Wild-Rice

Passing through the heart of San Marcos, Texas, a booming city halfway between Austin and San Antonio, the San Marcos River receives high recreational use year-round. In the summer, however, the crowds really start flowing. This is no more apparent than just after the day's float-tube rentals begin every morning at City Park, as masses of rivergoers embark on a one-mile tube ride to Rio Vista Dam.

During the annual, two-week Texas Wild-Rice Survey in August, I am among the dozen surveyors, several from my office, the San Marcos Aquatic Resources Center, who are firsthand witnesses to each day's initial wave of tubers. One morning, the father of a young family just entering the water asked me if they would loop back to their starting point. I hesitated, confused by his question until I realized he might have anticipated a looping tube ride like the one at a nearby big water park. I managed only a hurried no before the current pulled him away. Given the chance, I might have tried to convey some of the

river's unique attributes that would surely set this float apart from any others for him and his family.

The San Marcos River is perhaps the oldest river in central Texas and the only one in the region to have never gone dry. Constant spring discharges from the river's source, the Edwards Aquifer, and a stable water temperature—about seventy-two degrees Fahrenheit year-round—support a diverse array of species reliant on these conditions. Some, like the Texas blind salamander, live deep inside the dark recesses of the aquifer; others, like the riffle beetle, require microhabitats at spring openings; and still others, like the fountain darter and Texas wild-rice, depend on the crystal-clear flows of the main river.

For being endangered, Texas wild-rice is quite hardy in its home waters. There, this aquatic bunchgrass can exploit any water depth, from fast- to slow-flowing. Completely submerged, it grows large and leafy with long willowy blades swaying fluidly in deep, fast currents; in shallower, slower-moving water, it is

Stands of Texas wild-rice lie low in the smooth, clear currents of the San Marcos River. RYAN HAGERTY, USFWS

Botanist Leah Murray, San Marcos Aquatic Resources Center, collects Texas wild-rice seeds along the San Marcos River in Texas. RYAN HAGERTY, USFWS

emergent, staying shorter but sending up stout flowering panicles that produce seeds. Owing to its vigor, wild-rice generally even holds its own against aggressive exotic plant species that take over many parts of the river.

The plight of Texas wild-rice lies mainly in the small size of its natural range—only the first two miles of the San Marcos River, an area of roughly twenty-two acres. Although described as abundant throughout this area in the early twentieth century, Texas wild-rice had declined to only a few stands by the 1960s and '70s due, in large part, to active removal, through plowing and mowing, for recreation. To worsen matters, the few remaining plants did not appear to produce flowers and seeds, making the prospects for a future recovery bleak. Texas wild-rice was drifting into the abyss. What's more, the San Marcos River itself was doomed, according to credible sources, to extinction in twenty years—this because of intense, rapid demand by over two million people in the greater San Antonio area for water from the aquifer.

The tides turned for Texas wild-rice when it was listed as endangered in 1978, becoming the first Texas plant, and one of the first in the country, to

receive that designation since the passage of the Endangered Species Act of 1973. Removal and other activities destructive to Texas wild-rice were halted. The Act also led to new regulations on pumping from the Edwards Aquifer, averting the river's once-predicted demise.

Today, because of intensive human intervention—including propagation, river reintroductions, and protection of wild stands—the prominence of Texas wild-rice throughout much of its historical range has rebounded. Unlike in the past, it even flowers and seeds regularly in certain areas. Unfortunately, the species' ability to reproduce without help remains elusive, a sign that it is not self-sustaining. Finding ways to change this, by promoting natural production of seeds capable of sprouting into new plants in the river, could be the key to its long-term success. Otherwise, even if Texas wild-rice does not disappear altogether after the next scouring flood or other catastrophe, we might have to start from scratch in our restoration efforts, a very costly and long-term endeavor.

Texas wild-rice is a shining example of how endangered species and human use—in this case, recreation—can be compatible. Instead of cutting wild-rice to open more space for swimmers, the city of San Marcos is now part of a multi-agency partnership to protect it. Its near extinction also highlights the vulnerability of other rare, but less conspicuous, species reliant on the Edwards Aquifer. In the upper San Marcos River alone, there are at least four other species that occur nowhere else in the world, including the threatened San Marcos salamander, an endangered (possibly extinct) mosquitofish, a micro-caddisfly, and an amphipod (small crustacean) so new to science it remains unnamed. Though true testaments to the uniqueness of the aquifer and the aquatic ecosystems it supports, these species are unlikely to be observed by the casual rivergoer. Texas wild-rice, on the other hand, is experienced by nearly every visitor to the river, whether they know it or not. With proper management and protection, this understated symbol of the broader ecosystem might persist for future generations. If so, its story can continue to serve as a springboard in understanding for any new visitor to the San Marcos River, and a reminder to us all, that this place is much more than a recreational hot spot, with value far beyond what one will find on a looping tube ride at a big water park.

—Chris Hathcock

Wyoming Toad

A recently released Wyoming toad basks in the sun. MINDY MEADE, USFWS

I'm walking a transect within a designated survey plot in the high plains of Wyoming watching for the slightest movement in the tall grass. My partner, who wears a backpack filled with a clipboard, data sheets, scale, thermometer, swabs to detect disease, and a tag reader, walks the transect with me.

The sun beats down on us both, and I can hear the sound of a mosquito buzzing next to my ear.

With each step I take, my boot sinks into the marsh mud. A droplet of sweat runs down my cheek as I look at the ground with deep concentration. All of a sudden, my partner calls out, "Toad!" We pause our stopwatch and my heart races in anticipation to lay my eyes on our great find of the rare amphibian, the Wyoming toad.

The Wyoming toad is a unique species only found within the Laramie Basin—its historic range confined to a thirty-mile radius near Laramie, Wyoming. The toad is a glacial relict, a population that was left behind after the last ice age some ten thousand years ago. The toad's population once flourished in the flood plains, ponds, and small seepage lakes within the Laramie Basin until their population drastically crashed in the mid-1970s.

The cause remains unknown, but pesticides and habitat loss may figure large. Another serious matter is Chytridiomycosis, commonly called Chytrid, caused by a fungus. It's an infectious disease found to afflict amphibians and is linked to dramatic population declines of amphibians in several locations around the world.

A tool of the fish culture trade, egg pickers. These tongs allow biologists to remove dead fish eggs to prevent bacteria from affecting remaining live eggs. The object is preserved at the National Fish and Aquatic Conservation Archives.
SAM STUKEL, USFWS

In 1984, the U.S. Fish and Wildlife Service listed the toad as an endangered species, and shortly thereafter, declared extinct in the wild. In 1987, an isolated population of toads was discovered at Mortenson Lake, and those individuals were used to start a captive breeding program.

I first learned about the Wyoming toad in 2014 while attending the University of Wyoming. Seven years later I am fully immersed in Wyoming toad conservation at Saratoga National Fish Hatchery, where we keep a captive population in addition to working with Yellowstone cutthroat trout, lake trout, brown trout, and rainbow trout.

Since the toad's arrival to the hatchery in 1997, biologists have worked tirelessly to reintroduce tadpoles and juvenile toads to the wild at a handful of locations within the Laramie Basin. Mortenson Lake—where the last isolated population of toads was rediscovered—receives toads from Saratoga.

Years of monitoring the toads in the wild showed low survival rates and little evidence of breeding that has underscored the need for captive rearing. The toad does not reach sexual maturity until it reaches two or three years of age, and Wyoming's short summer season hinders its growth.

Management plans for the toad changed in 2016, and the national fish hatchery committed to keeping toads to just under one year of age before releasing them into the wild. Holding the toads for a longer period gives them a head start to being larger in size or even nearing breeding size when released.

Holding animals to a bigger size and older age also allows for research opportunities. Research on the toad will help us better understand the species' needs, and from that information we can hopefully reestablish enough toads to the wild that they will be able to survive on their own.

Meanwhile, we will keep walking transects in toad habitat beneath the vast Wyoming sky, looking down with great concentration for that subtle yet thrilling movement of a Wyoming toad in the wetland grasses.

—Ana Bode

Yazoo Darter

The Great Flood of 1927 in the lower Mississippi River and the Flood Control Act of 1928 could arguably be the most powerful natural disaster and resultant piece of legislation for enacting change on a major natural resource. Not only did those changes affect mainstem navigation depths and bank stability, take out sinuous bends, and shorten the river, there were also major changes to tributaries on the Lower Mississippi River.

The Yazoo River was not immune. It forms in northeast Mississippi and encompasses a 13,500-square-mile watershed, eventually emptying into the Mississippi near Vicksburg. Four flood control reservoirs were built from 1940 to 1954 on tributaries to the Yazoo.

As it turns out, the headwater areas above the two uppermost Enid and Sardis reservoirs serve as home, here and nowhere else on earth, to a two-and-a-half-inch fish called the Yazoo darter. The Yazoo darter was formally described for science in 1994 and is one of several snubnose darters in the loessial and clay hills of the eastern Mississippi Alluvial Valley.

Despite its relatively recent recognition, it has received some well-deserved research and attention from the U.S. Forest Service, the University of Southern Mississippi, the Natural Resource Conservation Service, and my station in the U.S. Fish and Wildlife Service, the Lower Mississippi Fish and Wildlife Conservation Office.

The Yazoo darter, a beautifully colored bottom-feeder, lives in the Little Tallahatchie River upstream of Sardis Reservoir and in the Yocona River upstream of Enid Reservoir. In-depth studies of the species are turning up new evidence that there could be two separate species, with the current thinking being that the Tallahatchie River fish is the true Yazoo darter.

Time will tell. Over the last twenty-five years, we have learned a great deal about distribution, habitat preferences, and genetic isolation across the species' range. There are locations within the Yocona and Little Tallahatchie basins where Yazoo darter cannot reach one another to breed due to habitat fragmentation. Their populations are isolated. The darter needs a way to better reach all available habitat to successfully reproduce with Yazoo darter populations from different creeks.

The problem, particularly in this part of Mississippi, is that many creeks are highly degraded. The building of the flood control reservoirs and clearing of land for agriculture, coupled with straightening streams to increase floodwater capacity, caused a lot of problems for streams in north Mississippi. Erosion and sediments choking fish habitat are a pervasive problem for the Yazoo darter.

So what can be done to help the Yazoo darter? Reconnect habitats and get darters back into improved waters within their natural range. A deteriorated culvert blocked the upstream passage of Yazoo darter on Smith Creek, which flows into Otoucalofa Creek. The U.S. Fish and Wildlife Service replaced the road crossing with a bottomless arch culvert—that is, a culvert where the natural stream bottom comprises the culvert bottom, allowing fish to freely swim through.

Biologists at Private John Allen National Fish Hatchery in Tupelo, Mississippi, spawned Yazoo darter and stocked them in Smith Creek three years running.

The journey of any length starts with the first step. Improving connectivity of the network of streams the Yazoo darters inhabit is that first step.

—Angeline Rodgers

Sicklefin Redhorse

The Eastern Band of Cherokee Indians call it *jung-hitla*, which means, wearing a red feather. It is an appropriate appellation as it describes a prominent physical feature on a fish native to southern streams of northern Georgia and western North Carolina: the sicklefin redhorse.

This fish is a member of the sucker family, fishes that typically dwell on the bottom of lakes and streams. Their fleshy lips are tactile organs that feel for food. Sucker species are important in the life and health of waters, living on a diet of microscopic crustaceans and insects. Redhorse are a group of suckers most commonly found in flowing waters, from small upland streams to bigger rivers, particularly in the Midwest and eastern U.S. Their head and nape, especially in older and bigger fish, looks like a horse's head. The fins of breeding males take on various hues of orange and brick to scarlet red.

The sicklefin redhorse's dorsal fin drapes up and over its back with some flair as if to call attention to itself like the panache in a military officer's headdress. And that is the origin of the fish's name used among the original people who populated the range of the sicklefin redhorse.

The sicklefin redhorse has long been known among Native people but only to biologists since 1937. Another fifty-five years later, fish expert Dr. Robert Jenkins at Roanoke College determined the sicklefin redhorse was likely a distinct species, one among many other redhorse species—except the sicklefin had a much more limited range.

Cherokee Indians harvested sicklefin redhorse. If you were to travel back in time to the creeks and rivers of western North Carolina, you would see V-shaped stone structures—weirs that spanned the breadth of streams with the point facing into the current. These large edifices concentrated fish in a narrow point, to spear or ensnare them. The sicklefin redhorse was particularly vulnerable as it moved upstream in spring to spawn. The fish were an important high-protein food source for the Cherokee.

Research on the sicklefin redhorse reveals that the fish has an affinity for rivers and creeks with moderate to fast currents. They grow up to two feet long and tip the scales at seven pounds. In the spring, adults around five to eight years old migrate to spawn over gravel and cobble. Eggs drop into clean gravels and fry emerge in a few days and drift on the currents until they find a soft eddy or drift into reservoirs.

Researchers concluded that the sicklefin redhorse's current range is greatly reduced from its former natural range in the southeast U.S. The fish is now only found in the Hiwassee River; its tributaries Brasstown Creek and Hanging Dog Creek, Valley River, and Nottely River. The Little Tennessee River and the Tuckasegee River and their large tributaries harbor populations of sicklefin redhorse.

Hydroelectric operations, erosion, pollution, habitat loss, and predation caused the reduction in their range.

In May 2005, the U.S. Fish and Wildlife Service declared the sicklefin redhorse a candidate for the federal endangered species list. Since then, numerous conservation measures have been employed, including removing a small hydropower dam on the Tuckasegee River—opening up miles of potential habitat to the redhorse.

Biologists at Warm Springs National Fish Hatchery, Warm Springs, Georgia, rear young sicklefin redhorse and plant them in home waters. In the spring if you happen by the Oconaluftee River, you will not see fish traps on stone weirs or anyone spearing sicklefin redhorse, but you might hear the low roar of a generator and boat engines as biologists ply the waters catching spawning adult redhorse by means of electric current that temporarily stuns the fish.

There in the boat, biologists collect eggs from ripe, gravid fish and then deliver fertilized eggs to the hatchery. It is not the same as six-year-old sicklefin redhorse maneuvering upstream to a gravel bed to procreate in swift water. But the resulting fry and fingerlings have a greater chance of successfully facing the rigors of the wild because of the care they have been given at the early life stage. The young fish go back into the Oconaluftee and Tuckasegee rivers and into habitats where the *junghitla*, the one wearing a red feather, has long been absent.

—Jaclyn Zelko

Colorado River Fishes

My early appreciation of fish was practical in nature. My grandfather Charles "Dode" Rogers schooled me on the two kinds of fish: those that you can eat and those that you can use to catch those you eat. There was no way to know that this early introduction to fish and the outdoors would lead to a vocation conserving native fishes, including four of the largest fish species native to the Colorado River basin. Were it not for the passion and understanding of two Arizona State University professors, W.L. Minckley and Paul Marsh, I may never have discovered the wonder of the incredible native desert fishes.

The four big river fishes—razorback sucker, Colorado pikeminnow, bonytail, and humpback chub—live naturally only in the Colorado River basin. All but the sucker are members of the minnow family. All four fish are long-lived, up to forty years or more, and have incredible body forms and other features that have aided their survival in the pre-dam Colorado basin. Theories for their body shapes include aids to navigating extreme river rapids and evading the mouth size of native predators. With unique shapes like these, naming most of these fish required little imagination.

I think about this turn of fate that steered me toward a career in conservation while perched on a rock ledge in yet another beautiful place. I'm grateful for the many amazing streams, some small and some quite large, that I have been privileged to explore. I have come to learn that a place's beauty also lies in the unseen—the native fish species residing in the murk, underwater, hidden from view.

This place, the Little Colorado River in Grand Canyon, defines beauty in its inspiring canyon walls cut by the timeless force of turquoise waters. Unseen and as beautiful are the healthy native fishes swimming its waters.

In striking contrast, other desert streams in the American Southwest face a constant onslaught of invading non-native fish. The lower Little Colorado River's native fish flourish. The non-native catfish, sunfish, and others that normally dominate and overrun warmwater streams are thankfully uncommon.

The minerals in the water of this river and the process of forming travertine produces high levels of carbon dioxide. The carbon dioxide level is sometimes higher than that used to clinically anesthetize fish. The gaseous water is thought to be a natural

Waters from the Little Colorado River join the bigger, darker flow of the Colorado River. Both are historic habitats of Colorado pikeminnow, humpback chub, razorback sucker, and bonytail. MIKE PILLOW, USFWS

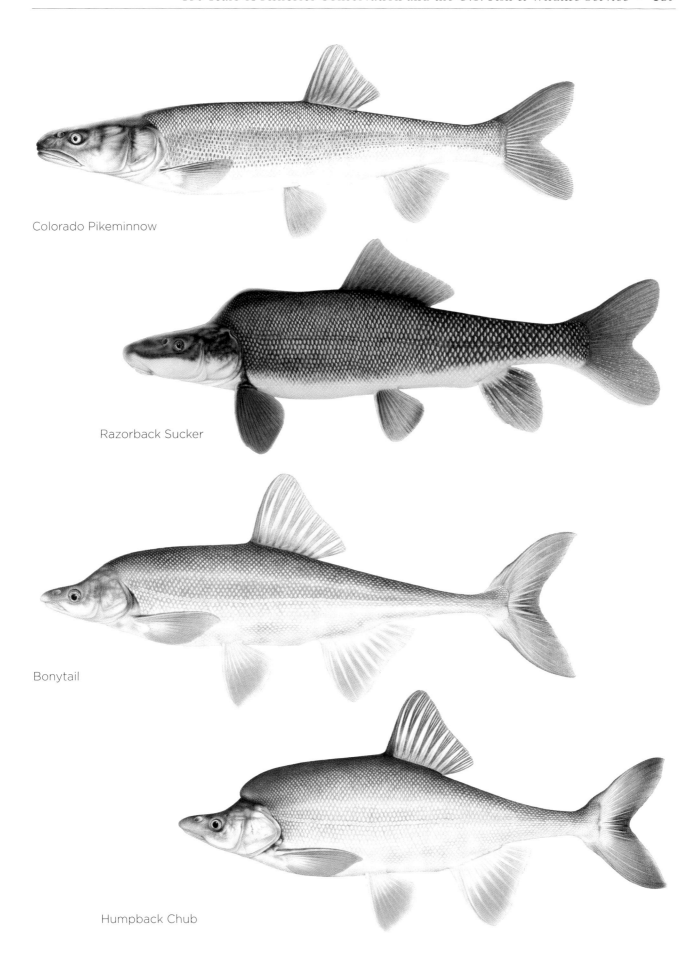

Colorado Pikeminnow

Razorback Sucker

Bonytail

Humpback Chub

Fish biologist Olivia Williams, Arizona Fish and Wildlife Conservation Office, has anchored the lead line of a hoop net and is about to toss it into the Little Colorado River. The net is designed to catch humpback chub.

MIKE PILLOW, USFWS

Fish biologist Kristy Manuell, Arizona Fish and Wildlife Conservation Office, weathers the spray of a Colorado River rapid in the Grand Canyon. Though rough and challenging, rafting to reaches of the reddish river is the easiest way for biologists to conduct their work. MIKE PILLOW, USFWS

Fish biologist Kirk Young, Arizona Fish and Wildlife Conservation Office, shows off a humpback chub wrested from the waters of the Colorado River inside Grand Canyon National Park. MIKE PILLOW, USFWS

Fish biologist Kirsten Tinning looks over Kirk Young's shoulder as he downloads data from antennas that have recorded the passing of tagged fish. MIKE PILLOW, USFWS

Fish health biologist Ashlie Peterson, Southwestern Native Aquatic Resources and Recovery Center, holds a razorback sucker at Willow Beach National Fish Hatchery. At the facility located on the banks of the Colorado River the native fish are raised to recover their depleted populations. Peterson and her colleagues check fish for parasites and diseases and prescribe remedies. CRAIG SPRINGER, USFWS

barrier to the non-native fishes. Our native fish are adaptable to these high levels, while the non-natives are not. The long-term dominance of native fish in a warmwater stream like this is rare.

The aptly named humpback chub is doing remarkably well in the Little Colorado and in the mainstem Colorado River in the Grand Canyon, and humpbacks may be as abundant now in this small area of the Little Colorado as they have ever been.

With a large and growing Grand Canyon population and four separate stabilizing populations in Utah and Colorado, biologists reason that the fish is worthy of downlisting from endangered to threatened under the Endangered Species Act. Its resurgence in western Grand Canyon is thought to be due to warming water and few warmwater non-native predators. My colleagues and I at the Arizona Fish and Wildlife Conservation Office closely monitor these fish as rising water temperatures benefit these natives but could also enable non-native predators to expand their range. For native fish in the Grand Canyon, a Goldilocks temperature is needed, where it's warm enough to enable spawning and growth, but cool enough to keep non-natives at bay.

The Colorado pikeminnow is the Southwest's native top predator and North America's largest of the minnow family as well. Widely used for food, the white salmon as some early settlers called them, grew to sizes up to a remarkable six feet and eighty pounds.

A young Utah boy holds a bonytail caught from the Green River circa 1905. Bonytail once occurred over much of the Colorado River Basin, particularly in the tributaries to the Colorado proper. USFWS NFACA

Hatchery manager Manuel Ulibarri, Southwestern Native Aquatic Resources and Recovery Center, checks up on incubating razorback sucker eggs. The eggs appear like gobs of farina cereal as cool water percolates over them in stacks of trays. The fish are destined for the Colorado River. CRAIG SPRINGER, USFWS

This is one of the native fishes my grandfather would have appreciated, as they were readily caught on hook and line with resourceful baits like rabbit heads. In the Grand Canyon, dynamite was the lure of choice perhaps due to the remote and extreme environment where fishing with traditional gear was difficult. Pikeminnow was the main course for Christmas dinner by the Stanton Expedition of the Grand Canyon in 1889.

Only their ghosts remain in Arizona, and they persist albeit in declining numbers today in the Green, Colorado, and San Juan rivers of Colorado, Utah, and New Mexico. In homage to granddad, I'd like to see them returned to the Grand Canyon with enough numbers to allow fishing for them again, without dynamite.

The razorback sucker, the first big river fish I ever held, is one of the larger suckers in North America. Sometimes bright yellow underneath with a fleshy reddish topside, razorbacks reach nearly three feet long and ten pounds in weight. Everyone who has held one is taken by the aptly named fish's exceeding large keel rising from behind their heads. These sailboatlike keels serve a stabilizing role similar to one on the many vessels that incorporate them in their hulls.

This young man pulled this impressive Colorado pikeminnow from the Green River near Vernal, Utah, circa 1905. It weighed thirty-two pounds. USFWS NFACA

Early in my career as a biologist, I collected hundreds of large wild razorbacks in a population that then numbered in the tens of thousands in Lake Mohave. These were large, muscular fish, a handful to hold on a measuring board when they thrashed about. The scene sometimes resembled an amateur wrestling match, rather than a scientist's measuring a rare and ancient fish.

Though we knew that unless some of their young survived to replace these large, old fish, they would not last, it is still hard to imagine that all of those wild fish in Lake Mohave have disappeared. The same went for wild razorbacks that persisted in the Green, Colorado, and San Juan rivers. The good news is that agencies and conservationists did not let this species disappear. They have maintained it across much of its range through stocking with fish raised at Willow Beach National Fish Hatchery, the Southwestern Native Aquatic Resources and Recovery Center, and other state and federal facilities.

Bonytail are the rarest of the four big river fish, and among the rarest of any fish on earth. Extinction was narrowly avoided for this fish when less than a dozen wild fish were collected and reproduced to establish a hatchery brood stock in the 1980s at the Southwestern Native Aquatic Resources and Recovery Center. Pencil-thin tails and large fins give this fish a streamlined sports car look. Interestingly, bonytail do well in waters without non-native predators—almost too well with production of thousands of young. But they do not survive long in the wild with predators like catfish, bass, and sunfish. Predator-free environments, in part, seem to be one solution to decrypting the recovery code, but more remains to be done for this fish.

Challenges remain for all the big river fish and much of that has to do with dwindling habitat and non-native fishes that prey upon the native species. Controlling non-native predators and maintaining important habitat are big tests of ingenuity and commitment. Recently proposed, a set of new dams in the heart of the Little Colorado River would destroy habitat and provide sanctuary for non-native predators that would no doubt devastate native fish including the humpback in Grand Canyon.

Professor Minckley once told me that the span of time needed for recovery of these long-lived big river fish would exceed the length of our careers. Being young, bulletproof, and tall as a pikeminnow is long, I didn't appreciate that idea. After all, I was here to make—and witness—a difference.

For fish that live longer than most careers, I now appreciate more than ever what the late professor was saying. While technical and scientific skills are important in conservation, there is something else that can't be measured or counted. That is tenacity, and it is vital. Einstein said, "Success comes from curiosity, concentration, perseverance and self-criticism." I'm comforted that the many committed fish biologists who persistently work and innovate are up to the task. I'm hopeful for a future with places where we and future generations can witness these incredible native species.

—Kirk Young

Colorado River anglers enjoy an outing catching what appear to be Colorado pikeminnow, razorback sucker, and flannelmouth sucker. Time and exact place are uncertain. USFWS NFACA

Channel Catfish

For food and for sport, few fish can beat the channel catfish. The iconic whiskered fish have a vast native range, grow large, and are great sport when fished with lure or bait. And on the plate, they are tops.

The channel catfish first became known to science by the work of Constantine Rafinesque, a professor of natural history at Kentucky's Transylvania College, when he traveled down the Ohio River collecting and describing fishes and plants and mollusks. Rafinesque named the catfish *Ictalurus punctatus* in his 1820 publication, *Ichthylogia Ohioensis*.

Greek for fish cat and Latin for spotted, the name is appropriate, as channel catfish are dotted with black spots over their slate gray sides at least through much of their younger years. As they age, the spots disappear and a big, spotless channel catfish might be mistaken for its next of kin, a blue catfish. Blue cat is in fact one of its nicknames, along with fiddler, chucklehead, and willow cat.

Channel catfish originally were found with much frequency through the Great Lakes and southeast Canada, and throughout the entire Mississippi River basin, in small streams, big rivers, and lakes and ponds. The catfish has been introduced throughout the entire U.S. including Hawaii and overseas in England. The British weekly periodical *Punch* published this protest in 1900:

"Oh, do not bring the catfish here! The catfish is a name I fear. Oh, spare each stream and spring, The Kennet swift, the Wandle clear. The lake, the loch, the broad, The mere, from that detested thing!"

The poem goes on in disapproval, "leave him in his western flood/ Where the Mississippi churns the mud."

While the blue catfish and related smaller bullhead catfishes prefer muddy waters, the channel catfish has a liking for cleaner, flowing waters. But they are adaptable and can live in streams and rivers, lakes and reservoirs, and even small farm ponds. If young anglers did not make a bluegill their first catch, it is likely a channel catfish—they are that common.

Fish biologist John Anderson, Austin National Fish Hatchery, Texas, shows off channel catfish broodstock circa 1960. The Austin facility was among the first national fish hatcheries to open shortly after the U.S. Bureau of Fisheries joined the Biological Survey to become the U.S. Fish and Wildlife Service. The hatchery closed in 1968. USFWS NFACA

J. C. Standifer holds a net while W. O. Cox lifts a channel catfish broodstock into a tub and Glenn F. Adams holds a spawning keg at Tishomingo National Fish Hatchery, Oklahoma, in 1955. The hatchery opened in 1929 and still raises catfish, as well as alligator gar, paddlefish, and alligator snapping turtles. USFWS NFACA

Anglers can catch channel catfish on an occasional spinner or lipped crankbait fished deep. But bait is by far the more common method. And they are not picky—they will chew on chicken liver, dough balls, or a gob of garden worms dangled beneath a red and white bobber. Their natural foods include bugs, crayfish, snails, and algae, but for the bigger channel catfish other fish are the favored fare.

You might say they have a taste for meat. The channel catfish has been called a swimming tongue, as they have approximately 670,000 taste buds spread over their entire body with the densest concentration around their gills and whiskers. You, by comparison, have about six thousand taste buds in your mouth.

Channel catfish have an acute sense of smell, too, being able to detect certain compounds at the most minute levels.

And this all makes sense if you consider the environment the fish lives in. For the most part, channel catfish live in waters that are dark and murky—and they are most active after the sun goes down. Having these heightened senses allows channel catfish to remain an efficient predator when its eyesight alone will not suffice.

And not only do channel catfish have increased taste and smell, they can communicate with each other. Channel catfish are capable of producing and recognizing individual specific scent pheromones. In fact, the fish not only recognizes the species and sex of another fish, but also its approximate age and size.

Channel catfish are spring spawners—when the daylight increases and the water warms, the fish are cued to procreate. They have the curious habit of spawning in natural nesting cavities found in rocky crevices or boulders, dense tangles of woody debris, muskrat runs, or undercut banks—all of which yield protection from currents and shelter from would-be predators.

At Inks Dam National Fish Hatchery, Burnet, Texas, and with so many other national fish hatcheries that raise channel catfish, we take advantage of that behavior and put out barrels in pond shallows. The adult

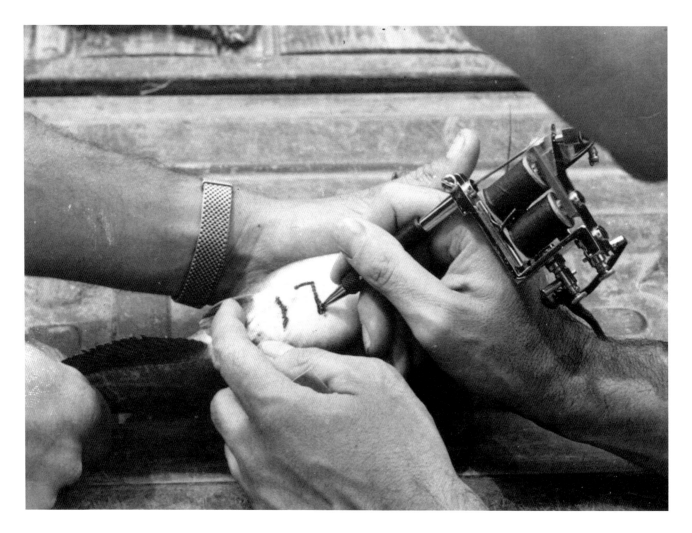

Above: Workers at Tishomingo National Fish Hatchery mark channel catfish broodstock by tattoo. Today, biologists use more refined, modern, and less time-consuming methods of tracking fish in captivity and in the wild. USFWS NFACA

Right: Because channel catfish prefer privacy, especially at spring spawning time, they hole up in submerged tree roots and logs, under rocks, and in undercut banks. Fish culturists take advantage of this behavior, using artificial cavities to attract them. This antique handmade clay keg formerly used at Inks Dam National Fish Hatchery is now preserved at the National Fish and Aquatic Conservation Archives. SAM STUKEL, USFWS

channel catfish take to the cavities as easily as a blue bird takes to a wooden nest box on a fence post over a grassy field. In Texas, channel catfish start spawning in late April. In Minnesota and Canada, around June.

And in both cases their behavior is the same: males clear a nest site and females lay upwards of twenty thousand yellowish sticky eggs smaller than a pea. The male

Channel catfish provide farm pond fun for anglers of all ages, as well as fine table fare. CRAIG SPRINGER, USFWS

hovers over the brood as they incubate for ten days. He continues to guard the young fry for several more days before they disperse to make it on their own.

These captive spawning techniques were first explored around 1916 to 1920 at our Fairport Fish-Cultural Station, in Iowa, along the Mississippi River. During that same period, Edgar Fearnow, inventor of the Fearnow pail and chief of the U.S. Bureau of Fisheries' rail car and messenger service, shepherded freshly fertilized channel catfish eggs spawned at Fairport all the way to the Panama Canal Zone where they were stocked in Gutan Lake.

Channel catfish get big—up to four feet long and sixty pounds. But a ten-pounder is a respectable fish. By day they sulk in the sinks of deep holes and around velocity breaks in flowing waters. When the crickets start chirping in the fading light of dusk, that's a sign that channel catfish are on the move, cruising into the shallows to feed under the cover of darkness. And channel catfish are known to move—sometimes great distances of a mile or two in a day's time over several days.

Channel catfish have had a home at Inks Dam National Fish Hatchery since its inception in 1938—one of several New Deal era hatcheries that are still in operation. This U.S. Bureau of Fisheries station was in the district of an up-and-coming congressman, Lyndon Baines Johnson. Channel catfish were raised to stock the chain of highland lakes created by dams on the Colorado River of Texas.

That mission changed slightly through the 1950s and 1960s when fish were raised for farm ponds. National fish hatchery trucks delivered stock to local pond owners who had applied for fish allotments—all to promote fishing and provide a source of protein.

The mission again changed during the 1980s when recreational sport fish stockings on Native American waters in the Southwest became the priority, and that work continues to this day.

There is an indescribable beauty to a cool summer morning at the hatchery during a channel catfish harvest. The sun rises over the rolling Texas hills and paints the sky red, orange, violet, and every shade in between. The hatchery crew prepares to seine a pond using methods their ancestors would recognize. The morning breeze brings with it the smell of a freshly drawn-down pond that most would say is unpleasant, but to me it's the reaffirming smell of life.

—Jeff Conway

Common Carp

The common carp is one of hundreds of minnow species worldwide and among the largest-growing of them all. It may be the most widely distributed of minnows, if not of all freshwater fish species, owing to its natural attributes and the works of mankind. The common carp is well established in North America and ranges from southern Canada through the U.S. and into Mexico, where it becomes not so common.

It is a fish known in antiquity, most likely because it has been a major source of food since probably the beginning of recorded time. The common carp appears in writing in China circa 500 BCE. Fast forward a thousand years to the Common Era and common carp show up in writing in a circular to government officials in the Ostrogothic Kingdom, circa 500 CE. Cassiodorus, the secretary to Theodoric, the king of the Ostrogoths, ordered high governing officials over present-day southern France, Italy, Austria, Hungary, and the Baltic states to advance the supply of common carp for the king's table.

Clearly, the big minnow had been domesticated by the time the fish arrived in the U.S. That was as early as 1830, by some accounts. Those early introductions did not take. The fish was probably established in the Hudson River basin by 1850. But the decade of the 1880s has been fixed as the most successful effort, one that tipped the scale in favor of the invasive minnow to take hold in American waters.

With the help of Spencer Baird, the first commissioner of the U.S. Fish Commission, common carp took hold in the U.S. Baird reasoned that the fish would be happily received given their popularity in Europe and Asian for millennia. Baird believed that common carp could feed the masses, that the fish could be grown for half the cost of poultry and on lands converted to ponds, land more suitable for water than for grains. The U.S. Fish Commission cultured common carp in the capital city in ponds at the base of the Washington Monument now covered with green grass and tourists. He made fingerlings available to congressional representatives to send to their constituents back home. Railroads veining over the landscape sent common carp overland.

If you think we would be better off without common carp, then Baird failed miserably. The fish may have been suitable for the king's table in a far-off land at a time far removed from nineteenth century America. But not so in this republic where the fish had come to swim in public waters. Common carp fell out of favor. Efforts to promote common carp as a culinary delight landed with a dull thud.

Common carp commonly occur just about anywhere you find water, flowing or flat, clean or polluted. They swim sloughs, irrigation canals, reservoirs, lakes, ponds, big rivers, or the smallest of headwaters. They live in every state in the lower forty-eight and owe their success to being generalists in diet and habitat.

If they had a habitat preference, it would be warm and muddy. If it is not muddy yet, they will make it so, wallowing and rooting up the bottoms looking for food, be it bugs, roots, or carrion. That creates a nuisance where it doesn't belong. Common carp will eat the eggs of native fishes and turn clear-water creeks into turbid torrents as they agitate the bottoms.

Above: Chelsea McKinney releases a Potomac River common carp. BRETT BILLINGS, USFWS

Left: Catch it, buy it, cook it, eat it—that's the message of this circa 1920 U.S. Bureau of Fisheries poster meant to encourage Americans to eat the introduced minnow first made widely available by the well-intentioned Spencer Baird and the U.S. Fish Commission. USFWS NFACA

PLEASE POST CONSPICUOUSLY

DEPARTMENT OF COMMERCE
U. S. BUREAU OF FISHERIES
WASHINGTON

EAT THE CARP!

The carp discovered America in 1877.

He found the land to his liking. He multiplied and filled the waters with his kind.

He is now big, abundant, useful. He converts useless vegetation and small animals into meat.

This meat is wholesome and nutritious. It contains as much protein as sirloin steak.

It is easily digestible.

It can be cooked in such a way as to remove the muddy taste. It can be boiled, baked, made into croquettes, or fish loaf. Carp jelly, an ancient Swedish dish, is delicious.

There are millions of carp in the United States. The last census shows that 43,000,000 pounds were marketed in one year. Nearly all this came from a few states in the Middle West.

Somebody ate those 43,000,000 pounds of carp.

Therefore the carp must be good to eat.

The carp is good to eat. Carp has not only been eaten, but has been cultivated in Europe for centuries. Europeans know how to cook it.

Catch the carp; buy the carp; cook the carp properly and eat it. Eat the roe; can the roe. Make carp jelly. Can the fish. Smoke it, too.

For information and recipes write to

UNITED STATES BUREAU OF FISHERIES
DIVISION F, WASHINGTON, D. C.

PRINTED BY
GOVERNMENT PRINTING OFFICE
WASHINGTON

Natural sight feeders such as smallmouth bass and northern pike don't favor muddy water because they can't see as well. Another serious factor working against common carp is that they compete directly for food, particularly at a young age. Small carp can grow to eight inches in their first year, piling on the weight. They compete for microscopic animals that native fishes need to make it to their next life stage.

Common carp spawn in the spring, usually by May in the South, and later in the spring as you move north. Both sexes gather in the shallows of streams or lakes where they roil en masse in weedy bays or shoals or in the backwaters in big rivers, fouling habitats of more desirable fishes.

We would probably be better off without common carp infesting our waters, most anglers and

Above: U.S. Fish Commission workers harvest common carp from ponds near the base of the Washington Monument in Washington, D.C., circa 1890. USFWS NFACA

Right: Anglers catch common carp by fly, bait, bow, or spear. This stringer of carp came from the Rio Grande at Bosque del Apache National Wildlife Refuge in New Mexico in 1957. USFWS MA

conservationists agree. There is much to dislike about them, and that shows up in the vernacular, with names like sewer bass, buglemouth bass, and the likes. But the fish are here to stay; they could never be eradicated in any practical matter, and you should take care not to spread them, or any other fish species, elsewhere.

Where water is reasonably clear, common carp are great sport. They are a surprisingly wary fish, not easily caught where they have the advantage of sight. You can stalk them on the flats in shallow lake water and sight-fish them with a wet fly imitating a mayfly, bloodworm, leech, or a mulberry. They take live bait and dough balls. Common carp grow quite large—nearly ninety pounds. A full-grown heavy-shouldered common carp is great sport on any tackle.

—Craig Springer

Largemouth Bass

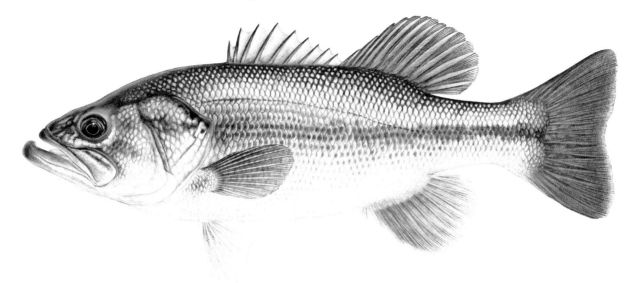

argemouth bass is by far the most popular sport fish in the U.S. It is certainly my favorite. I have had the good fortune to work at several stations throughout my career with the U.S. Fish and Wildlife Service, and no matter where that has been, I have sought out largemouth bass, often with my wife and

The largemouth bass is today among the most popular sport fish species. You can catch them in reservoirs, sluggish big rivers, small lowland streams, water storage tanks, and farm ponds. The fish is appropriately named if you note the size of the man's gripping fist on its jaw. USFWS MA

daughters. I have fished reservoirs, creeks, and ponds in Puerto Rico, Arkansas, Texas, New Mexico, Virginia, and Mexico. I have tossed spinnerbaits, crankbaits, and plastics baits, and now I make my own or paint my own lures. Largemouth bass have been an object of affection with me for decades and I can tell you this one thing: they are a great sport fish.

If ever there were to be a national sport fish, the largemouth bass might well be the one. The great conservationist and contemporary of Theodore Roosevelt, William T. Hornaday, wrote in 1920, "You can catch an eight-pound pike-perch and think you have hooked a bunch of weeds; but if you hook a two-pound largemouth bass you know at once you have engaged a fish."

The vast regard for largemouth bass today borders on a secular religion. The species has enormous importance to the American economy as it occurs throughout the continental U.S. It is maybe the most recognizable of any fish in the country.

And here is a striking artifact of history. The largemouth bass was originally misnamed, and remains so. Its common name referring to its massive maw is most appropriate, but its scientific nomenclature, as U.S. Fish Commission biologist James Henshall wrote in his classic 1881 *Book of the Black Bass*, is unsatisfactory. Henshall lamented that its scientific name, *Micropterus salmoides*, was owing to a train of accidental circumstances.

The renowned French scientist Bernard de Lacépède first described our uniquely North American sport fish for science around 1800. The Frenchman relied on skins of fish with broken fins

Illustration labeled *An Expert Learns a Lesson* shows two largemouth bass outwitted by a lure drawn by Bob Hines. BRETT BILLINGS, USFWS

sent to him from South Carolina. The fragmented fins appeared naturally small. The scientific name granted by him means lake-dwelling trout with small fins. Two hundred years ago, bass in the South were commonly called trout.

This may seem like minutiae. With the accepted rules in the sciences for naming organisms, the largemouth's label is one scientists have had to live with—though not without resistance. David Starr Jordan, a fish biologist who had done much work for the U.S. Fish Commission, was impelled to write a story in an 1878 issue of *Forest & Stream*, then a leading national publication read by anglers and hunters and naturalists. Jordan resisted the notion that the largemouth bass's scientific name should be "stamped out," and he explained why to America's anglers.

Largemouth bass nowhere resemble trout or salmon. But they are indeed lake-dwellers, mainly. They also thrive in sloughs and bayous, slow-flowing streams of all sizes, and farm ponds. In fact, the U.S. Bureau of Fisheries and later today's U.S. Fish and Wildlife Service were steeped in promoting largemouth bass in what we called the farm pond program.

A good many of our national fish hatcheries, mostly in the mid- to southern-tier states, were waist-deep in raising largemouth bass for stocking both private and public waters—in both cases with the intent to promote angling and to yield a reliable source of protein. In the case of farm ponds, our fisheries workers often worked in concert with the Soil Conservation Service, an agency in the U.S. Department of Agriculture that had its rise during the New Deal and Great Depression era. Ponds were part and parcel of staving soil erosion and served double duty in providing a place to fish.

Our farm pond work is no longer. Much of that ceased in the late 1970s and early 1980s before my

This fine stringer of largemouth bass put a smile on this angler's face and sure has the attention of the terrier. Largemouth bass have been an important source of protein. USFWS MA

These U.S. Fish and Wildlife Service researchers, forerunners of today's Fish and Wildlife Conservation Office staff, are assessing a largemouth bass population. There appear to be five sizes or ages present on the board. Envelopes on the man's knee to the right hold fish scales that he will examine to determine age, growth, population health, and perhaps future fishing regulations. USFWS NFACA

time. But I understand from conversations I have had with veteran employees when I was the assistant director for fisheries that our interactions with anglers and landowners was always positive. Farmers applied for fish and would get a post card from a national fish hatchery assigning a time and place to meet—anywhere from the town square outside the hardware store to a four-way gravel crossroads out in the county.

This conjures in my mind a bucolic scene worthy of a Rockwell painting on a *Saturday Evening Post.* I can see myself in it, too, sitting on a pond bank with my kids patiently waiting under the shade of an old willow, watching for a bobber to jog sideways then dunk completely under. The hookset—then the taut tug in my forearm—what will it be, a largemouth bass, a bluegill, or a channel catfish. No matter the case, the experiences—even if I relive them only in my mind—are an elixir to the anguish of the day. This is universal language.

Something else that is universal is that no matter where largemouth bass reside, you will find them mostly on the shallow side rather than deep open water. They take up station around rocks and weeds and stumps usually over mud or sand in water anywhere from ten inches to forty feet deep. Given the choice to hide or swim open water, they will choose the former. Rooted vegetation strongly favors largemouth bass. Think about it: they are ambush predators relying on sight to locate food, and mostly let the food come to them—sunfish, minnows, bugs, frogs, and birds.

Largemouth bass are not as social as, say, bluegill or crappie. But come springtime when they turn thoughts toward spawning, they necessarily form loose aggregations. Sexual maturity might be reached as early as the first year, but later in their third or fourth year is more common. When water warms to around sixty-five degrees in spring, males set about

Largemouth bass illustration in pen and ink by U.S. Fish and Wildlife Service artist, Bob Hines. USFWS MA

finding a place to build a nest, sweeping away silt and debris in a concave depression near shore. Males court gravid females and they swim synchronously over the nest. Fertilized eggs rest in the depression under the intense guard of the male. Some minnow and sucker species take advantage of the male's fidelity to the nest and lay their own eggs in the nest, and then move along on their way.

Largemouth bass, and actually most any fish species, lay an enormous number of eggs. Few will make it to adulthood. Largemouth bass have the capability of a long life, living twenty-plus years, but that is not the norm. Sizewise, an eighteen-inch, five-pound largemouth bass teased out of a weed bed on a surface plug makes for a memorable outing. They can grow much bigger, more than twenty pounds.

While the U.S. Fish and Wildlife Service's fisheries field stations are no longer immersed in largemouth bass culture to any large degree, we still have essential roles in their conservation. Our fish health practitioners assess the well-being of largemouth bass stocks held in state hatcheries as well with wild stocks in rivers and reservoirs. And we play a role in habitat conservation benefitting bass—and many other species. A few of our national fish hatcheries still raise largemouth bass, fish that go to state-managed and tribal waters.

I was pleased to learn that in 2020, the South Dakota largemouth bass state record was broken. The fish that looked more like a football with fins and scales was caught on the Rosebud Indian Reservation. Our national fish hatcheries stock tribal waters. That is most gratifying and motivates me to get on the water again and again.

When speaking on the reason for writing *Book of the Black Bass*, Henshall said: "This book owes its origin to a long-cherished desire to give the black bass its proper place among game fishes, and to create among anglers and the public generally, an interest in a fish that has never been fully appreciated as its merits deserve, because of the want for suitable tackle for its capture, on the one hand, and lack of information regarding its habits and economic value on the other."

Dr. Henshall's desires came through. We have billions of dollars in economic activity tied to this football-shaped beauty of a sport fish.

—Bryan Arroyo

Largemouth bass stocked into Lake Mead, Nevada, from Las Vegas Fish-Cultural Station seemed to have done well as evidenced by these stringers. The photo was taken circa 1942. The Las Vegas station operated from 1939 to 1944. USFWS NFACA

Fish stocking always draws a crowd—especially when the fish are big bass. These U.S. Bureau of Fisheries workers from Lakeland Fish-Cultural Station released these fish in a twenty-five-acre lake in Greenbelt, Maryland, in 1936. Greenbelt was a product of FDR's New Deal, under the short-lived Resettlement Administration that relocated citizens to planned communities. COURTESY LIBRARY OF CONGRESS

Cast-iron largemouth bass finials adorned U.S. Bureau of Fisheries' fish-cultural station entranceways starting in the 1930s. This one is on display in the foyer of the U.S. Fish and Wildlife Service's National Conservation Training Center in Shepherdstown, West Virginia. BRETT BILLINGS, USFWS

Neosho National Fish Hatchery in Missouri is among the oldest operating hatcheries in the U.S. It produced a great number of largemouth bass through the years and offered early insight completely by accident into how fish behave when shocked. The station's superintendent witnessed lightning striking bass ponds and temporarily stunning some fish, while others expired. Today, biologists use electrofishing gear to safely stun and catch fish in streams and lakes. USFWS NFACA

Dr. James Alexander Henshall (1836–1925)

Dr. James Alexander Henshall was one of the most famous fishing writers of his day, referred to even in his time as the Apostle of the Black Bass and the Dean of American Anglers. Overshadowed by his other work, Henshall himself felt that his work on fish culture for the U.S. Fish Commission was among his most important contributions to American angling.

Henshall was born in 1836 in Baltimore, Maryland, to English immigrants Clarissa and Rev. James G. Henshall and by age seven was firmly hooked on the sport of fishing. He finished high school and followed his family to Cincinnati, a city that he would call home off and on for the remainder of his life. In 1855, he began his medical studies and finished in 1859, opening an office first in Cincinnati and then joining the Union Army as part of the medical corps. His *Autobiography* details many interesting events that he was a part of during the Civil War in Kentucky, especially his run-in with Morgan's Raiders, and upon the war's conclusion, he settled into practice in New York City and became interested in fish culture.

The last decades of the nineteenth century were the golden age of fish culture, and Henshall was among the earliest American experts. He was a frequent contributor to both *Forest & Stream* and *The American Angler*, the premier outdoor journals of their day, contributing dozens of full-length articles and hundreds of letters to the editor—many of them on the subject of fish culture.

Henshall's name will forever be connected to bass, in large part because nearly a half million copies of his magnum opus—*Book of the Black Bass*—first published in 1881, has been reprinted in recent years. Yet, his experience at an Oconomowoc, Wisconsin, brook trout hatchery in the late 1860s was one of the most formative events in his life. "I was a frequent visitor at this hatchery," Henshall wrote in his *Autobiography*, "and became pretty well versed in the method of trout culture." Beginning in 1868, he

DR. JAMES ALEXANDER HENSHALL. COURTESY TODD LARSON

took this knowledge and applied it to the breeding of bass.

Although he is better known today as a promoter and historian of fishing tackle and techniques, much of the last half of his life was spent in earnest study of various fish and their artificial breeding. He wrote on a multiplicity of subjects, from exploding the myth of the Gogebic Razor-Back (emaciated smallmouth bass suffering from tapeworms) to discourses on the peculiarities of the ova of fishes. In 1888, he was named secretary of the Ohio Fish Commission and would soon become its president; during this same time, he was also an officer of the Cincinnati Society of Natural History and edited this organization's prestigious journal in the 1890s.

Having been an active member of the American Fisheries Society since its founding in 1870, he read important papers at its national conferences for many years and eventually served as president (1891–1892). Henshall served aboard the U.S.F.C. *Grampus* collecting fishes for study on coastal Florida. He took charge of the legendary exhibit of the U.S. Fish Commission at the Columbian Exhibition in 1893. The success of this World's Fair exhibition further added to Henshall's fame and perhaps led to his nomination to fill the post of U.S. Fish Commissioner in 1896. Backed by three cabinet members, five governors, and dozens of other political luminaries, he expected President Grover Cleveland to rubber-stamp the appointment. But that was not to be: the job was given to Captain John Brice, the cousin of the influential Senator Calvin Brice of Ohio. Henshall never let on if he was embittered and recorded in his *Autobiography* that he "simply said *sic transit gloria*, and wrote a letter of congratulations to my friend Captain Brice."

His disappointment may have been tempered when in late 1896 Brice asked him to rejoin the U.S. Fish Commission, now operating under civil service jurisdiction that required Henshall to take a series of exams. He was offered his choice of three new

Smallmouth bass was a favorite fish of Henshall's, evidenced by his writings of the species in books and magazines. U.S. Fish and Wildlife Service artist Bob Hines created this pen-and-ink illustration adeptly catching the fish's pugnacious disposition. USFWS MA

James Henshall (center) during his first U.S. Fish Commission appointment aboard the *Grampus*. USFWS MA

stations—Texas, Iowa, or Montana—and perhaps to the surprise of some chose to become superintendent of the Bozeman Fish-Cultural Station in Montana in January 1897.

It was during his twelve years in Bozeman that Dr. Henshall did significant research on the Montana grayling. With the Michigan grayling on the verge of extinction, many feared the Montana grayling was similarly marked for oblivion. Henshall

concentrated his considerable acumen on finding a way to artificially propagate it. He overcame many of the peculiarities of grayling breeding, and when he finally discerned that the only food grayling fry eat are naturally occurring minute crustaceans, he successfully bred the species.

As gratifying as this was—and he was lauded by contemporaries like Theodore Gordon for his work—Dr. Henshall was getting older and the

U. S. Fish Hatchery, Tupelo, Miss.

James Henshall cultured largemouth bass and sunfishes at Tupelo Fish-Cultural Station in Mississippi until he retired and returned to Cincinnati, Ohio. USFWS NFACA

bitterly cold winters were taking their toll. At age seventy-three, he transferred to the Tupelo Fish-Cultural Station in Mississippi (today's Pvt. John Allen National Fish Hatchery) in October 1909, and for the next seven years successfully raised largemouth bass that were shipped throughout the south and as far away as Cuba. Sadly, his eyesight began to fail, and on March 31, 1917, he resigned his position after nearly a quarter century of service.

Henshall was prolific and it is a challenge to put together a bibliography of his writings. Author Clyde Drury spent six decades tirelessly working on this project, which remains incomplete today. In addition to *Book of the Black Bass* (1881), which went through multiple revisions and editions, Henshall wrote *Camping and Cruising in Florida* (1884), *More About the Black Bass* (1889), *Ye Gods and Little Fishes* (1900), *Favorite Fish & Fishing* (1908), and *Bass, Pike, Perch, and Others* (1903). His *Autobiography* was originally published in serialized form from 1919 to 1921 in *Forest & Stream*. Sadly, Henshall lost his eyesight during the proofing of this book and passed away in 1925 before it could go to print.

He published two major works on fish culture, *Life of the Fishes of Montana* (1906) and *Culture of the Montana Grayling* (1907), both of which highlighted his unpretentious theories on the subject. "The simplest devices give better practical results than those of more elaborate and complicated structure," he noted in an address to the American Fisheries Society in 1901. "In fish culture, especially, is this true, and the more we endeavor to follow the methods of nature, and rely on the simplest means to that end, the greater will likely be our success." He always sought the simplest answer to even the most complicated question, and perhaps this is his legacy in the field of fish culture.

Fittingly, there was one more appellation Henshall was given that is as descriptive as any, as it represents his tireless efforts in the field he loved. For the last decade of his life, whenever his name appeared in print it was often followed by the words the Father of the Grayling. For a man who spent so much time promoting fish culture, it must have been the most gratifying nickname of all.

—Dr. Todd E.A. Larson

Smallmouth Bass

Dr. James Henshall and I had common experiences with smallmouth bass. We both caught our first on an Independence Day outing in southwestern Ohio—120 years apart.

Henshall caught his in the Little Miami River. He and a pal on break from medical school in 1855 went by train to the little town of Morrow, thirty miles northeast of his Cincinnati home. He documented the outing at length in his *Autobiography*. Fishing with live minnows, Henshall remembered:

"I cast again toward the flat rock, and when the minnow floated to the end of its tether I began reeling as rapidly as I could when the bass made a vicious lunge and seized the bait. Then followed a battle that I will never forget, so vividly was it impressed on my senses. His quick rushes and sudden twisting and turnings reminded me of the brook trout of the Pennsylvania hills; but his frantic leaps and violent shaking and whirling of his strong body in mid-air, with wide open mouth and the rotary play of his powerful tail were characteristic, unique and unequalled."

I caught my first smallmouth bass some forty miles north of Cincinnati near Oxford in Four Mile Creek while on a family picnic. I was twelve years old. Outfitted with a Zebco 202 and a white Rooster Tail spinner, I laid the lure crossways into the current and pulled it upstream, feeling the tense vibration of the shiny, spinning blade against the swift flow. Four Mile Creek was full of two-inch-thick limestone slabs colored like glazier's putty, each one profusely littered with Ordovician bivalve fossils frozen in time. I pulled

the spinner past a stand of water willows at the head of a small stack of stones that must have slowed the velocity to carve a lair for a fish.

What followed impressed my senses. An eight-inch smallmouth bass hit the spinner with a ferocity the likes of which I had never before witnessed; it leaped out of the water in three successive turns, head shaking each time, and its whole body pulsating. The silvery glint of summer sunlight coming upon the white spinner and the crystalline spray of creek water burned into my retina. The taut tug of the smallmouth bass transmuted from the water to my skinny forearm. Writhing in my small hands, the bass had a brick red iris and was barred in greenish bronze along its sides while its cheeks were streaked in green over an opalescent pale white, all beneath a chrome veneer. Its lip felt raspy like the bristles of a hard toothbrush. That marvel molded into my memory.

Henshall went on to doctor injured soldiers in the Civil War and later pursued a storied career with my antecedent U.S. Fish Commission. The man was a prodigious writer on all things fishes, including his famous *Book of the Black Bass*, the seeds of which likely germinated on Independence Day 1855.

I endeavored to learn all that I could about Four Mile Creek, its small tributaries that fed it near the Indiana state line, and the history of the area.

Turns out the military named Four Mile Creek for a practical purpose: mere yards downstream from the pool where I caught my first smallmouth, the U.S. Army passed by in October 1791. The soldiers cut a wide road into the wilderness and bivouacked along the stream for one night, four miles from the gates of Fort Hamilton, then an outpost in the wilderness. Three miles on, they crossed Seven Mile Creek. A month later, the tattered and scattered remnants of our nation's army crossed Four Mile again, seeking sanctuary. The army took a shellacking at the hands of the confederated Miami and Shawnee tribes.

The naming of Four Mile Creek during the march to a massacre seemed antithetical to the stream's placid nature. The creek meandered between glacial moraines piled up in a Pleistocene winter when the mile-thick ice sheets retreated to the north. As a teen, one of my favorite places to catch smallmouth bass and rock bass and longear sunfish was along a lengthy, sweeping bend in the creek that elbowed into the toe of a hill.

The primeval, the historic, and the present all seemed to coincide here in bucolic harmony.

An ancient elaborate Adena earthwork, large and ovate, laid over a great flat tongue of land, one hundred acres or more, abutting the creek bank. Gravity and modern agriculture reduced the walls of a large abode to meager drawings in books on archeology. These Mound Builders must have found something attractive about the site, as did the first European settlers. A long-abandoned three-story mill made of stone situated at the creek's edge was evidence of another time. The water was after all the mill's power source; the millrace long since filled in. A gray-black unstriped coarsely paved road conveyed an occasional car and farm implement. Beneath a steel-truss bridge, the creek's erosive forces exposed the earth's basement—Ordovician bedrock, dolomitic limestone slabs encrusted with fossilized seashells.

Beneath those slabs lived a profusion of blacknose dace flecked with pepper spots, greenside darters painted a verdant dayglow deserving their own Pantone swatch, and creek chubs with a maw wide enough to take a spinner

or a worm. They lived in common with crayfish that preferred the shade by day, but wandered about in search of carrion on which to dine by night.

And smallmouth bass sought crayfish. Any ardent smallmouth bass angler knows that crayfish are a favored fare. I came to better understand that when I conducted my research for a master's degree in fish ecology at the University of Arizona where I had the great fortune to study under the late Dr. O. Eugene Maughan, who led the U.S. Fish and Wildlife Service's Cooperative Fishery Research Unit.

Smallmouth bass were introduced into Arizona's Black River on the San Carlos Apache Indian

Sycamore tree roots keep Four Mile Creek in place, slow the water, and provide habitat for fish. CRAIG SPRINGER, USFWS

Reservation decades ago. I examined how the bass used various parts of the river at different times. Wearing a dry suit, snorkel, and mask, I watched smallmouth bass by day, by night—and at dusk and dawn. What I learned felt like peering behind a curtain into the workings of nature.

During the day, the bass stayed on the edge of faster water, letting the groceries come drifting to them. At dusk and dawn, the fish went on the prowl into crayfish habitat, hunting prey—a behavior that lasted only until full daylight or until complete darkness fell upon the water.

What I discovered about their nocturnal behavior was most unexpected given that I had caught a fair share of them on top-water stickbaits after dark. In the cover of darkness, smallmouth bass moved into the shallowest and slowest flows to rest, hiding in logjams, wedging themselves in rock crevices, and even moving into slack water next to the bank beneath alder trees, their backs mere inches from the surface.

In the 112 years between Henshall's *Book of the Black Bass* and my master's thesis, a lot of hefty work went into smallmouth bass conservation in the U.S. Fish Commission, U.S. Bureau of Fisheries, and the U.S. Fish and Wildlife Service. Smallmouth bass were among the first species of fish transported by airplane in 1928 by the U.S. Bureau of Fisheries, flown from Northville Fish-Cultural Station in Michigan to Dayton, Ohio. Fish biologist John Van Oosten researched smallmouth bass in the Sandusky area of Lake Erie in the 1920s. Put-in-Bay Fish-Cultural Station in Ohio produced smallmouth for Lake Erie and points well beyond. Many U.S. Fish and Wildlife Service national fish hatcheries raised smallmouth bass, and some still do, including Genoa, Gavins Point, and Warm Springs National Fish Hatcheries in Wisconsin, South Dakota, and Georgia.

Not only are these fish stocked for anglers, but they also serve essential roles as host fish in conserving imperiled mussels in captivity. Smallmouth

Male smallmouth bass have a strong paternal instinct. They guard fertilized eggs and newly hatched black fry seen here wafting over the nest. Smallmouth bass nest over clean gravels in shallows along edges of creeks often near a boulder, log, or overhanging tree limbs, all of which offer some protection against predators. USFWS MA

Four Mile Creek elbows into the toe of a moraine at the site of an old mill near Oxford, Ohio.
COURTESY R. KIRK MEE FAMILY AND SMITH LIBRARY OF REGIONAL HISTORY

bass are essential in advancing our understanding of therapeutants in fish culture at our Aquatic Animal Drug Approval Partnership attached to Bozeman National Fish Hatchery—where Henshall coincidentally wrote some of his books. Biologists at our fish and wildlife conservation offices restore habitats by removing blockages to fish passage for the betterment of smallmouth bass and its kind. Smallmouth bass move about, especially in the spring when their instincts turn toward procreation. More habitat means more fish.

Henshall wrote in his *Autobiography* about catching smallmouth bass in 1856 in the Great Miami River fed by Four Mile and in a stream that laid near the dividing line between Ohio and Indiana. I figure that was Four Mile Creek. I have pondered on the prospect that both he and I waded the same reaches, casting for one more bronzeback—more than a century apart. He was the contemplative sort and I figure that

he, like me, had remembrances that rested gentle on the mind.

Smallmouth bass tug the mystic cords of memory. I am calf-deep in Four Mile at the sweeping bend near the old mill next to the Adena earthworks. A car glides down a moraine and crosses the grated bridge, its sound growing faint with distance. Yellow-breasted chats sing their last in the fading light of dusk in massive sycamores that lean over the bank. Their roots reach into the water in pale gray twisted masses that make dark voids where the fish will lie. As day bleeds into night, that is where the smallmouth bass will head, to the slow water and the protection afforded by the trees. A well-placed floating lure laid in the flat water next to a sycamore, twitched just so, will turn a calm smallmouth bass into an irascible creature sure to remain in memory for decades to come.

—Craig Springer

Dusk is a time of accelerated feeding activity by smallmouth bass. MATTHEW PATTERSON, USFWS

Spotted Bass

The spotted bass has long had an identity crisis. Despite being collected from Kentucky's Licking River and formally described in 1819 by eccentric naturalist and Transylvania University professor of natural history Constantine Rafinesque, it took more than another century before the fish was scientifically recognized and given its own Latin name, *Micropterus punctulatus.*

The genus name, *Micropterus,* meaning, "little wing," refers to the entire group of black basses—the most important sport fishes in the U.S. The species name, *punctulatus,* meaning dotted, was given by Rafinesque. In the 1949 book *North American Freshwater Sport Fish,* Lou Caine explains, "The blackish markings below the lateral line have a jagged sawtooth effect while the markings above the lateral line and just below the dorsal fin are a series of diamond-shaped splotches. The general combined effect of these two give this fish its name and its spotted appearance." These characteristics along with an upper jaw that extends only to the middle of the eye, and a small patch of teeth on the tongue, differentiate the species.

Among the fourteen species of black bass, spotted bass, along with the largemouth and smallmouth basses, are the most wide-ranging. Spots, as some anglers refer to them, are native to the lower Ohio River Valley, lower Mississippi River drainages, and areas along the Gulf Coast. The state of Kentucky lies at the heart of the fish's range. In 1956, the Kentucky state legislature made a joint resolution proclaiming, "Whereas . . . it is native to the streams of the Commonwealth of Kentucky and was initially found in waters of the Commonwealth, . . . the Kentucky Bass is universally acclaimed for its gameness and fighting qualities and also as a dish prized by connoisseurs of fine food." Thus, it was named the state fish.

The spotted bass, also called the Kentucky spotted bass or Kentucky bass, is an enigma, defined largely by what it is not. It is not a largemouth bass, though a cursory glance may lead one to label it as such. Nor is it that coolwater cousin, the smallmouth bass, with which it shares some physical features and the preference for a rocky residence. Even the writers of its Kentucky state fish resolution tried to distinguish it. "Whereas it appears that many people are unaware of the distinction which should be made between the Kentucky Bass and the other black basses," they wrote, "it appears desirable that this distinction be maintained and impressed with vigor upon the uninitiated."

In that gold standard of scholarly fish works *The Fishes of Ohio,* acclaimed fisheries scientist Milton Trautman noted, "Although ichthyologists and sport fishermen may not have recognized the Spotted Blackbass, the commercial fishermen of the Ohio River long believed it to be a distinct species, calling it 'Speckled,' 'Yellow' or 'Spotted bass,' 'perch' or 'trout.' They agree it was the most abundant bass in the Ohio River since and before 1900."

Modern fishery managers still wager that spotted bass are more abundant than people realize. Retired Kentucky Fish and Wildlife biologist Jim Axon says even creel surveys don't do the fish justice: "You can't

For a lure to work, it first has to catch the angler. This well-stocked tackle box full of eye-catching lures has much to choose from for catching spotted bass, largemouth bass, smallmouth bass, and more. BRETT BILLINGS, USFWS

go by creel surveys because fishermen will concentrate along the shoreline and they're more likely to catch largemouth and smallmouth and not give you a true depiction of it."

The spotted bass's preference for large expanses of clear water makes it difficult for fish biologists to collect for research. The best lakes for this species tend to be deep and cool with lots of rocks. Axon goes on to note a pattern in Kentucky's highland reservoirs. "There's a transition from largemouth to spotted bass to smallmouth from headwater down to the lower end of the lake in larger impoundments," Axon said. "Spotted bass dominate in terms of numbers because they take advantage of the open-water pelagic conditions in our larger impoundments. They have more room for the population to take advantage of."

Current eastern fishery district biologist for Kentucky, Kevin Frey, concurs. "In the same lakes where you'll find largemouth and spotted bass, generally in these east Kentucky lakes, the better numbers of spotted bass will be in mid-lake to lower lake nearest the dam. The upper lake is usually more shallow, more mud, and tends to go toward largemouth," Frey

states. "With the spotted bass, usually the rocky habitat works better."

Large reservoirs give spots many of the things they like—deep, clear water and rocky structure. Whereas largemouths are usually caught in ten feet of water or less, anglers have reported catching spotted bass ninety feet deep in places like Table Rock Lake, Arkansas. Unlike their largemouth brethren, who prefer lily pad–infested gumbos with tangles of tree limbs, these speckled cousins are creatures of deep, clear, open waters. That's not to say that spotted bass won't come shallow, on occasion, if the water is clear and baitfish plentiful. However, in big lakes, they generally opt for river channels, steep drop-offs, and main points, especially if coupled with boulders. There, if you find one fish, you will likely find a school—especially in fall.

Before the region's large reservoirs were impounded in the mid-1900s, the spotted bass was mainly a fish of mid-sized streams and lazy rivers. In *The Fishes of Ohio*, Trautman presented an anecdote that clearly showed the preferred locations of spotted, largemouth, and smallmouth bass in an Ohio stream. "On August 17,

1930, I collected the three species of black basses within a hundred feet of each other. . . . the small-mouths were on the riffle, the spotted bass were in the sluggish pool, and the few largemouth bass were in a connecting and weedy oxbow," he observed.

Retired biologist Jim Axon has noticed that spots enjoy the same type of streams in eastern Kentucky as do muskellunge. Axon recalls, "Most of our muskie streams are dominated by pool habitat—about 89 percent. A very small portion was riffles, so the spotted bass dominated. They provide a major fishery in our streams."

Generally considered less selective than either the smallmouth or largemouth, spots are widely known to chase shad and other soft-bodied minnows in the middle of large lakes. When near the surface, schools of baitfish leap out of the water en masse to escape the finny predators corralling them below. Fishing these jumps with stickbaits, popping cork combos, and rubber finesse swimbaits is an action-packed way to catch these fast, aggressive sport fish.

When not at the surface or mid-depths, there's another prime target spotted bass may be hunting . . . on the bottom. Biologist Kevin Frey observes, "I've always thought a main type of forage for them, similar to smallmouth, was crayfish . . . and it might have to do with why they like rocky habitat so much." Any of the dozens of smallish crayfish-mimicking baits makes a serviceable offering for these fish when they're foraging on the bottom.

With all baits, size is important when fishing for spotted bass. It has been said that largemouth bass want one big meal, but their speckled cousins like to eat multiple smaller helpings. Remember that a spot's mouth is much smaller than a similar-sized largemouth's. As it grows, the spotted bass's head stays about the same size, but the belly gets chubbier. Thus, a two-pounder and a six-pounder both have nearly the same sized mouth. It is suggested anglers limit themselves to three-inch or smaller lures for spots, as opposed to the half-foot monstrosities used to entice largemouth.

Another notable difference in the two similar black bass is obvious upon hooking them. While largemouth typically go up—with those iconic gill-flaring leaps and jumps—spotted bass dive down. The wise angler knows to keep a light drag for these fish. After a slashing strike and some violent head-shaking,

most spotted bass will dive-bomb the bottom once they see the boat or angler. That last-chance run has cost many an angler a trophy fish.

Fishing for spotted bass can lengthen the fishing season. These fish tolerate the cold better than either of their tournament fish counterparts and are easier to catch in winter. Opposite of many fish, spots move shallow in the fall and winter from November through February, making them more available. Then, after the spawn, they head back deep for the summer. A good rule-of-thumb is to anchor the boat deep and fish shallow in the late fall and winter, then park the boat shallow and fish deep from spring through early fall. When fish are deep, vertical jigging, Alabama rigs, and heavy spoons cast on light spinning gear can reach them quickly. Using six-pound test fluorocarbon line allows the best action from small baits and a measure of invisibility in the fish's preferred clear water.

Anglers who have gotten to know the spotted bass appreciate its eagerness to bite and its aggressive nature. Many would say that a spot fights harder than a largemouth of equal or even slightly larger size. Add to this that, as table fare, they rank well above the other black bass species, being favorably compared to crappie in both taste and texture. That's a high honor.

The University of Michigan ichthyologist Dr. Carl Hubbs brought the spotted bass out from obscurity in 1927. He wrote about the newly recognized black bass in a 1932 issue of *Field & Stream* with high praise: "This least-known of all game fishes, but best-appreciated when once you become acquainted with it, is none other than the spotted small-mouth bass of Southern spring-fed waters. This creature is literally bedecked with diamonds from stem to stern, and should be recognized at once as 'the king of diamonds' of the finny pack."

Lastly, for fisheries managers, the feisty spotted bass provides a hardy sport fish that is more tolerant of hatchery life than its better-known cousins. In areas where dams and poor water quality have reduced smallmouth bass, the tough little spot has proven a worthy addition to fill the gap. Perhaps, at last, this unsung fish is getting a measure of respect.

—Brett Billings

Edgar C. Fearnow (1875–1944)

In 1921, Edgar C. Fearnow was nineteen years into his career with the U.S. Bureau of Fisheries and had worked his way up to superintendent of fish distribution. He oversaw shipments of fish and fish eggs in specially designed fish cars—rail cars owned and operated by the U.S. Bureau of Fisheries. Fearnow's position provided him with ample access to study and experiment with improving the survival rates of live fish and fish eggs shipped across the country and around the world.

Improving shipping methods came to Fearnow's attention early in his career when he accompanied a shipment of live fish from New York to Gatun and Gamboa. Soon after setting sail, he realized the supply of ice would run out before they reached their destination. Ice was crucial for keeping the water temperature suitable for the fish to survive. Fearnow grouped all of the containers closely together and wrapped them in a saturated sail. His idea conserved ice and the fish were delivered "without undue loss."

Fearnow continued to experiment with improved ways to move live fish, and by 1922 he had patented several of his inventions. One of them, a shipping container bearing Fearnow's name, quickly became a mainstay at fisheries facilities and remained so for many decades. The Fearnow pail, patent #1419549, lists the invention as the "Fearnow self-aerating fish transportation pail with canvas jacket." Wildly successful, the pail carried the same amount of fish that commonly used milk cans did, but five Fearnow pails took the same amount of space as three milk cans and increased the carrying capacity in the specialty fish rail cars by more than 66 percent. The Fearnow pails, wider and shallower than milk cans, provided more surface area for water, which improved oxygen for the fish and used less water per container. A specially designed inset lid with holes permitted aeration in two ways: when the water in the pail splashed around during transport it went through the holes and increased aeration. Ice could also be put into the lid; the melting ice dripped into the water and added more oxygen. The canvas cover had wicks that extended into the water, creating a "sweating" package that was air-cooled. The 1922 Bureau of Fisheries Report noted, "The device is especially useful in shipping fish for considerable distances without an attendant. It also affords a practical means of transporting fish to the headwaters of

Fearnow pails efficiently transported small fish over distances short and long. These pails are held at the National Fish and Aquatic Conservation Archives.

SAM STUKEL, USFWS

Edgar Fearnow earned a patent on his namesake pails in 1922. USFWS NFACA

streams that have heretofore been neglected on account of their inaccessibility."

The Fearnow pail provided another benefit—improved economic efficiencies. Fearnow wanted to improve fish survival rates but also decrease the costs of shipping fish. He wrote in a 1922 paper for the American Fisheries Society, ". . . the allotment of funds for distribution purposes has remained practically the same for a number of years notwithstanding an enormous increase of applications (for fish) received annually. . . . If the transportation problem could be solved there would be corresponding benefits in other phases of fish-cultural work."

According to a presentation given in 1922, it cost the Bureau $1.57 to distribute a milk can of fish and the Fearnow pails cost only ninety cents per can. Fearnow's invention made the ten-gallon milk cans obsolete. An ad that was "Used and Approved by the Bureau of Fisheries" read "The fry of today are the fish of Tomorrow! For Economy and Safety in transporting living fish use the Fearnow Pail."

The pail was not Fearnow's only invention—he also patented a fishway in 1925 to move migratory fish over dams in response to the increase in dams being constructed. He was highly concerned over the threat to fish species that migrate from salt to fresh water to reproduce. His fish elevator was designed to move anadromous fishes over these high dams. Many variations of fish ladders are still in use today.

Fearnow pails in use aboard a U.S. Bureau of Fisheries truck at Creede Fish-Cultural Station, Colorado. The station operated from 1929 to 1965 and raised rainbow trout, Yellowstone cutthroat trout, and Rio Grande cutthroat trout. USFWS NFACA

Fearnow was also charged with writing a substantial portion of the annual Report of the United States Commissioner of Fisheries dealing with distribution. His knowledge of fisheries was vast and many of his recommendations and considerations are relevant one hundred years later.

Fearnow made another contribution to fisheries conservation. Son Theodore C. "Ted" Fearnow (1905–1982) followed his father into the profession. Ted started his career at the White Sulphur Springs National Fish Hatchery in 1920 as a high school summer intern. While completing his formal education, he worked at the Bureau of Fisheries headquarters in Washington, D.C., and on the fish rail cars transporting fish around the nation.

In 1926, Ted was hired as a full-time Bureau employee and two years later, the West Virginia Fisheries Division hired him as its first chief. In that position he scouted, designed, and superintended construction of state hatcheries. He returned to the U.S. Bureau of Fisheries in 1934, two years after his father retired. A year later the U.S. Forest Service hired Ted to serve as the regional biologist in charge of game and fish management for fourteen eastern states.

Ted remained with the Forest Service for thirty years until he retired in 1965. Father and son shared a love for West Virginia—they both were born in Berkley Springs and lived out much of their lives there. Ted honored his father with a son he named Edgar C. Fearnow II.

Edgar C. Fearnow II carefully kept his grandfather's original patents for many years. In 2004, he attended a U.S. Fish and Wildlife Service retirees' reunion in West Virginia and gave a presentation about the lives of his father and grandfather. He presented the patents to the U.S. Fish and Wildlife Service to be preserved in the National Fish and Aquatic Conservation Archives in Spearfish, South Dakota, where they help tell the story of the many creative innovations of fisheries pioneers.

—April Gregory

Bluegill

Bluegill is the quintessential first catch of many neophyte anglers and goes on to provide dependable catches throughout an angler's life. During the twilight of a fisher's time, when mobility and reflexes may soften, the amiable bluegill holds no grudge and will continue to provide well-suited sport. What other fish can be so enjoyed from one's first day of fishing until the last?

The bluegill's size is dwarfed by its importance. Bream, to use one of its many colloquial names, is the largest member of the sunfish clan and it's claimed to be the most important gamefish in the U.S. Sometimes thought of as a kid's fish, small and prone to stunting, a mature disc-shaped bluegill can grow well over four pounds.

Lou Caine in his 1949 work, *North American Freshwater Sport Fish*, elaborates on the fish's many endearing traits, observing, "They seem to school readily, strike vigorously, and feed often—a most inviting combination for angling sport."

No wonder early U.S. Fish Commission biologists David Starr Jordan and coauthor Barton Warren Evermann asserted in their 1902 book, *American Food & Game Fishes*, that bluegill deserved the moniker "the gamest of all fishes for its size." That holds true today. Hook one at the surface or suspended ten feet deep and your quarry will invariably tilt sideways and scurry and jog side to side.

The bluegill's attraction is its simplicity. No costly equipment needed, and no boat required—though custom panfish boats are now available from many manufacturers. With minimal gear and a few minutes' time, anyone can enjoy a serious outing for what Caine referred to as, "ounce for ounce . . . the most concentrated package of fun in the entire fish family."

Adding to the bluegill's attractiveness is its palette of vivid colors—from powder blue to vermillion. True to its entry-level reputation, identifying the bluegill is a cinch. The North American Fishing Club's guide, *Panfishing*, points out the marks to look for. "The tiny mouth, entirely black 'ear flaps' and sky-blue throat are this sunfish's distinguishing characteristics." If still in doubt, check the pectoral fins. While some sunfish have short, rounded fins on their sides, if you pull the pectoral fin forward and the point extends past the eye, then it's a bluegill. One last unmistakable field mark is a dark splotch at the rear of the soft dorsal fin.

Bluegills are also beloved by national fish hatchery managers for their robust hardiness and tolerance of handling, crowding, and about any other issue that would make a lesser fish go belly-up. This hardiness is part of why the bluegill is arguably the most widely distributed fish in the nation. It filled a new niche created by an explosion of farm ponds across the nation from the 1930s onward.

These bluegill in a Fearnow pail were destined for a farm pond. USFWS NFACA

Bluegill were long the mainstay alongside largemouth bass in the U.S. Fish and Wildlife Service's immensely popular farm pond stocking programs. For decades, national fish hatcheries at Hebron, Ohio; Louisville, Kentucky; Corning, Arkansas; Cedar Bluff, Kansas; Austin, Texas; and Millen, Georgia, only to name a few, provided the warmwater pond-dwellers through formal application to landowners. Community gatherings centered on the moments that hatchery trucks and landowners showed up at the appointed time and place, often at wide spots along the thinnest lines on a road map, to receive fish destined for a farm pond. Farm-pond bluegills eat the bugs and the bass eat the bluegill. The Fairport, Iowa, Fish-Cultural Station proved significant in furthering our understanding of pond fish ecology, particularly bluegill. Many states still continue growing out bluegills as part of their own farm pond programs.

Chances are that bluegill are as close to you as the nearest park, farm pond, or municipal lake. For many a rural kid, this is the highlight of summer vacation—catching countless bluegills while experimenting with the higher art forms of spin fishing, bait casting, or fly rodding. Adults destined to fight giant muskies and lunker bass first built, then honed, their skills on the backs of countless bluegills.

Nothing is a more welcome sight to the panfisher than dozens of bowl-shaped depressions in the shallows

of a favorite pond as the spring spawn begins. A big female 'gill may lay upwards of sixty thousand eggs into such nests annually. Looking like the topside of a dimpled golf ball, a cluster of bluegill beds can increase the heart rate of the most jaded fisher. I remember one such area in our family lake when I was ten.

I watched in amazement as my fly-fishing uncle worked over a cove of bedded bluegill. He'd zap a cast out with a seemingly invisible fly, wait about two seconds, and then set the hook on a beefy hand-sized bream. I, too, yearned, to catch scores of bluegills without having to chase jumpy crickets or pinch worms in two. A hastily called family meeting ended with my uncle's promise to teach me how to fly fish, and I soon became that odd kid, madly chasing local bluegill, a fly rod clutched across the handle bars of a BMX bike as I careened from one pond to the next. Such is the spell cast by a fisher's first finny love.

How many parents have held their young child on a dock, pier, or farm pond bank, with pole in hand, ready for that first catch? As new recruits learn basic angling skills—from baiting hooks to throwing out lines—the bluegill teaches them to love fishing.

Some may eventually pursue more challenging piscatorial adventures. But, as kids begin to show up, those same adults often return to their fishing roots—just as sunfish return to the shallows each May.

—Brett Billings

Farm ponds if properly managed grow big bluegill.
CRAIG SPRINGER, USFWS

Farming and fishing may have been the topics of the day as a group of Iowa farmers awaited a truck from Guttenberg National Fish Hatchery. Milk cans filled with water were ready for bluegill and other warmwater fishes. Ponds were often created in cooperation with the Soil Conservation Service to stave erosion. USFWS NFACA

Farm pond owners over much of the U.S. could apply for and receive bluegill, channel catfish, largemouth bass, and more. These applicants lived near Guttenburg National Fish Hatchery in Iowa. The cards are preserved at the National Fish and Aquatic Conservation Archives. SAM STUKEL, USFWS

Robert Thoesen (1927–2010)

He skipped his high school graduation to go to the front lines in the European Theatre in World War II. Seventeen-year-old Robert Thoesen served in General George Patton's Third Army and suffered serious injury. By war's end, he reached the rank of sergeant and stayed on as a guard during the Nuremburg Trials.

Post-war, Thoesen took advantage of the G.I. Bill and earned a degree in zoology at Colorado State University. He hired on with the U.S. Fish and Wildlife Service in 1952, already a father to a son, John, who followed in his footsteps as a fish biologist. Robert's first assignment took him to Eagle Nest, New Mexico, a seasonal rainbow trout egg-collection station auxiliary to Leadville National Fish Hatchery in Colorado, where fertilized eggs were shipped to incubate and hatch.

Thoesen immersed himself in trout conservation at his next station, Williams Creek National Fish Hatchery in Arizona, located on the Fort Apache Indian Reservation. The crew raised rainbow, brook, and brown trout and tried raising rare Apache trout, found only in the White Mountains of Arizona.

In the 1950s, feeding hatchery fish was a crude endeavor; feral horsemeat rendered with pinto beans into pellets did not prove nutritious for fish. Thoesen experimented and innovated trout diets that improved fish health and reduced labor costs and energy consumption by eliminating the need for refrigeration.

Thoesen went east from Arizona, with a stint at Dexter National Fish Hatchery in New Mexico, then Cortland National Fish Hatchery in New York where he worked with warmwater sport fish such as largemouth bass and bluegill. He continued innovating fish feed as well as modernizing fish-hauling trucks, pumps, and aerators. At his next stop, Washington, D.C., headquarters, he developed new national fish hatcheries to offset losses to fisheries upset by water development projects, many of them in the Southeast.

Thoesen standardized fish-hauling methods for trucks, with hatcheries using nearly all the same technology that minimized mortalities. More fish could safely travel longer distances. He also designed systems for aerial hauling, so that

Robert Thoesen innovated fish hauling methods, including aerial stocking. Fish from Uvalde National Fish Hatchery are loaded onto a plane that will drop them into Lake Powell, behind Glen Canyon Dam on the Colorado River. USFWS NFACA

A plane drops fish into Lake Powell. USFWS NFACA

Robert Thoesen holds a broodstock brown trout at Williams Creek National Fish Hatchery, Arizona.

COURTESY JOHN THOESEN

large airplanes could efficiently stock large or remote waters with relative ease, technology still in use today.

The man who started at the bottom worked his way to the top as chief of the National Fish Hatchery System. His son John, who retired as a fish health biologist in 2009 after nearly thirty-one years of service, recalled as a boy watching his dad build concept models from balsa wood that became metal tanks on trucks.

"In my view, two of my dad's greatest accomplishments were his dedication to improving fish distribution systems on both land and in the air and mentoring employees both young and old," said John. "He saw the future and encouraged employees to get college educations and continue their education throughout their careers."

In 1999, Robert Thoesen was inducted into the Fish Culture Hall of Fame in Spearfish, South Dakota.

—Craig Springer

Redbreast Sunfish

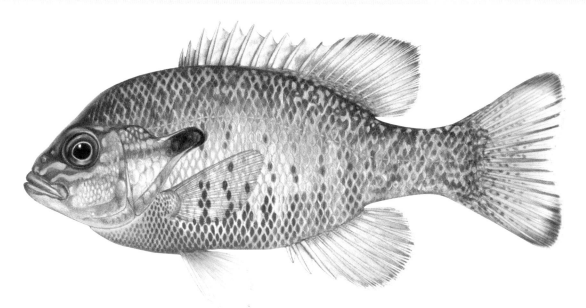

The redbreast sunfish might just be the most colorful of our native sport fish. Its striking breast ranges from yellow or golden orange to bright scarlet. Wavy turquoise lines ornament its face and a big, silvery blue teardrop splash on the side gives contrast to its olive brown backs and namesake rosy blush below. Robin is this red-breasted panfish's nickname.

The fish's Latin species name, *auritus*, refers to the large ear flap. This extension of the gill cover is extremely long and completely black and distinguishes it from other colorful sunfish with which it may be confused. The orangish belly may extend all the way up to the fish's eyes and that color can often be seen in the lobes of the tail fin as well as the top of the soft dorsal fin.

These spunky, chunky sunfish are voracious eaters. With mouths considerably larger than a bluegill's they can take on heftier prey such as crayfish and minnows, but their bread and butter foods are small aquatic insects, including mayfly, dragonfly, and damselfly larvae, as well as various bugs that accidentally fall into the water. This makes live bait—crickets, mealworms, and earthworms—deadly for the fish known as rooster in the waters of South Carolina's Santee Cooper Reservoir.

In *The Fishes of Tennessee*, noted fisheries scientists David Etnier and Wayne Starnes observe that the redbreast is ". . . generally more aggressive, more surface oriented and more active in cool waters than is the bluegill." Anglers have observed that these fish will move for a lure in water so cold that bluegill are immobilized. Redbreast sunfish are also more nocturnal than other panfish, which makes angling for them in the cool of evening a way to beat the summer heat.

An Atlantic slope fish, redbreasts are native to waters from Nova Scotia to Florida, with size generally increasing the further south one goes. In the northern part of their range, they are associated with smallmouth bass streams and medium-sized rivers. Scott Smith, biologist with Virginia's Department of Game and Inland Fisheries, explains their niche in the Mid-Atlantic region. "Typically, in our small lakes and larger reservoirs, bluegill are the dominant sunfish," he begins. "Redbreast and rock bass are the dominant sunfish in most of our rivers." Further south, the fish locals refer to as "redheaded bream" or "tobacco box," inhabits blackwater swamps. Warm, sluggish rivers, like Florida's Suwannee, harbor some of the largest specimens. Pound-plus redbreasts are possible there.

According to the North American Fishing Club's guide, *Panfishing*, "In streams, redbreasts are usually found in deep pools out of fast current. They often hide behind boulders and logs and in undercut banks around tree roots. In lakes and ponds, they prefer deep, weedy areas with sand or mud bottoms." Redbreasts are homesteaders. Once they find a place they like, they can often be found there time and again. Etnier and Starnes point out, "Nests are constructed in flowing portions of streams in areas of sandy substrate and usually near some obstruction." Look for communal honeycombs of spawning beds near logs, large rocks, or masses of vegetation. Males,

Orangeburg National Fish Hatchery opened in 1912 and continues operations today. USFWS NFACA

who protect the eggs, can often be caught multiple times as they return to the nest upon release.

Kurt Eversman, a fisheries biologist for the U.S. Fish and Wildlife Service and manager at Orangeburg National Fish Hatchery in South Carolina—long a redbreast sunfish powerhouse—writes, "There are a ton of fishers in this area that fish for redbreasts using cane poles. They wade in and put their cane pole over some cattails and drop them right into a hole . . . and pick them off their beds. The beds are typically three feet or less deep."

Eversman and his staff are tasked with raising two million of the panfish annually, using the area's climate to advantage. "I've gone to a wintertime production," says Eversman. "In the wintertime my photoperiod (daylight) is less, and my water is cooler, so I don't have as many nuisance algaes or weeds in the pond. This makes it easier when time comes to harvest." Kurt and his staff are the only national fish hatchery producing redbreasts.

Fish coming out of Orangeburg are bound for several destinations. Some go to stock rivers that have had recent population declines of the fish. Eversman gives one such example, "The redbreast program in the Edisto River is actually a restoration program to mitigate damages caused by invasive flathead catfish." Anglers there are now reporting good catches of redbreasts, likely due to his staff's hard work. In addition, Orangeburg's sunfish progeny also make their way to

ponds at Harris Neck and Carolina Sandhills National Wildlife Refuges. In those locations and some nearby Audubon properties, the fish provides a ready food source for the federally threatened wood stork.

This spirited panfish also assists in the recovery of certain endangered native mussels. Orangeburg's mussel biologist, Jonathan Wardell, explains, "We're a big redbreast sunfish facility, and we've been one for decades. We produce lots of fish for the Edisto, but we can also use redbreasts as a host for imperiled mussel species." Larval mussels must hitch a ride on a host fish in order to develop. After noticing several of the fish in areas where mussel broodstock were collected, Wardell had an idea. "We decided to keep some redbreast sunfish for hosts for the brook floater mussel, and they did really well."

The redbreast, along with bluegill and redear make up the "Big Trio" of panfishing—the largest members of the *Lepomis* group. Despite their smaller size, relative to bass, panfish account for a huge part of the fishing economy. Panfish anglers—about 8.4 million—are second only to bass anglers (9.6 million) in numbers. According to the 2016 Survey of Hunting and Fishing, published by the Wildlife and Sport Fish Restoration Program, U.S. panfishers spent 110 million angler-days pursuing these tasty fish, just shy of the 117 million days put in by bass anglers.

—Brett Billings

Dr. Stanislas F. Snieszko
(1902–1984)

Dr. Stanislas F. "Doc" Snieszko was born in Krzyz, Poland, in 1902 and reared on a farm that included a carp pond. He was educated in bacteriology and chemistry at Jagellonian University in Krakow, where he later became a professor in 1937. His research travels took him to Cornell University in 1939 and he remained in the United States when Nazi Germany invaded Poland.

Snieszko was appointed visiting research bacteriologist at the University of Maine where he worked on bacterial lobster diseases until conscripted into the U.S. Army's Chemical Warfare Service. Stationed at Camp Detrick, Maryland, Dr. Snieszko served the war years as a microbiologist at the U.S. Army Biological Warfare Laboratories attaining the rank of captain. By war's end, Snieszko was naturalized an American citizen.

In 1946, Snieszko joined the U.S. Fish and Wildlife Service at the Microbiological Laboratory of the Fisheries Experimental Station at Leetown, West Virginia. Snieszko was in charge of a small staff that worked on fish health diagnostics of salmon and trout and a variety of warmwater species, and within a few years he became the station's director. The National Fish Hatchery System and aquaculture for conservation benefitted greatly with solutions for bacterial problems, parasite control, egg disinfection, and drug efficacy. Snieszko acknowledged a lack of training related to fish health and encouraged seminars and formal training programs for fish hatchery biologists and fish health practitioners. Hundreds of American and foreign fishery personnel attended his workshops and comprehensive long courses, and Snieszko developed his laboratory in Leetown into the world's foremost institution of technical training of its type.

Snieszko authored more than two hundred publications on prevention and control of bacterial fish diseases—many still used by aquaculturists worldwide. He retired in 1972 but maintained an office until his death in 1984. Throughout his career Dr. Stanislas F. Snieszko received numerous accolades including his entry in 1991 into the National Fish Culture Hall of Fame in Spearfish, South Dakota.

—Carlos R. Martinez

Above: Dr. Stanislas F. Snieszko joined the U.S. Fish and Wildlife Service after serving in the U.S. Army during WWII. He became renowned for his knowledge of fish diseases. USFWS NFACA

Crappie

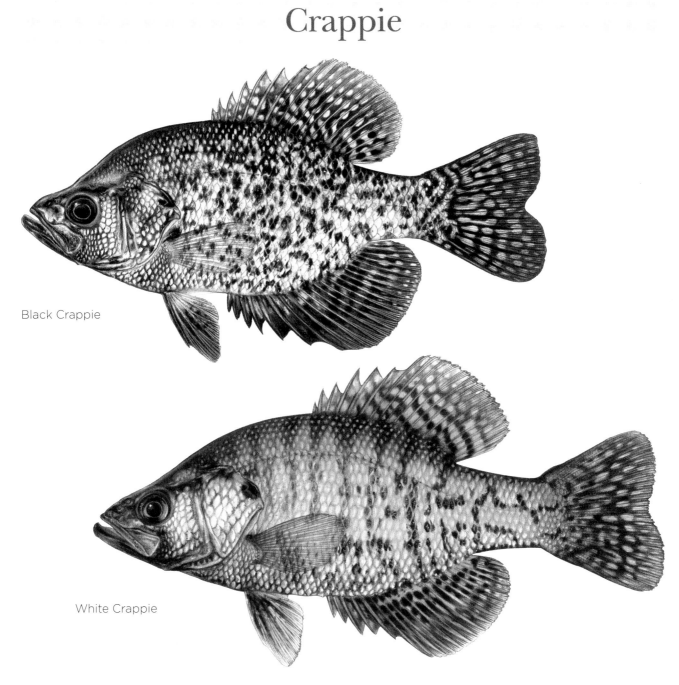

Black Crappie

White Crappie

No fish has as many nicknames as the crappie. Local monikers, such as calico bream, strawberry bass, and bank-lick bass hint at the crappie's storied place in rural America. Early U.S. Fish Commission biologists David Starr Jordan and Barton Warren Evermann give a sampling of names used in the early 1900s in their encyclopedic work, *American Food & Game Fishes*. "It is called bachelor in the Ohio Valley, Campbellite, croppie, and Newlight in Illinois, Indiana and Kentucky; tin-mouth or paper-mouth in northern Indiana and Illinois, and sac-à-lait, and chinquapin perch in the lower Mississippi, Louisiana, and Texas."

U.S. Fish Commission biologist James Henshall included the assortment of names and their origins in his 1903 book, *Bass, Pike, Perch and Others*, and noted that croppie derived from their crepe-shaped body and Campbellite from a religious sect founded by Alexander Campbell in central Kentucky. The sect members were known as Newlights—and so were crappie. Cajuns called the fish sac-à-lait, or bag of milk, the origin of which Henshall did not offer.

Regardless of what you call it, crappie is a local favorite on many big lakes, including the well-known Reelfoot Lake, which straddles the Kentucky-Tennessee border. It is the home water of crappie enthusiast

Ronnie Capps, who has studied and fished for crappie from every angle for over half a century. Ronnie won his first crappie tournament well before he turned ten. He recalls, "I fished on Reelfoot with my grandfather. We used to sell crappie commercially on Reelfoot. The fish were actually sold in the restaurants locally. People would come from everywhere to eat 'em."

Though the lake's commercial crappie market is now a thing of the past, Ronnie still has a few of the old metal tags that had to be clipped to the fish's lips before taking them to the check station. Unlike the average bassmaster and many a trout aficionado, who practice catch-and-release, the non-tournament crappie fisher is all about eating golden, deep-fried fillets.

In high school Capps worked as a musselshell diver. He learned a lot about where to find these notoriously tough-to-locate fish from crawling around on the bottom substrate. "It's always a soft bottom for a big female in the spring," he recalls, "and a lot of the males will definitely be on harder, sandier gravel or pea gravel."

After college, he worked with crappie for three decades as part of the Tennessee Wildlife Resources Agency, learning the science and professional management of his favorite sport fish. Recently retired, he is now a full-time tournament crappie fisherman with eight national crappie championships and half-dozen runner-up prizes to his credit.

The two species—black crappie and white crappie—were separated out in the scientific literature in 1875. Many anglers still have difficulty telling them apart, especially since the two regularly hybridize, producing offspring with an intermediate appearance, and fisheries managers have had to consider the two as one in most fishing regulations. Bag limits are almost always an aggregate of both. Managers usually set size limits for whatever length the crappie will reach in its third year, be that ten inches in Kentucky and nearby Barkley Lake or twelve inches in more southerly waters. After the third year, a downshift in growth means the crappie, already a short-lived fish, may not live long enough to make the next benchmark.

Body shape is a clue in distinguishing the two species. Black crappie tend to be stockier with random black markings over their silvery or olive sides. White crappie are more elongated, often with dark vertical bars—a camouflage hint that they often hide in standing timber, rooted vegetation, and brush piles where the longitudinal markings help break up their outline.

According to Ronnie Capps, "The black crappie gets shallower and swampier if possible, versus a white crappie—a deeper open-water kind of fish. The way they relate to current is different, too. You usually don't associate very much of a current flow with a black crappie. They will not migrate with a current in their face compared to a white crappie."

There are also differences in food habits. Western district fisheries biologist for Kentucky, Adam Martin, explains that all crappie depend on tiny zooplankton for most of the first two years of their life. Their anatomy attests to this. In their 2000 book, *Fishes: An Introduction to Ichthyology*, Moyle and Cech point out, "The longest and finest gill rakers in the family (Centrarchidae) are those of the crappies, reflecting the importance of zooplankton in their diets, which they pick individually from the water column." Biologist Martin says they feed on plankton up to an unusual size: "Both species can rely just on zooplankton up to about eight inches in length.

Once crappie are ready for bigger foods, Martin attests, "You'll often see that white crappie switch over to feeding on fish earlier than the black crappie." That earlier switch accounts for slightly larger white crappie than black crappie of the same age. Plus, black crappie tend to feed on crayfish, insects, and other bottom-dwelling invertebrates more so than their white crappie counterparts. However, once fish hit the ten- to twelve-inch range, their diet is mainly soft-bodied fish prey for both species.

Hardly any other freshwater gamefish is pursued with live bait as much as crappie. Ronnie Capps swears by live bait, saying, "I've won more championships fishing live bait with a double minnow rig . . . some people call it a Reelfoot rig. It's basically an egg sinker two-thirds down from the top and a top hook." For the past thirty years "spider-rigging"—fishing multiple poles, usually with live bait—has been king. Research has supported that up to four rods, more lines meant more fish in the boat.

"We're entering a new era of crappie fishing these days," says Capps. "That multi-pole setup will be pretty popular for a good while, but fast gaining ground is the electronics and the technology we're using now. We're catching fish with just one pole since we can identify them." Ronnie remembers the old days: "When we started we just had a lead ball and a piece of string and a cork." Fishing with his grandfather on Reelfoot, the young Capps learned to triangulate to remember where sunken trees and other structures were located in the muddy water. That was important, because crappie love structure—be it brush piles, downed trees, or stumps.

Then, early sonar technology called "flashers" allowed anglers to see the bottom in a rudimentary way. "Fish finders" in the 1970s and '80s made huge

These cane pole anglers are taking home a stringer of crappie in Natchitoches, Louisiana, circa 1940, likely stocked by still-operational Natchitoches National Fish Hatchery, which opened in 1931. These panfish in Cajun country go by the curious name of sac-à-lait which means "bag of milk" in French. COURTESY LIBRARY OF CONGRESS

leaps forward in understanding fish movement. The advent of non-land-based GPS in the '90s allowed anglers to consistently relocate structure and brush piles—keys to crappie success. Then sidescan and 360-degree sonar gave even more coverage and better resolution.

Currently, Garmin's "Livescope" technology allows the person in the boat to see the fish and structure below in real time, and that's been a game-changer. Technology that lets the angler pinpoint a fish and put a bait on its nose is making fishermen better and more confident. At a recent tourney on Mississippi's hallowed crappie water of Grenada Lake, Ronnie caught forty-three fish. "There was only five of the forty-three I didn't know I was gonna catch." This high-tech sonar has even confirmed that crappie can feel the pressure of a boat coming and move out of the way. The result? Many crappie anglers are now opting for longer rods of twelve feet or more in length.

The U.S. Fish and Wildlife Service has a long history with crappie, dating back to the U.S. Fish Commission days of the 1880s, when its workers raised them at hatcheries. Crappie were among the several fish species that U.S. Bureau of Fisheries employees in the upper Mississippi River reaches around La Crosse, Wisconsin, and Homer, Minnesota, endeavored to rescue from backwaters through the 1920s and 1930s.

Crappie were repatriated in the Mississippi-proper or taken to hatcheries to be distributed by rail car to points well beyond. In 1921, 37 million crappie were repatriated in the Mississippi and another 75,000 crappie stocked elsewhere.

Considering the ease of raising crappie in a hatchery, it is a very low investment—high return type culture. In addition to providing fish for tribal and public lands partners, the U.S. Fish and Wildlife Service now has another reason for raising crappie—saving native mussels.

Native freshwater mussels are one of the most imperiled groups of animals in the world. The damming of rivers and loss of native fish have pushed many of the country's mussel species to the brink of extinction. Approximately three-quarters of our host-dependent native mussel species are in trouble. Many freshwater mussels require native fish hosts, on which their larvae must hitch a ride, in order to develop and disperse. Crappie are an ideal host fish for many mussel species being propagated in the nation's federal and state hatcheries. Mussels such as the black sandshell, fat mucket, and white heelsplitter are just a few relying, in part, on crappie for their continued existence.

—Brett Billings

Atlantic Salmon

My team and I were not just going for a late autumn stroll in a beautiful, cold Maine stream for fun or to soak up the little light left on the shortening days. We were continuing on a long-term study to investigate the freshwater ecology of the endangered Atlantic salmon.

This was the second day of our trip, catching fish. The backpack did not feel as heavy as it would by the eighth or ninth day. My legs were still fresh and so I could still hop from rock to rock with ease. I knew the stream, the rocks, the logs, the riffle, and pools, just as well as I knew the fish. Over the five years of doing Ph.D. dissertation research, I had collected Atlantic salmon in the same half-mile stretch of Shorey Brook dozens of time.

Slowly and methodically, time after time we would sample thirty-foot section by thirty-foot section with a thirty-five-pound backpack electrofisher. Three or four times a year, I would sample the stream and attempt to catch every fish along the way. We used a low electrical current to stun the fish for a moment so that the team could scoop them up to give them a full biological work up. Every salmon captured, we sedated and handled the same way. We took a length, a weight, a picture, and each fish longer than two and a quarter inches got a tag approximately the size of a grain of rice and a fin clip. The tags are not unlike a microchip a veterinarian might place on your pet in case it gets lost. The Atlantic salmon, once recovered from the sedation, was placed back to within a few steps of where we captured it. These rice-sized tags called passive integrated transponders would stay in the fish for the rest of their lives so each time we recaught a fish we had the chance to record how it had grown and where it may have moved.

The stream had several monitoring stations where, if passed, the station would automatically detect the tag and record the time and code of the fish that passed through. Our intensive focus over the years gave us great insight into growth and life history patterns of individual fish, with an understanding of the entire community of fish nearby and the seasonal changes that occurred from season to season.

All the salmon in our little stream originated as inch-long fry from Craig Brook National Fish Hatchery, Maine. The hatchery has led the way in Atlantic salmon conservation since the 1890s, with Charles G. Atkins at the helm for nearly five decades. Mr. Atkins helped develop many of the practices the U.S. Fish and Wildlife Service still uses today with hatchery rearing. He published papers on bettering hatchery feed for Atlantic salmon and conducted early studies with tagging salmon to learn more about their growth and movement. Atkins was prescient in that he concerned himself with some of the first fishway designs, understanding that conservation also meant ensuring or restoring access to habitat.

We have come a long way with hatchery management and restoration, but many of Mr. Atkins's ideas are still at the heart of Maine Atlantic salmon restoration. One cannot help but wonder what he would think if he could see current technology—the advanced electronic tags and the modern level of hydraulic engineering and our understanding of how water flows that goes into fishway design today.

Our November fish collection endeavor was always a rush to squeeze in before the stream froze up, but that last fall foray was important to learn what fish might do after the winter's thaw in the coming spring. Atlantic salmon have flexible lives. They normally

Fertilized Atlantic salmon eggs packed in wet moss in wooden crates are about to be shipped. USFWS MA

An Atlantic salmon broodstock at Craig Brook National Fish Hatchery. USFWS MA

A moment of levity during routine maintenance of troughs at Craig Brook Fish-Cultural Station circa 1950. The sign marks a transitional period before "National Fish Hatchery" became the standard still used today. USFWS MA

Women were often hired on a short-term basis to pick eggs or, in this case, apply tags to small Atlantic salmon for migrations studies. USFWS MA

Geneticist Dr. Meredith Bartron, Northeast Fisheries Center in Pennsylvania, analyzes Atlantic salmon tissues. Genetic data is used to monitor the diversity of hatchery and natural-origin broodstock spawned at Craig Brook National Fish Hatchery and Green Lake National Fish Hatchery as part of Maine Atlantic salmon restoration work. RYAN HAGERTY, USFWS

spend about two to three years in freshwater growing to about five inches, then during spring they go through a process of smoltification and move out to sea for one to two years.

But there are more dynamic choices than what is normal. The males that grow fastest in their first year of life will often make a switch from growing fast and getting longer to staying put in a river and becoming a precocious parr. Their hurried growth ceases; these precocious parr—small fish—become reproductively viable even as they are only a mere few inches long.

Instead of the long sea migrations most fish take, these precocious parr instead act as stealthy spawners. They will wait in the streams for large sea-run males and females to return and to pair up in the fall, make gravel nests, or redds as they are commonly called, and then spawn. They then will dart into the midst of the mating pair and sneakily fertilize a few eggs at a time, all while the large sea-run fish are spawning.

Finding the precocious parr in the fall always helped answer several questions. How many fish are going to migrate out to sea next year? What is the average growth this summer? What is the variation in growth this year?

Some questions were even more in the moment, though. With the sea-run salmon adult returns so low in the stream, we would only see one of our many stocked fry return to spawn as an adult. Seeing the variation of life history expressed in the precocious parr gives hope to the resilient nature of Atlantic salmon. These parr who are normally cryptic and skittish become brave and colorful trying to ensure their genes are passed on to the next generation. Their adaptation to this river system helped us understand the current growth regime of our imperiled Atlantic salmon population.

Our hope is that Atlantic salmon return in greater numbers to their nascent waters, eventually becoming self-sustaining, driven by a transcendent, restless urge to create the next generation.

—Michael Bailey, Ph.D.

Landlocked Salmon

Fall of 2015, three members of the landlocked salmon restoration team and I arrive at the ferry dock in Charlotte, Vermont. We are headed to the Boquet River on the New York side of Lake Champlain, to check a trap we set the night before to catch landlocked Atlantic salmon.

On the ferry ride I look out over the long horizon and imagine how the land must have looked when the cold crush of glaciers a mile thick slowly gouged the Champlain Sea and connected what is now Lake Champlain to the Atlantic Ocean. The continuous waterway allowed migratory salmon unfettered access to the freshwater lake.

But that did not last. Approximately ten thousand years ago when these glaciers retreated, this connection between lake and the ocean was cut off and salmon became landlocked—blocked from the ocean and their seafaring counterparts.

Atlantic salmon also became landlocked during this time in lakes and rivers in Norway, Sweden, Russia, and the British Isles. In North America, landlocked salmon naturally occurred from New York to the Maritime Provinces and westward to Ontario. In fact, most populations of landlocked salmon are located north of Lake Champlain in Quebec and Newfoundland where they are called ouananiche. Scientists call them *Salmo salar*, leaping salmon. Their sporting qualities are renowned. They grow to twenty-plus pounds.

At least ten rivers pouring into Lake Champlain historically supported landlocked salmon populations, with fish up to twenty pounds returning to spawn. For landlocked salmon, the lake was their ocean. Historical records document that British soldiers harvested large numbers of landlocked salmon

from Lake Champlain rivers during the Revolutionary War. That bounty did not last; by the mid-1800s dam building and deforestation caused the extirpation of landlocked salmon from the lake. Then, in 1972, the U.S. Fish and Wildlife Service collaborated with New York and Vermont state agencies to restore landlocked salmon to Lake Champlain and proceeded apace.

But more is to be done. Arriving at the Boquet River, I look at the Willsboro Dam and take gratification knowing that the town has been working with the U.S. Fish and Wildlife Service and other conservation partners to remove it to benefit salmon. With this wooden edifice out of the way, landlocked salmon can swim up into more than eighty miles of habitat upstream.

Landlocked salmon need connected lake and river habitats. They hatch in the river and remain there for approximately two years before heading out to the lake in a life stage called smolts. They take up house in the lake for approximately two more years foraging on native smelt and non-native alewife, growing to sexual maturity.

In the autumn of their fourth year, they are compelled to reproduce, river-bound, drawn to the streams of their origin. Adults "home" back to the river where they hatched using river-specific odors like a beacon, which they imprinted on in their early life.

Two people are fly-fishing in a large pool just upstream of our trap. We put on our waders and start toward the trap. We see a small amount of foam on top of the net indicating we have fish—eleven landlocked salmon, in total. We transport them to the shore where we measure their length and weight,

U.S. Fish Commission workers spawn landlocked salmon at Grand Lake Fish-Cultural Station in Maine circa 1895. The station operated from 1891 to 1933 when it was transferred to the state of Maine as a federal cost-saving measure during the Great Depression. USFWS NFACA

Landlocked salmon in the hands of a biologist at Berlin National Fish Hatchery. The facility opened in 1930 and was transferred to the state of New Hampshire in 1982. FRANK DUFRESNE, USFWS

remove a few scales to determine their age, and examine them for sea lamprey wounds and fin clips.

Sea lamprey are parasitic and attach to landlocked salmon while they are in the lake. Wounds from the parasite can lead to death. Fortunately, the U.S. Fish and Wildlife Service's sea lamprey control endeavors have recently reduced the wounding rate to levels in favor of the salmon. We are still in the early stages of restoration where fish from the Dwight David Eisenhower National Fish Hatchery are reintroduced to the river to jumpstart the establishment of a natural population.

As we expected, most of the fish have a fin clip indicating they were stocked into the Boquet River as smolts. A few of them have no clips indicating they were stocked into the Boquet soon after hatching as unfed fry. This is good news—the stocked salmon have imprinted to the Boquet River and have returned from the lake to reproduce and start a natural population. All trapped salmon are fitted with radio tags to allow us to track their movements.

Fast forward to 2020: the Willsboro Dam is now for five years an artifact of the past. Landlocked salmon lay their eggs in gravelly redds above the former dam site. We have documented fry emerging from these redds, and this was no small matter. It was the first time natural reproduction of landlocked salmon occurred in a Lake Champlain tributary in more than 150 years. We will continue to work upstream. Now the focus is on habitat restoration in the upper Boquet River and tributaries to allow for higher survival of fry and natural production of smolts.

—William Ardren, Ph.D.

Charles Atkins raised landlocked salmon at Grand Lake and Craig Brook Fish-Cultural Stations in Maine. He described the Grand Lake station in the 1884 Bulletin of the U.S. Fish Commission. "Our best hatching house stands on the lake shore and is a very substantial structure, partly underground, with massive stone walls; it has capacity for developing 4,000,000 eggs or hatching 1,000,000. We pack eggs in sphagnum moss, wet to embed the eggs, and dry to surround this mass. Surrounded by 3-inches dry moss they go on a sled, in the morning, with the temperature 10 to 15 degrees below zero, 28 miles (taking the whole forenoon), without the frost penetrating to them." USFWS MA

Dr. Mamie Parker (1957–)

The trek of a thousand miles starts with the first step. Dr. Mamie Parker began her journey in humble beginnings in rural southern Arkansas, on a path that made its way into Washington, D.C., and the upper stratum of leadership in the U.S. Fish and Wildlife Service, as the assistant director for fisheries.

Mamie was blessed with a strong foundation—a loving mother, Cora, who saw to it that Mamie possessed a strong work ethic infused with a love of the outdoors.

"If any one person influenced me," said Mamie, "it was my mother. I was the last of eleven children and the outdoors was our common bond right near Overflow Creek National Wildlife Refuge. Mom taught me to fish for bowfin—grinners, we called them—and catfish and carp."

Fishing was fun, but a practical matter. "We fished for food—we practiced catch-and-release, without the 'release' part," she giggled. "I was not familiar with the term 'rough fish.'"

Education was paramount to Cora and Mamie did not disappoint—she attended the University of Arkansas and the University of Wisconsin earning a B.S. in biology, an M.S. in fisheries, and a Ph.D. in limnology (the biological character of freshwater). She began her U.S. Fish and Wildlife Service career in 1977, when there were few female scientists and even fewer African-Americans employed in the profession. Wisconsin was a long way from Arkansas—and that's where she landed as a fish health biological trainee at Genoa National Fish Hatchery and the Fish Health Laboratory, diagnosing, preventing, and controlling infectious diseases on the hatchery that reared smallmouth bass, walleye, brook trout, and lake trout, as well as performing health assessments on fish hatcheries over an eight-state area.

"I was a southerner in the North and next headed further north, to New London National Fish Hatchery in Minnesota," said Mamie. "I was headed in the wrong direction, I thought; I deviated from my desires but grew personally and professionally and encouraged everyone to think outside their comforts."

It was a cultural experience for a southerner in the Great Lakes states, one that cut both ways. "A lot of people had no experience with a pioneer Black woman, and it was isolating at times, like living in a little house on the prairie," said Mamie. "But I felt like an ambassador, and for me it germinated an interest where conservation and human dynamics meet—and that is where my heart has been ever since."

Dr. Mamie Parker, former U.S. Fish and Wildlife Service assistant director, during a 2005 visit to Iron River National Fish Hatchery in Wisconsin.
COURTESY DUDLEY EDMONDSON

She made moves back southward, working on federal permits and with private landowners in Missouri to promote fish and wildlife conservation on their lands and waters. In Atlanta, in a U.S. Fish and Wildlife Service regional office, she supervised national fish hatcheries, field offices, and national wildlife refuges in three states. She advanced in managerial positions and got called north again to serve as regional director for the U.S. Fish and Wildlife Service's thirteen-state Northeast Region based in Massachusetts, where she earned the respect of state fish and game agencies as well as Canadian authorities. Atlantic salmon conservation rose to great concern during her tenure.

Mamie wrapped up her U.S. Fish and Wildlife Service career in 2007 as the assistant director for fisheries, in headquarters leading the staff in completing the National Fish Habitat Action Plan. Her home state's governor inducted her into the Arkansas Outdoor Hall of Fame in 2005. The Virginia governor appointed her to the Board of Game and Inland Fisheries in 2017, subsequently being elected chair.

"That was a moving experience for me, to be the first African-American appointed to the board," said Mamie. "I wept as I thought of my ancestor, my great-great grandmother Ann—approximately thirty years a slave and thirty years a free woman—when they handed me the gavel. The sense of how far we have come was stirring."

The past is prelude: "On the face of it, the years seem long and the miles great—and so far removed from my rural Arkansas upbringing," she said with contemplation, "but that's not so. Fishing the bayous and creeks of Ashley County, Arkansas, made me. Nature makes us human and it made me whole."

—Craig Springer

Fisheries employee Mary Westfall, stationed in Alaska, painted two watercolor concepts in 1950 for the eventual U.S. Fish and Wildlife Service crest. Her images included a leaping king salmon with a Canada goose, and the leaping salmon with a drake mallard. The goose triumphed and artist Bob Hines polished off the design, which was which was first used on uniforms in 1952. CARLOS R. MARTINEZ, USFWS

American Shad

Having come more than a thousand miles from Canadian and New England coastal waters, these sleek fish flash like the glint of a freshly minted silver coin in the turbid, dark waters of Carolina rivers. Driven by the competing urges of safety and spawning, they are adept at avoiding the long-handled nets of fish biologists who sweep the river surface, leveraging themselves upon the stout rails on an electrofishing boat plying against flowing waters.

Biologists net American shad. Scientists know them as *Alossa sapidissima*. They are the largest member of the herring family and sometimes known locally as white salmon for the way they leap when hooked. A slab-sided five-pound muscular American shad can put up quite a tussle caught on a spinner or a fly.

For food and for sport, the U.S. Fish and Wildlife Service has been involved in American shad conservation since shortly after its 1871 founding as the antecedent U.S. Fish Commission. The American shad has long been a part of our cultural and economic history. In colonial and early American times, American shad landings often exceeded a million pounds per year on the East Coast, and they were an important protein source for the population of our young nation.

In the winter of 1778, George Washington was on the verge of sending his beleaguered Army home from Valley Forge because he could not feed them. Then the American shad came up the Schuylkill River finning their way upstream to spawn. Starving soldiers waded out into the frigid river with pitchforks and crude nets and harvested the densely stacked fish. American shad allowed Washington to keep the Continental Army together and continue the fight for independence. Perhaps you have read about this in John McPhee's *The Founding Fish.*

In 1865, the Confederates lost the Battle of Five Forks in Virginia in part because General George Pickett had left to attend a shad bake, supposedly with whiskey aplenty, without telling anyone. When Federal troops in Phil Sheridan's V Corps attacked, Pickett's staff could not find him; there was no second in command in his absence. The Federal troops rolled up Pickett's four brigades and won the battle and shad helped to secure the Union.

In June 1873, the two-year-old U.S. Fish Commission sought to plant American shad in western waters and succeeded, but not first without some painful travail. Commission employee Livingston Stone shepherded Hudson River shad aboard a train westward. It derailed in Nebraska and the fish were lost.

Not dissuaded, Stone tried again a month later planting American shad in the Sacramento River. The U.S. Fish Commission planted American shad in Pacific waters into the 1880s. The fish subsequently spread up the West Coast, creating a tremendous run on the Columbia River and have even extended their range to Kamchatka, Russia. They have done so well that early shad restoration programs on the East Coast used eggs and fry from these introduced Pacific populations, which were much easier to obtain. The U.S. Bureau of Fisheries's Clackamas Fish-Cultural Station workers in Oregon immersed themselves in American shad culture in the 1910s.

Shad numbers in their native East Coast range noticeably declined in the late 1800s as fishing

American shad were spawned and incubated aboard the floating hatchery the U.S.F.C. *Fish Hawk*. It's seen here at Bryan Point, Maryland, where the U.S. Fish Commission operated a station from 1892 to 1928. The *Fish Hawk* sailed from 1880 to 1912. USFWS NFACA

U.S. Bureau of Fisheries workers release American shad near Washington, D.C. USFWS MA

Right: American shad has long been an important food source on the east coast of North America, sought by commercial operators and by anglers. COURTESY LIBRARY OF CONGRESS

Below: A U.S. Fish and Wildlife Service biologist expresses eggs from a ripe American shad at Edenton National Fish Hatchery, North Carolina. USFWS MA

became more efficient and harvests increased. Interest in American shad conservation ramped up. In 1939, the U.S. Fish and Wildlife Service's first female scientist, Dr. Louella Cable, fully immersed herself in shad investigation, a topic she published in the popular and scientific presses through the 1940s. Following a spike of 11 million pounds harvested in 1957, the populations crashed, and the commercial harvest reached its nadir of zero by 2005. Overfishing and dams that stymied passage to spawning grounds caused serious depletions in shad runs. To restore the fishery, national fish hatcheries in

Edenton, North Carolina, and Bryan Point, Maryland, engaged in raising American shad around the turn of the twentieth century. The Bryan Point station closed in 1928 and essentially moved to Ft. Belvoir, Virginia.

Rearing this species is challenging, exhilarating, and thoroughly rewarding. There are early spring days on the rivers and time collecting broodstock and acclimatizing them to their spawning tanks. As the manager, you watch every parameter, coming in late at night in utter darkness to make sure the water and aeration are set properly. Unable to see a thing, you keep the lights off to avoid spooking the fish. You place your hand on the outside of the twelve-foot circular tanks and feel the adult shad thrumming along the inner edges. It is rewarding to know that despite the stress of capture, shad are spawning in this space that you and your crew have set up. In the morning, your reward is a liter or more of richly golden fertilized eggs collected in the oyster spat bags placed over the tank outflows.

Fertilized shad eggs drift with water flow. You'll get a half liter or more every night for the next month. Some ninety thousand eggs will fill a liter and that may yield fifty thousand tiny fry if you have every aspect set right: finely adjusted water flow, oxygenation, removal of dead eggs and treatment for fungal growth, feeding of fry with newly hatched brine shrimp at the optimal densities, and cleaning of debris from the tanks.

Do all this properly and the number of hatchery-reared fry that go back out into the wild may exceed the number of naturally spawned fry by a hundred times. Hatchery-spawned shad do not have to contend

Barriers to upstream movement of spawning American shad hamper the species. Fish biologist Julie Devers, Maryland Fish and Wildlife Conservation Office, takes landform measurements for an eventual shad-friendly culvert that will open miles of fish habitat to migratory fishes. STEVE DROTER, USFWS

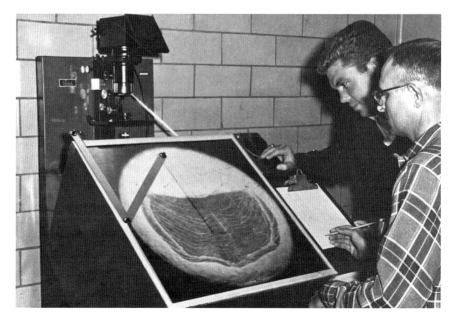

As trees leave rings as records of growth, so do fish. An amplified American shad scale is easy to read. USFWS MA

with suffocating silt or heavy predation in the first few crucial days of life. The hatchery spares them that.

The shad and their cousins the river herrings are a foundational part of the food web in the coastal rivers, estuaries, and the ocean. It is no coincidence that striped bass numbers dropped precipitously after American shad populations crashed; American shad constitute a forage base for stripers.

American shad restoration benefits the larger food web as well as people and economies associated with fishing and commercial harvest. American shad conservation is an American story. Restoring the fish is, in a way, restoring ourselves.

—Stephen Jackson

Striped Bass

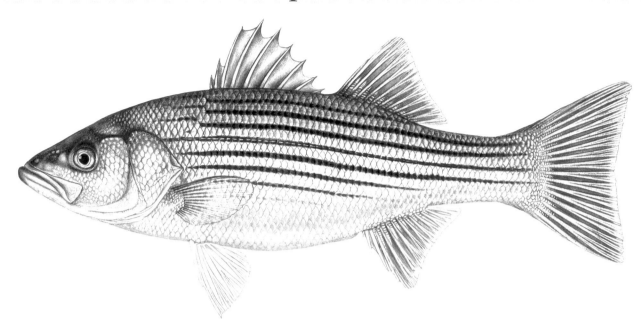

The U.S. Fish and Wildlife Service's history with the striped bass dates to 1879, through its antecedent U.S. Fish Commission. Commission biologists made early attempts at culturing them in captivity and planting the fish to bolster depleted populations or expand the fish's range. My history with striped bass began nearly a century later, after I had passed a few mileposts along the way.

I came of age in the Scioto Valley near Columbus, Ohio, fishing Big Darby Creek and other upland streams that veined the land like a silver maple's leaf, pouring successively southward toward the Ohio River. There were no striped bass there, but Big Darby drained gentle undulating hills and meandered through uplands that favored smallmouth bass. Rock bass abounded, too, taking up in the shadows cast by the roots of sycamore trees that knotted the stream banks in place. The creek was home to the nearly mythical Scioto madtom, a tiny catfish species last seen there in 1957.

When I was a boy, my dad who was a biology major made a small-mesh seine net and introduced me to the marvels that lay beneath the burbling riffles of Ohio's upland waters. We kicked shallow stony riffles and turned up disagreeable hellgrammites as long as a finger that would transform into elegant dobsonflies with transparent wings, all told, as big as your hand.

Under the cover of darkness, the hellgrammites foraged on caddis and mayfly larvae in the swift water combing through the recesses between stones. Darters waited downstream to partake of what the

hellgrammites dislodged but could not grasp. The creeks' rainbow and orangethroat darters—colored as advertised—were lit like neon signs in the spring. Dad owned a 1957 first edition of Milton Trautman's *The Fishes of Ohio* and I pored through its pages.

In a complete role reversal, the fishes caught me. I figured early on that I was going to be a fish biologist.

Along the way there, I worked short-term gigs at Senecaville National Fish Hatchery in southeastern Ohio, which foreshadowed my eventual full immersion into striped bass conservation. The federal fisheries facility was a home base for me as I conducted independent research on eastern Ohio darters. Shortly after buttoning up my academic credentials at University of Wisconsin–Stevens Point, I landed work with the U.S. Fish and Wildlife Service in the Kenai Fisheries Resources Office.

Alaska was a tremendous proving ground for what was to follow. I worked under the tutelage of veteran fish biologist Ed Crateau, catching and tagging Pacific salmon in a long-term management study. Our work carried us throughout southern Alaska, the Kenai Moose Range, today's Kenai National Wildlife Refuge, and out into the Aleutians—it was a great introduction to the Fish and Wildlife Service.

When Ed left Alaska to take on a striped bass investigation, I followed him to Panama City, Florida. He hired me on full-time and I waded chest-deep into striped bass research along the Gulf Coast.

Striped bass have long had a following in the U.S. and Canada. It has been of great value for food and for

U.S. Fish and Wildlife Service biologists collect data from striped bass caught in a purse seine on the North Carolina coast in 1958. USFWS MA

Tagged striped bass, caught again at a later date, reveals much about migration patterns, habitat needs, and the fitness of populations overall. USFWS MA

Allan Brown, then manager of the Welaka National Fish Hatchery in Florida, moves an adult striped bass between tanks. USFWS

sport for two centuries. The American affinity dates to the colonial period where observers remarked on the great abundance of the fish in coastal streams as they came in to spawn. U.S. Fish Commission biologists David Starr Jordan and Barton Warren Evermann in *American Food & Game Fishes* recounted the words of an early New England colonist. "There is a fish called a basse, a most sweet and wholesome fish as ever I did eat; it is altogether as good as our fresh sammon and the season of their coming was begun when we came first to New England in June and so continued about three months space."

Striped bass was described for science as a distinct species in 1792 and by then already running headlong into problems. The father of the U.S. Fish Commission, Robert Roosevelt, commented on their biology and conservation in his 1862 book, *The Game Fish of the Northern States of America and British Provinces*. "The Striped Bass becomes an object of the angler's attention in April, when he runs up the rivers to spawn.

He ascends into cool fresh water, until arrested by a natural, or all too frequently, an artificial barrier."

A profusion of low-head barriers and millpond dams and pollution coupled with overharvest sent striped bass numbers downward over the years. The fish became fewer and the fish became smaller. James Henshall, the Civil War surgeon turned U.S. Fish Commission biologist, wrote about seeing huge striped bass at fish markets in his boyhood Baltimore. In *Bass, Pike, Perch, and Others*, which he wrote in 1903 while superintendent at our present-day Bozeman National Fish Hatchery, Henshall remembered standing on a balance scale as a 103-pound youth. A single striped bass on the other side outweighed him.

Striped bass that big became a rare exception, and by the time I landed in Florida in 1978, striped bass were in serious trouble. Why, and what to do about it, was our primary charge.

We surveyed waters in Florida and Georgia for striped bass using all methods old and new. We

Striped bass anglers buy rods, lures, and boats, and travel some distances to catch fish. Angling was and remains important to the economy, as evidenced by the offerings at this Deal Island boarding house on the shores of Chesapeake Bay, Wenona, Maryland, circa 1945. USFWS MA

Fish biologist Charles Wooley heads off to striped bass habitat in an electrofishing boat in 1978. USFWS

employed beach seines and trawls and built electro-fishing boats to stun and capture striped bass. Radio telemetry for fish was somewhat new at the time and that was an eye-opening experience. The radios revealed the habits and habitats of striped bass; we followed radioed fish by boat and airplane. From our research, we published several scientific journal articles about striped bass and co-occurring gulf sturgeon.

In the mid-1980s, the Maryland Department of Natural Resources asked the U.S. Fish and Wildlife Service for assistance with the striped bass fishery in Chesapeake Bay. The fishery was feeble. I jumped at the chance to work on the project and Maryland folks insisted I station myself in their headquarters office next to their fisheries chief.

Literally, alongside Maryland DNR fish biologists, we dug into a cause and remedy for the poor state of striped bass. We tagged thousands of striped bass and our federal fisheries facilities were put to full use in striped bass conservation. My former haunt, Senecaville National Fish Hatchery, reared striped bass as did national fish hatcheries at Warm Springs, Georgia; McKinney Lake and Harrison Lake in Virginia; and Edenton in North Carolina. Maryland's Joseph Manning Hatchery proved quite useful, too.

All the tag returns illuminated the life history of striped bass. It was such a thrill to learn where eighty-pound females stacked up, staging for an upstream spawning run. We learned that striped bass possess a strong fidelity to return to their natal coastal streams to spawn. We know the adults cruise near the seashore, but they are far-ranging animals of great magnitude. Stripers stocked in Maryland waters were caught as far away as Nova Scotia.

One tag return came back to me in the oddest way. The patron of a Montreal restaurant complained to the maître d' about an anchor tag in his bass on his plate. The maître d' to my good fortune was an angler and had the presence of mind to send the tag information to me.

All of our research, coupled with the population augmented by the hatchery fish, jumpstarted striped bass recovery. But the two-year moratorium placed on harvest by the Maryland governor had great effect.

Today, striped bass are a great prize for anglers in the surf, in coastal rivers during their spring migration and you can find them in many big inland reservoirs from South Carolina to New Mexico. They are well established on the West Coast from plantings made by the U.S. Fish Commission decades ago.

The future for the fish is much brighter now because of science and technology and genetics—and perhaps most of all, for the good people, the scientists and the anglers, dedicated to their conservation. The mountain of knowledge accumulated since the 1970s lends itself to responsible management.

It has been such a great privilege to peer into the workings of striped bass, to come to better know how they make their living. It is almost spiritual—and not unlike the wonder I experienced as a boy turning over stones in a riffle in an Ohio creek.

—Charles "Charlie" Wooley

Fishing is recreation. It re-creates our souls and opens us up to the beauty and workings of nature.

Epilogue

Deep in the hills of eastern Kentucky, the Cumberland River begins its downhill westward trek to the Ohio in a small stream that flows through Harlan. I grew up on that river and learned how to turn over rocks in riffles and catch crawdads and grampuses, the local parlance for hellgrammites, to use for fish bait to go along with the redworms we'd dig up and keep in a tin can. Our boat was an old coupe car top from the junk yard. Inverted, it kept us afloat as we rested our cane poles in the struts that had once attached the top to the car. It was on this river that I spent many summer days, and a few nights fishing for catfish by a campfire on the sandbar. I enjoyed being on the river and loved catching sunfish, bass, catfish, and redhorse suckers. In our culture, fishing wasn't just for enjoyment—it put food on the table.

There weren't many luxuries growing up in the home of a totally disabled veteran and a short-order cook. But if we were poor, we didn't know it. We thought we were rich because we could float the river for fish, set trotlines, and be free. Hill people understand the great gifts the Creator has given us, and they are woven into the fabric of everyday life. As I grew into manhood and left the Appalachian hills, I began to see that I wasn't that different from people all across America. We Americans love our natural treasures, and especially our fishing.

I began my career in conservation managing catfish farms in the Mississippi Delta and learned just how important fish culture is to our economy and in meeting the challenges of feeding people. For Americans, the inalienable rights of life, liberty, and the pursuit of happiness are not just words. People came to America not only for religious freedom, but for the right to catch fish and harvest game to feed their families. In England, these natural resources were considered owned by the Crown, and to harvest fish and game was considered poaching—taking the Crown's game without permission. The fierce belief in freedom that characterizes Americans is one of survival, and demands that these natural resources belong to the people, not the government.

It is this very belief that underpinned the beginning of the U.S. Fish Commission and the eventual planting of bass, trout, catfish, walleye, salmon, and sunfish across the country during the fish rail car era. The belief germinated the ideas that turned fisheries management from an art into science and the creation of federal and state fish hatcheries; these convictions were manifest at the passage of the Sport Fish Restoration Act and the willingness of anglers and boaters to pay for the conservation so important to healthy fisheries.

The people who dedicated their lives to this quest are the real subjects of this book, those living and those long passed. Those whose bylines appear in the preceding pages write about the places, fishes, mussels, plants, and amphibians that they know best. Their words exemplify the enduring dedication to conservation. National Fish Hatchery workers and their families lived in some of the most remote places in America because that's where the good water for raising fish was found. Privations were many. Some were housebound throughout the winter because the snow would block the passes. Others fought mosquitoes and black flies as well as the critters that also wanted to have fish for dinner. There were no set hours. They worked until the job was done, then got up the next day and started again. By doing so, they ensured that America would always have healthy fish populations and a means to survive. Though I speak in an historical sense, this is still true in many cases today.

With the increase in human population, so was the increase in demand for healthy and abundant fish to feed them and provide recreation. In the beginning, many hatchery managers were "fish men," but were not college-educated scientists. They were successful at growing fish because they could "feel" that the fish were in trouble and intuitively knew what to do. They may not have been able to tell you the biology of why, but they knew how. As disease control and genetics became increasingly important, more fisheries scientists were recruited to join the work and help provide the sound science necessary to keep fish healthy, as well as genetically fit.

The Fisheries Assistance program was born and worked closely with the federal hatcheries and states to manage migratory as well as non-migratory fish stocks. Together, they worked to increasingly build on science to deal with the challenges facing aquaculture and free-run stocks. But inherent in both the self-made fish men and the new breed of fisheries scientists was a rich sense of humor. People like Neal Ward, Monty "The Shadow" Millard, Hannibal Bolton, and John Forester were always ready with a quick wit and an injection of fun into daily work. They loved what they did and couldn't separate their personal lives from their professional ones. The assistance work is carried out today in Fish and Wildlife Conservation Offices spread across the country housing some of the best fisheries scientists you'll find, men and women strongly trained in genetics, physiology, population ecology, statistics, hydrology, and habitat restoration.

Commercial fishing operations began to increase substantially to provide a hungry and recovering world with protein. The catch per unit effort, a long-standing measure of fishing gear efficiency, began to change dramatically with new gear and new technology. In some cases, the ability of the gear to harvest fish exceeded the ability of nature to replace and sustain it. Increased demand for stocking fish strapped the ability of hatcheries to keep up, especially when ecosystem-altering dams and other structures were built on free-flowing rivers for hydropower, flood protection, and irrigation. Fishermen responded by once again being willing to pay for the conservation and management of the fishery resources. While these stresses on the system are significant, they are not the real enemy.

The only real enemy of fishery conservation is a public that is ignorant about what we do, why we do it, and what's in it for them. As we move into the future, recruiting anglers, boaters, and aquatic conservationists into the movement is critical, and we must emphasize the importance of clean water.

We are making great strides in this effort but competing with personal electronics and the quick answer on Google is a formidable challenge. We must not only address this challenge, it must be *included* in the solution. We must weave hand-held electronics into the way we message and we must make it fun. Our society, and especially our youth, are ready and willing to become the next Arden Trandahl but we have to realize that their world is one of instant communication, and thought deflection is just a text away. Significant progress is being made in the joint efforts of conservationists through the R3 movement to recruit, retain, and reactivate anglers and hunters—an organized endeavor to bring future conservationists in the fold.

Water has increased in its role as a highly significant issue around the world. Coupling clean, drinkable water to fishing is not new. The Clean Water Act of 1972 had as its goal to have "fishable, swimmable waters" by 1983. By taking the powerful history we have inherited and moving it to the future through our talented and energetic young people, we will achieve the most important goal of all: reinstituting fishing and our aquatic resources as an *American value*, along with family, faith, and country.

I know there are today young people turning over rocks, floating the river, setting trotlines, and feeling the fight of a three-pound largemouth bass caught on a hellgrammite. The future is in very capable hands. We must do our part and see that they have the support they need to assume their rightful place.

I don't live my life with hopes, I live with beliefs. When we hope something will happen, we expect someone else to do it. But when we believe something will happen, we accept personal responsibility to ensure success. I am grateful for all those who came before us, and what they did to build our fisheries tradition. I *believe* our younger generations will carry it forward into a bright future.

—H. Dale Hall

Editor's Note

I offer to you that no great dichotomy exists between art and science. Both emanate in the same place—the wellspring of a creative mind. Beauty is the blossom of inner goodness, posited the ancient Greek philosophers, and I agree. Beauty rouses love, and my colleagues express their deep affections for fishes and the aquatic world between the lines in their stories, if not written directly upon them. I am grateful to have worked with each contributor of this book. An unyielding concern for the conservation of nature's perfect creatures binds us all.

The genesis of this book came about twenty years ago when my colleague Stewart Jacks and I first bandied about where we might be in the year of the sesquicentennial and how we might commemorate 150 years of art and science applied to fisheries conservation. You hold that outcome in your hands, thanks in no small part to Stewart for shepherding the project among his peers Allan Brown, Dan Castleberry, Mary Colligan, Roy Elicker, Greg Gerlich, Judy Gordon, Dave Miko, John Schmerfeld, Todd Turner, Sherry White, Nathan Wilke, and Aaron Woldt.

America's Bountiful Waters has the bylines and photo credits of forty-eight people, all but five of them current or former U.S. Fish and Wildlife Service professionals. Other agency colleagues who don't have a byline proved indispensable in seeing the manuscript from tip-off to the buzzer: Joshua Anderson, Miguel Cordova, John Fisher, Pamela Hicks, Corey Hitt, Alexi McPherren, Robert Pos, John Seals, Jamie Stoner, Denise Wagner, and Andy White.

I am especially grateful for my immediate supervisor, Mary Elder, for her willingness to allow me to edit this book, and her coaching along the way.

Some things cannot by measured and put in a box, but you know the matter has intrinsic value when you see it or experience it. Such has been the collegiality between Carlos R. Martinez and me. We both have an enduring interest in conservation and in history. I write about both. He lives both as the director of the D.C. Booth Historic National Fish Hatchery, home to the National Fish and Aquatic Conservation Archives, in Spearfish, South Dakota. This book is our second such collaboration born of our common interests and a great amount of the material in the preceding pages came from the archives.

Carlos and his staff treated me like kin. April Gregory, the archives' curator, steered me to the files needed for this book and contributed not only her writing, but offered critical assessment of the book prospectus. The comprehensive list of field stations past and present that we present is much of her doing. April and Susanne Nuemiller scanned scads of archival images. Spearfish residents Kyle and Heather Doerges welcomed me into their home while I worked in the archives. Thanks, also, to Karen Holzer and the Booth Society for their interest in this book.

My colleagues Brett Billings, Katrina Liebich, Mark Madison, Tait Ronningen, and Tim Smigielski leave an imprint well beyond their bylines and photo credits, and I am most appreciative.

The following people and institutions helped me gather material for this book: Tara Bell, Alexis Fintel, John Thompson, and Michelle Bouchard, U.S. Geological Survey; Ava Freeman, American Fly Fishing Museum; Bob Lyngos, Alpena County George N. Fletcher Public Library; Walter Bennick, Winona County Historical Society; Jay Thompson, Shasta Historical Society; Doug Austen and Aaron Lerner, American Fisheries Society and members of its Fisheries History Section; Benjamin Harrison Presidential Site; Herbert Hoover Presidential Library and Museum; Montana State University Library; Clackamas County Historical Society; North Carolina State Archives; Ed Jones, Alaska Department of Fish and Game; Put-in-Bay, Police Department, Ohio; W. H. "Chip" Gross; Michelle Fecht; Stanford University Archives; and all the people who make the Library of Congress website work so well.

I thank Stackpole's publisher and editor Judith Schnell and her editorial assistant, Stephanie Otto, for the guidance along the way. Judith and I spent a great deal of time communicating the old-fashioned way, via telephone, and the book is the better for it.

My wife, Felicia, and our children, Carson, Willow, and Ava witnessed this book come together during The Great Hunkering of 2020. I hope they hold fond memories of this endeavor and happily recall our weekend forays to outwit Rio Grande cutthroat trout on dry flies in the high country. Kids, your dad never felt more alive.

I am grateful for my late father, Ernie, a blue-collar man, for taking me fishing and instilling in me that I should earn my money. I appreciate my late mother, Delores, a rebellious soul, for home-schooling me when its lawfulness was murky. It was an act of love— and desperation, to be truthful. She impressed upon me the value of intellectual pursuits, and I inherited her sense of history. They both encouraged me to pursue a career in fisheries conservation.

Abraham Lincoln wrote these words on the matter of patents: "Writing, the art of communicating thoughts to the mind through the eye, is the great invention of the world—enabling us to converse with the dead, the absent, and the unborn at all distances of time and space."

America's Bountiful Waters transcends the living and the dead and speaks to conservation opportunities that await the unborn. Beauty opens the soul's attention to the loveworthy. What is good is intrinsically most worthy of love—and so it is with nature's perfect creatures.

—Craig Springer

A Rio Grande cutthroat trout fell for a dry fly in New Mexico's Sangre de Cristo Mountains. Rio Grande cutthroats were the first trout documented in the New World in 1541.
CRAIG SPRINGER, USFWS

Map of Fisheries Field Stations 1871–2021

The February 1, 1921, issue of the Fisheries Services Bulletin, published by the U.S. Bureau of Fisheries, noted that in eight days it would celebrate its semicentennial, having its start as the U.S. Fish Commission in 1871. The article reflected on the first functions of the agency. Early fisheries work was chiefly investigatory. The bureau's fisheries professionals immersed themselves in scientific research as an essential aid to fish culture, producing fish for food and for sport. Congress added new functions, and growth of the bureau was rapid. By 1921, practical fisheries assistance was by large measure a bureau function.

Fish culture and fishery management assistance remained in the newly formed U.S. Fish and Wildlife Service in 1940 and does so today in its Fish and Aquatic Conservation Program.

In the list that follows, we attempt to record every fisheries field station that has existed in some lasting permanence in the span of 150 years. A lack of standard names as well as name changes for the same station over time confound the endeavor. The earliest fisheries field stations were called in the vernacular U.S. Fishery, U.S. Hatchery, or simply Station preceded by a location. Congressional records circa 1910 began to refer to hatcheries as Fish-Cultural Stations. That practice lasted into the 1950s, when the present term, National Fish Hatchery, became the common parlance. The practical assistance stations have gone by variations of Fisheries Assistance, Fishery Management Services, and Fishery Resources Offices, dating from the early 1950s. They are today the Fish and Wildlife Conservation Offices.

To compile this list, we relied on reports, bulletins, letters, logs, and memoranda in the National Fish and Aquatic Conservation Archives as well as congressional records and resources in the National Archives and the Library of Congress. We purposely excluded most egg-collecting stations and cooperative ponds by virtue of their temporary or seasonal nature, though they have existed in great number through the years.

On the map that follows, the National Fish Hatcheries symbols represent cultural-stations, fish hatcheries, fish technology centers, fish health centers, genetics labs, diet and nutrition centers, and Washington, DC sites.

Fishery Management Assistance symbols represent fisheries assistance offices, cooperative research units, fishery management services, fishery services field stations, fishery resources offices, fish and wildlife conservation offices, and research vessels.

Where multiple stations occur in one place, a single icon appears on the map. Unintentional omissions and mistakes may exist.

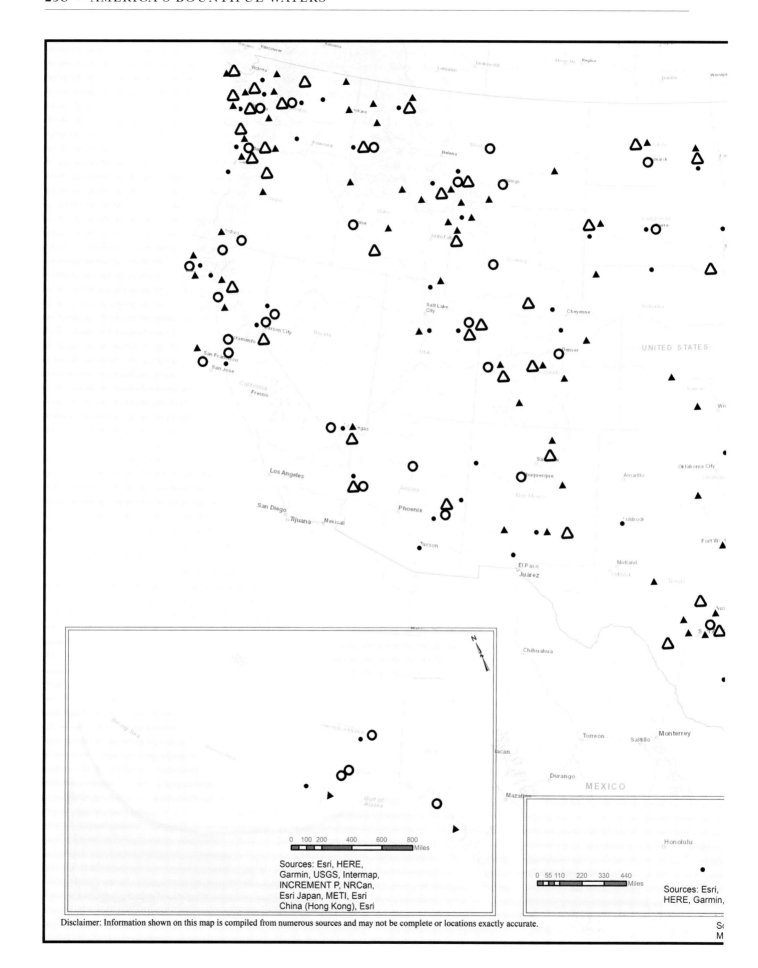

Sources: Esri, HERE,
Garmin, USGS, Intermap,
INCREMENT P, NRCan,
Esri Japan, METI, Esri
China (Hong Kong), Esri

0   100 200   400   600   800
Miles

Sources: Esri,
HERE, Garmin,

0   55 110   220   330   440
Miles

Disclaimer: Information shown on this map is compiled from numerous sources and may not be complete or locations exactly accurate.

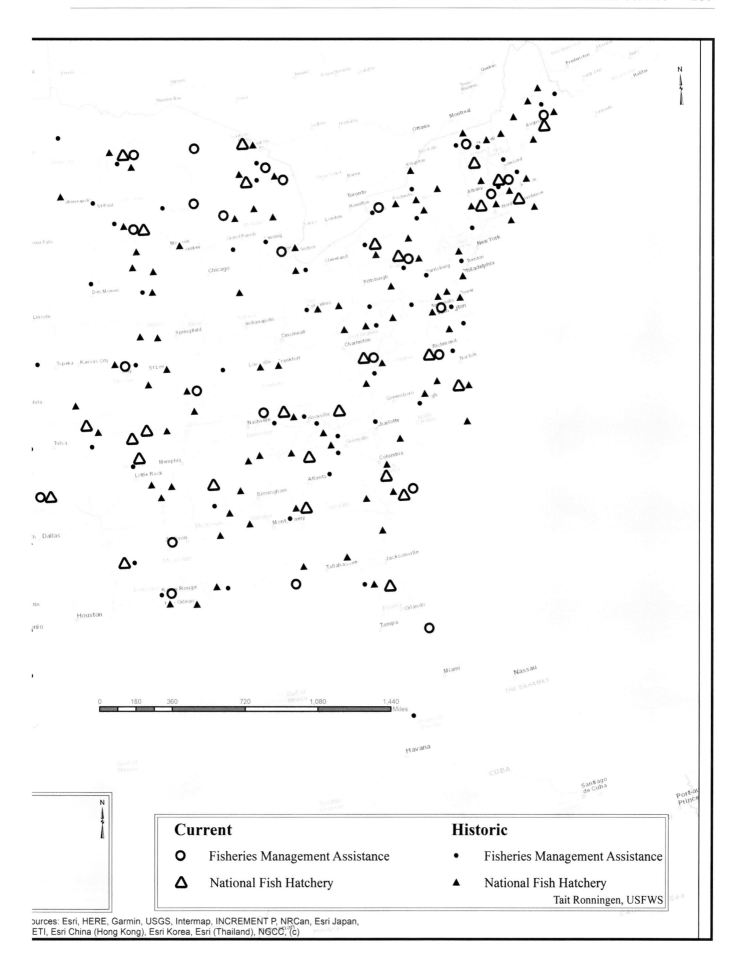

Current

○   Fisheries Management Assistance

△   National Fish Hatchery

Historic

•   Fisheries Management Assistance

▲   National Fish Hatchery

Tait Ronningen, USFWS

Sources: Esri, HERE, Garmin, USGS, Intermap, INCREMENT P, NRCan, Esri Japan,
METI, Esri China (Hong Kong), Esri Korea, Esri (Thailand), NGCC, (c)

List of Current and Former USFWS Fisheries Facilities

Compiled by April Gregory
*Indicates former USFWS facility

Alabama
*Alabama Cooperative Fish and Wildlife Research Unit, Auburn
*Aliceville Fish-Cultural Station, Aliceville
*Carbon Hill National Fish Hatchery, Carbon Hill
*Elk River Fish-Cultural Station, Elkmont
*Marion National Fish Hatchery, Marion
*Southeastern Fish Culture Laboratory, Marion

Alaska
*Afognak Fish-Cultural Station, Afognak
*Afognak Forest and Fish Culture Reserve, Afognak
*Alaska Cooperative Fish and Wildlife Research Unit, Fairbanks
Anchorage Fish and Wildlife Conservation Office, Anchorage
Conservation Genetics Laboratory, Anchorage
Fairbanks Fish and Wildlife Conservation Office, Fairbanks
*Juneau Fish and Wildlife Conservation Office, Juneau
Kenai Fish and Wildlife Conservation Office, Soldotna
*King Salmon Fish and Wildlife Conservation Office, King Salmon
*Yes Bay Fish-Cultural Station, McDonald Lake

Arizona
Achii Hanyo Native Fish Rearing Facility, Parker
Alchesay National Fish Hatchery, Whiteriver
*Arizona Cooperative Fish and Wildlife Research Unit, Tucson
Arizona Fish and Wildlife Conservation Office, Flagstaff, Parker, Whiteriver
*Arizona Fishery Resources Office, San Carlos
*Fisheries Assistance Office, Parker
*Fishery Management Services, Springerville
Williams Creek National Fish Hatchery, McNary
Willow Beach National Fish Hatchery, Willow Beach

Arkansas
*Arkansas Cooperative Fish and Wildlife Research Unit, Fayetteville
*Benzal Fish-Cultural Station, Benzal
*Corning National Fish Hatchery, Corning
*Fish Farming Experimental Laboratory, Stuttgart
*Fishery Assistance Office, Heber Springs

Greers Ferry National Fish Hatchery, Heber Springs
Mammoth Spring National Fish Hatchery, Mammoth Spring
Norfork National Fish Hatchery, Mountain Home

California
Arcata Fish and Wildlife Office, Arcata
*Baird Fish-Cultural Station, Shasta Lake
*Battle Creek Fish-Cultural Station, Battle Creek
Bay-Delta Fish and Wildlife Office, Sacramento
*California Cooperative Fishery Research Unit, Arcata
California-Nevada Fish Health Center, Anderson
Coleman National Fish Hatchery, Anderson
*Crooks Creek Fish-Cultural Station, Shasta County
*Fisheries Assistance Office, Stockton
*Fort Gaston Fish-Cultural Station, Humboldt County
Klamath Fish and Wildlife Office, Yreka
*Korbel Fish-Cultural Station, Korbel
Livingston Stone National Fish Hatchery, Shasta Lake
Lodi Fish and Wildlife Office, Stockton
*Mill Creek Fish-Cultural Station, Los Molinos
*Olema Experimental Station, Olema
Red Bluff Fish and Wildlife Office, Red Bluff
*Redwood Creek Egg Collecting Station, Humboldt County
San Francisco Bay-Delta Fish and Wildlife Office, San Francisco
*Tehama-Colusa Spawning Channels, Red Bluff
*Trinity River Fish Management Office, Weaverville
Yreka Fish and Wildlife Office, Yreka

Colorado
*Colorado Cooperative Fish and Wildlife Research Unit, Ft. Collins
Colorado Fish and Wildlife Conservation Office, Lakewood
*Colorado Springs Rearing Ponds, Colorado Springs
*Creede Fish-Cultural Station, Creede
*Crystal Lake Fish-Cultural Station, Crystal Lake
*Fish Research Office of Information Transfer, Fort Collins
*Fishery Services Field Station, Ft. Collins
*Fort Morgan Fish Health, Fort Morgan
*Grand Mesa Fishery Station, Grand Mesa
Hotchkiss National Fish Hatchery, Hotchkiss
Leadville National Fish Hatchery, Leadville
*National Ecology Research Center, Fort Collins

Connecticut
*Noank Fishery Station, Noank

Delaware
*Dover Cooperative Ponds, Dover

Florida
*Florida Cooperative Fish and Wildlife Research Unit, Gainesville
*Gainesville National Fishery Research Laboratory, Gainesville
*Key West Biological Laboratory, Key West
*Marianna Pondfish Fish Hatchery, Marianna
Panama City Fish and Wildlife Conservation Office, Panama City
Peninsular Fish and Wildlife Conservation Office, Vero Beach
Welaka National Fish Hatchery, Welaka

Georgia
Chattahoochee Forest National Fish Hatchery, Suches
*Cold Spring Fish-Cultural Station, Townsend
*Cohutta National Fish Hatchery, Cohutta
*Fishery Services Field Station, Athens
*Georgia Cooperative Fish and Wildlife Research Unit, Athens
*Harris Ponds, Townsend
*Lake Park Fish-Cultural Station, Valdosta
*Millen (BoGinn) National Fish Hatchery, Millen
*Southeastern Fish Control Laboratory, Warm Springs
Warm Springs Fish Health Center, Warm Springs
Warm Springs Fish Technology Center, Warm Springs
Warm Springs National Fish Hatchery, Warm Springs

Hawaii
*Hawaii Cooperative Fishery Research Unit, Hilo

Idaho
*Ashton Fish-Cultural Station, Ashton
*Clark Fork Fish-Cultural Station, Clark Fork
Dworshak National Fish Hatchery, Orofino
*Fisheries Assistance Office, Ahsahka
Hagerman National Fish Hatchery, Hagerman
*Idaho Cooperative Fish and Wildlife Research Unit, Moscow
Idaho Fish and Wildlife Conservation Office, Orofino
Idaho Fish Health Center, Orofino
Kooskia National Fish Hatchery, Kooskia
Lower Snake River Compensation Plan, Boise
*Mullan Fish-Cultural Station, Mullan
*Paris Whitefish Hatching Station, Paris
*Salmon Fish-Cultural Station, Salmon
*Sun Valley Fish-Cultural Station, Sun Valley
*Warm River Fish-Cultural Station, Gerrit

Illinois
*Cairo Fish-Cultural Station, Cairo
Carterville-Marion Fish and Wildlife Conservation Office, Marion
*Carterville National Fish Hatchery, Marion
Large Rivers Coordination Office, Marion
*Meredosia Fish Rescue Station, Meredosia
*Quincy Fish-Cultural Station, Quincy
*Rock Island Fish-Cultural Station, Rock Island

Upper Mississippi River Wildlife and Fish Refuge, Thomson

Indiana
*Argos National Fish Hatchery, Argos
*Central States Fishery Station, Princeton
*Rochester National Fish Hatchery, Rochester

Iowa
*Bellevue Fish-Cultural Station, Bellevue
*Fairport Fish-Cultural Station, Fairport
*Fishery Services Field Station, Davenport
*Guttenberg National Fish Hatchery, Guttenberg
*Iowa Cooperative Fish and Wildlife Research Unit, Ames
*Manchester National Fish Hatchery, Manchester
*Marquette Fish-Cultural Station, Marquette
*North McGregor Fish-Cultural Station, North McGregor

Kansas
*Cedar Bluff National Fish Hatchery, Ellis
*Farlington National Fish Hatchery, Farlington
*Kansas Cooperative Fish and Wildlife Research Unit, Manhattan
*Langdon Fish-Cultural Station, Langdon

Kentucky
*Frankfort Fish-Cultural Station, Frankfort
*Louisville Fish-Cultural Station, Louisville
Wolf Creek National Fish Hatchery, Jamestown

Louisiana
*Atchafalaya Fish-Cultural Station, Plaquemine
Baton Rouge Fish and Wildlife Conservation Office, Baton Rouge
*Fisheries Assistance Office, Natchitoches
*Louisiana Cooperative Fish and Wildlife Research Unit, Baton Rouge
*Marquette Fish-Cultural Station, New Orleans
Natchitoches National Fish Hatchery, Natchitoches

Maine
*Boothbay Harbor Fish-Cultural Station, Boothbay
*Bucksport Fish-Cultural Station, Bucksport
Craig Brook National Fish Hatchery, Craig Brook
*East Orland Station, East Orland
*Grand Lake Salmon Station, Schoodic
*Green Lake Fish-Cultural Station, Dedham
Green Lake National Fish Hatchery, Ellsworth
*Maine Cooperative Fish and Wildlife Research Unit, Orono
Maine Fish and Wildlife Conservation Office, East Orland
*Penobscot Station, East Orland
*Salem Feeding Station, Salem
*Sebec Lake Fish-Cultural Station, Sebec Lake
*Upper Penobscot Fishery Station, Brook Medway

Maryland
*Battery Island Fish-Cultural Station, Battery Island
*Bryans Point Fish-Cultural Station, Bryan
*Chesapeake Bay Fishery Coordinator, Annapolis
*Fort Washington Fish-Cultural Station, Fort Washington
*Havre de Grace Fish-Cultural Station, Havre de Grace
*Lakeland Ponds Fish-Cultural Station, College Park

*Maryland Cooperative Fish and Wildlife Research Unit, Prince Anne
Maryland Fish and Wildlife Conservation Office, Annapolis
* Spesutie Narrows Fish-Cultural Station, Spesutie Narrows
*St. Jerome Oyster Ponds, St Inigoes

Massachusetts
Berkshire National Fish Hatchery, New Marlborough
*Berlin National Fish Hatchery, Berlin
Connecticut River Fish and Wildlife Conservation Office, Sunderland
*Fisheries Assistance Office, Hadley
*Fishery Services Field Station, Amherst
*Gloucester Fish-Cultural Station, Gloucester
*Hartsville Fish-Cultural Station, Hartsville
*Massachusetts Cooperative Fish and Wildlife Research Unit, Amherst
North Attleboro National Fish Hatchery, North Attleboro
Northeast Anadromous Fish Research Laboratory, Turners Falls
Richard Cronin Aquatic Resource Center, Sunderland
*South Hadley Falls Fish-Cultural Station, South Hadley
Sunderland National Salmon Station, Sunderland
*Woods Hole Research Laboratory, Woods Hole

Michigan
*Alpena Fish-Cultural Station, Alpena
Alpena Fish and Wildlife Conservation Office, Alpena
*Bay City Fish-Cultural Station, Bay City
*Charlevoix National Fish Hatchery, Charlevoix
*Clare County Nursery Ponds, Harrison
*Detroit Fish-Cultural Station, Detroit
*Fisheries Assistance Office, Elmira
*Great Lakes Fishery Laboratory, Ann Arbor
*Hammond Bay Biological Station, Millerburg
*Huron National Forest Hatchery, Lilley Township
Jordan River National Fish Hatchery, Elmira
Ludington Biological Station, Ludington
M/V Spencer F. Baird, Alpena
Marquette Biological Station, Marquette
*Marquette National Forest Fish-Cultural Station, Raco
*Northville National Fish Hatchery, Northville
Pendills Creek National Fish Hatchery, Brimley
*Research Vessel Cisco, Saugatuck
*Research Vessel Grayling, Cheboygan
Research Vessel Stanford H. Smith, Rogers City
Sullivan Creek National Fish Hatchery, Brimley

Minnesota
*Cascade Rearing Ponds, Duluth
*Duluth Fish-Cultural Station, Duluth
*Fisheries Assistance Office, Bemidji
*Fisheries Assistance Office, Winona
*Homer National Fish Hatchery, Homer
*New London National Fish Hatchery, New London
*Minnesota Cooperative Fish and Wildlife Research Unit, St. Paul

Mississippi
*Friars Point Fish Rescue Station, Friars Point
*Gulf Coast Fisheries Resource Office, Ocean Springs

Lower Mississippi River Fish and Wildlife Conservation Office, Vicksburg
*Lyman National Fish Hatchery, Lyman
*Meridian National Fish Hatchery, Meridian
*Mississippi Cooperative Fish and Wildlife Research Unit, Starkville
Private John Allen National Fish Hatchery, Tupelo

Missouri
*Bourbon Fish-Cultural Station, Bourbon
Columbia Fish and Wildlife Conservation Office, Columbia
*Columbia National Fisheries Laboratory, Columbia
*Forest Park Fish-Cultural Station, Forest Park
*Missouri Cooperative Fish and Wildlife Research Unit, Columbia
Neosho National Fish Hatchery, Neosho
*Roaring River Fish-Cultural Station, Roaring River

Montana
Aquatic Animal Drug Approval Partnership, Bozeman
*Blaine Springs Fish-Cultural Station, Blaine Springs
Bozeman Fish Health Center, Bozeman
Bozeman Fish Technology Center, Bozeman
Bozeman National Fish Hatchery, Bozeman
*Creston Fishery Center, Kalispell
Creston National Fish Hatchery, Kalispell
*Elk Lake Egg Collecting Station, Red Rock
Ennis National Fish Hatchery, Ennis
*Glacier Park Fish-Cultural Station, Glacier
*Madison Point Station, Twin Bridges
*Montana Cooperative Fishery Research Unit, Bozeman
*Meadow Creek Fish-Cultural Station, Ennis
*Miles City National Fish Hatchery, Miles City
Montana Fish and Wildlife Conservation Office, Billings, Bozeman
*Mystic Lake Fish-Cultural Station, Red Lodge

Nebraska
*Crawford National Fish Hatchery, Crawford
*Valentine Fish and Wildlife Management Assistance Office, Valentine

Nevada
*Fishery Services Field Station, Las Vegas
Lahontan Fish and Wildlife Conservation Office, Reno
Lahontan National Fish Hatchery, Gardnerville
*Las Vegas Fish-Cultural Station, Las Vegas
Marble Bluff Fish Passage Facility, Marble Bluff
*Pyramid Lake Project, Reno
Southern Nevada Fish and Wildlife Conservation Office, Las Vegas
*Truckee River Fish Management Office, Truckee

New Hampshire
*Berlin National Fish Hatchery, Berlin
Central New England Fish and Wildlife Conservation Office, Nashua
*Laconia Fishery Resources Office, Laconia
*Merrimack River Fish Management Office, Nashua
Nashua National Fish Hatchery, Nashua

New Jersey
*Delaware River Coordinator, West Trenton
*Fishery Services Field Station, Rosemont
*Fishery Services Field Station, Trenton
*Gloucester City Fish-Cultural Station, Gloucester City
*Gloucester City Fishery Assistance Office, Gloucester City
*Lambertville Fish-Cultural Station, Lambertville
*Pequest National Fish Hatchery, Oxford

New Mexico
*Eagle Nest Fish-Cultural Station, Eagle Nest
*Fisheries Assistance Office, Gallup
*Fishery Services Field Station, Mescalero
*Hot Springs National Fish Hatchery, Elephant Butte
*Mescalero National Fish Hatchery, Mescalero
Mora National Fish Hatchery, Mora
*New Mexico Cooperative Fish and Wildlife Research Unit, Las Cruces
New Mexico Fish and Wildlife Conservation Office, Albuquerque
*Santa Rosa National Fish Hatchery, Santa Rosa
Southwestern Fish Health Unit, Dexter
Southwestern Native Aquatic Resources and Recovery Center, Dexter

New York
*Barneveld Fish-Cultural Station, Trenton
*Cape Vincent National Fish Hatchery, Cape Vincent
*Carpenters Brook National Fish Hatchery, Elbridge
*Cortland National Fish Hatchery, Cortland
*Fishery Services Field Station, New Windsor
*Lower Great Lakes Fishery Resources Office, Amherst
Lower Great Lakes Fish and Wildlife Conservation Office, Basom
*Oswego Biological Station, Oswego
*New York Cooperative Fish and Wildlife Research Unit, Ithaca
*Powder Mill Park Cooperative Fish Hatchery, Pittsford
*Research Vessel Kaho, Oswego
*Tunison Laboratory of Aquatic Science, Cortland
*Watertown Fish-Cultural Station, Watertown

North Carolina
*Avoca Fish-Cultural Station, Avoca
*Beaufort Fish Laboratory, Beaufort
*Davidson River Station, Raleigh
*Edenton Fish-Cultural Station, Edenton
Edenton National Fish Hatchery, Edenton
*Fisheries Assistance Office, Cherokee
*Fishery Management Services, Pisgah Forest
*Franklin County Hatchery, Franklin County
*McKinney Lake National Fish Hatchery, Hoffman
*North Carolina Cooperative Fish and Wildlife Research Unit, Raleigh
*Pisgah Forest National Fish Hatchery, Asheville
*Smokemont Fish-Cultural Station, Cherokee
*South Atlantic Fisheries Coordination Office, Raleigh
*Weldon Fish-Cultural Station, Weldon

North Dakota
*Audubon National Fish Hatchery, Coleharbor
*Baldhill Dam National Fish Hatchery, Valley City
Garrison Dam National Fish Hatchery, Riverdale
Missouri River Fish and Wildlife Conservation Office, Bismarck
*Fisheries Assistance Office, Valley City
Valley City National Fish Hatchery, Valley City

Ohio
*Hebron National Fish Hatchery, Hebron
*Ohio Cooperative Fish and Wildlife Research Unit, Columbus
*Put-In-Bay Fish-Cultural Station, Put-In-Bay
*Research Vessel Musky II, Sandusky
*Sandusky Fish-Cultural Station, Sandusky
*Senecaville National Fish Hatchery, Senecaville

Oklahoma
*Lawton Fish-Cultural Station, Lawton
*Oklahoma Cooperative Fish and Wildlife Research Unit, Stillwater
Oklahoma Fish and Wildlife Conservation Office, Tishomingo
Tishomingo National Fish Hatchery, Tishomingo
*Wichita Mountain Falls Rearing Ponds, Indiehoma

Oregon
*Applegate Fish-Cultural Station, Applegate
*Butte Falls National Fish Hatchery, Butte Falls
*Cazadero Fish-Cultural Station, Cazadero
*Clackamas Fish-Cultural Station, Estacada
*Delph Creek Fish-Cultural Station, Estacada
*Deschutes Fish-Cultural Station, Deschutes
Eagle Creek National Fish Hatchery, Estacada
*Grants Pass Hatching Station, Grants Pass
Klamath Falls Fish and Wildlife Conservation Office, Klamath Falls
*Oregon Cooperative Fishery Research Unit, Corvallis
*Rogue River Fish-Cultural Station, Central Point
*Salmon River Fish-Cultural Station, Salmon River
*Sandy River Fish-Cultural Station, Sandy
*Snake River Fish-Cultural Station, Snake River
*St. Helens Fish-Cultural Station, St. Helens
*Upper Clackamas Fish-Cultural Station, Eagle Creek
Warm Springs National Fish Hatchery, Warm Springs
*Willamette Falls Fish-Cultural Station, Oregon City

Pennsylvania
Allegheny Forest National Fish Hatchery, Clarendon
*Fisheries Assistance Office, Warren
*Fishery Services Field Station, Lamar
Lamar Fish Health Center, Lamar
Lamar Fish Technology Center, Lamar
Lamar National Fish Hatchery, Lamar
Mid-Atlantic Fishery Resources Office, Lamar
*National Fishery Research and Development Center, Wellsboro
*Ogletown Fish-Cultural Station, Ogletown
*Pennsylvania Cooperative Fish and Wildlife Research Unit, University Park

*Philadelphia Fisheries Research Station, Philadelphia
*Sheffield Fish-Cultural Station, Sheffield
*Susquehanna River Coordinator, Harrisburg
*Tylersville National Fish Hatchery, Loganton

Rhode Island
*Arcadia National Fish Hatchery, Arcadia

South Carolina
Bears Bluff National Fish Hatchery, Wadmalaw Island
*Cheraw National Fish Hatchery, Cheraw
*Jacksonboro Fish-Cultural Station, Jacksonboro
*Orangeburg County Fish Hatchery, Orangeburg
Orangeburg National Fish Hatchery, Orangeburg
*South Carolina Cooperative Fish and Wildlife Research
    Unit, Clemson
*St. Matthews Fish-Cultural Station, St. Matthews
Wadmalaw Island Fish and Wildlife Conservation Office,
    Wadmalaw Island
*Walhalla National Fish Hatchery, Mountain Rest

South Dakota
D.C. Booth Historic National Fish Hatchery & National Fish
    and Aquatic Conservation Archives, Spearfish
*Fishery Management Services, Spearfish
Gavins Point National Fish Hatchery, Yankton
Great Plains Fish and Wildlife Conservation Office, Pierre
*McNenny National Fish Hatchery, Spearfish
*Oahe Fishery Research Laboratory, Pierre
*South Dakota Cooperative Fish and Wildlife Research
    Unit, Brookings

Tennessee
Appalachian Fish and Wildlife Conservation Office, Celina
Dale Hollow National Fish Hatchery, Celina
Erwin National Fish Hatchery, Erwin
*Fishery Services Field Station, Gatlinburg
*Fishery Services Field Station, Maryville
*Fishery Services Field Station, Norris
*Flintville Fish-Cultural Station, Flintville
*Norris Fish-Cultural Station, Norris
*Tennessee Cooperative Fishery Research Unit, Cookeville

Texas
*Austin National Fish Hatchery, Austin
*Corpus Christi Fish Management Office, Corpus Christi
*Fort Worth National Fish Hatchery, Fort Worth
Inks Dam National Fish Hatchery, Marble Falls
*Kerrville Fish-Cultural Station, Kerrville
*Medina Lake Fish-Cultural Station, Medina Lake
*New Braunfels Ponds, New Braunfels
*San Angelo Fish-Cultural Station, San Angelo
San Marcos Aquatic Resources Center, San Marcos
*San Marcos Fish-Cultural Station, San Marcos
*Texas Cooperative Fish and Wildlife Research
    Unit, Lubbock
Texas Fish and Wildlife Conservation Office, San Marcos
Uvalde National Fish Hatchery, Uvalde

Utah
*Bear Lake Fish-Cultural Station, Bear Lake
*Fishery Management Services, Springville
Green River Basin Fish and Wildlife Conservation
    Office, Vernal
Jones Hole National Fish Hatchery, Vernal
Ouray National Fish Hatchery, Ouray
*Roosevelt Fish and Wildlife Assistance Office, Roosevelt
*Springville National Fish Hatchery, Springville
*Utah Cooperative Fish and Wildlife Research Unit, Logan
Utah Fish and Wildlife Conservation Office, Vernal

Vermont
Dwight D. Eisenhower National Fish Hatchery, North
    Chittenden
*Fisheries Assistance Office, Montpelier
*Holden Fish-Cultural Station, Holden
Lake Champlain Fish and Wildlife Conservation Office,
    Essex Junction
*Scranton Fish-Cultural Station, Scranton
*St. Johnsbury National Fish Hatchery, St. Johnsbury
*Swanton Fish-Cultural Station, Swanton
*Vermont Cooperative Fish and Wildlife Research Unit,
    Burlington
White River National Fish Hatchery, Bethel

Virginia
*Fisheries Assistance Office, Gloucester Point
*Fishery Services Field Station, Yorktown
*Fort Belvoir (Fort Humphreys) Hatchery, Fort Belvoir
*Gloucester Fishery Resources Office, White Marsh
Harrison Lake National Fish Hatchery, Charles City
*New Castle National Fish Hatchery, New Castle
*Paint Bank National Fish Hatchery, Paint Bank
*Virginia Cooperative Fish and Wildlife Research Unit,
    Blacksburg
Virginia Fish and Wildlife Conservation Office, Charles City
*Wytheville Fish-Cultural Station, Wytheville
*Wytheville National Fish Hatchery, Max Meadows

Washington
Abernathy Fish Technology Center, Longview
*Baker Lake Fish-Cultural Station, Baker Lake
*Big White Salmon Ponds, Spring Creek
*Birdsview Fish-Cultural Station, Birdsview
*Brinnon Fish-Cultural Station, Brinnon
Carson National Fish Hatchery, Carson
Columbia River Fish and Wildlife Conservation
    Office, Vancouver
Columbia River Gorge National Fish Hatchery
    Complex, Cook
*Darrington Fish-Cultural Station, Darrington
*Day Creek Fish-Cultural Station, Day Creek
*Duckabush Fish-Cultural Station, Duckabush
Entiat National Fish Hatchery, Entiat
*Fisheries Assistance Office, Coulee
*Fisheries Assistance Office, Leavenworth
*Fisheries Assistance Office, Olympia
*Fisheries Assistance Office, Vancouver
*Fishery Services Field Station, Tumwater
*Illabot Creek Egg Collection Station, Corkindale

Leavenworth National Fish Hatchery, Leavenworth
Little White Salmon National Fish Hatchery, Cook
Lower Columbia River Fish Health Center, Cook
Makah National Fish Hatchery, Clallam Bay
*Marrowstone Field Station, Nordland
*Marrowstone Point Fishery Research Station, Nordland
Mid-Columbia River Fish and Wildlife Conservation Office, Leavenworth
Mid-Columbia River Fish Management, Leavenworth
*Mount Rainier Fish-Cultural Station, Mt. Rainer
Olympia Fish Health Center, Olympia
*Ozette Fish-Cultural Station, Ozette Lake
*Phalon Fish-Cultural Station, Phalon
*Phinney Creek Egg Collection Station, Phinney Creek
Quilcene National Fish Hatchery, Quilcene
Quinault National Fish Hatchery, Humptulips
*Seattle National Fishery Research Center, Seattle
*Spokane Fish-Cultural Station, Spokane
Spring Creek National Fish Hatchery, Underwood
*Sultan Fish-Cultural Station, Sultan
*Washington Cooperative Fish and Wildlife Research Unit, Seattle
*Washougal River Fish-Cultural Station, Washougal River
Western Washington Fish and Wildlife Conservation Office, Lacey
Willard National Fish Hatchery, Cook
*Wind River Fish-Cultural Station, Wind River
Winthrop National Fish Hatchery, Winthrop
*Yakima Fish Screens, Yakima Valley

Washington D.C.
*Arsenal Carp Ponds
*Central Station-National Aquarium
*Washington Monument Ponds
*Potomac Station
*Washington Navy Yard

West Virginia
Appalachian Partnership Coordination Office, White Sulphur Springs
*Bowden National Fish Hatchery, Elkins
*Fishery Services Field Station, Elkins

*Leetown National Fisheries Center, Leetown
*Moorefield Fish-Cultural Station, Moorefield
*Palestine Fish-Cultural Station, Palestine
*West Virginia Cooperative Fish and Wildlife Research Unit, Morgantown
White Sulphur Springs National Fish Hatchery, White Sulphur Springs

Wisconsin
Ashland Fish and Wildlife Conservation Office, Ashland
*Chequamegon National Forest Fish-Cultural Station, Chequamegon
*Fisheries Assistance Office, Iron River
Genoa National Fish Hatchery, Genoa
Green Bay Fish and Wildlife Conservation Office, Green Bay
Iron River National Fish Hatchery, Iron River
LaCrosse Fish Health Center, Onalaska
LaCrosse Fish and Wildlife Conservation Office, Onalaska
*LaCrosse Fish-Cultural Station, LaCrosse
*Lake Mills National Fish Hatchery, Lake Mills
*Lynxville Fish-Cultural Station, Lynxville
*Trempealeau Ponds, Trempealeau
Whitney Genetics Laboratory, Onalaska
*Wisconsin Cooperative Fish and Wildlife Research Unit, Stevens Point

Wyoming
*Black Island Station, Yellowstone
*Fisheries Assistance Office, Yellowstone
*Grebe Lake Fish-Cultural Station, Yellowstone
*Jackson Fish-Cultural Station, Jackson Hole
Jackson National Fish Hatchery, Jackson Hole
Lander Fish and Wildlife Conservation Office, Lander
*Lost Creek Fish-Cultural Station, Moose
*Ranch "A" Diet Development Center, Beulah
*Ranch "A" Fish Genetics Laboratory, Beulah
*Mammoth Hot Springs Fish-Cultural Station, Yellowstone
Saratoga National Fish Hatchery, Saratoga
*Wyoming Cooperative Fish and Wildlife Research Unit, Laramie
*Yellowstone Fish-Cultural Station, Yellowstone Lake

About the Contributors

Doug Aloisi is the supervisor of the Genoa National Fish Hatchery in Wisconsin. The thirty-six-year U.S. Fish and Wildlife Service veteran has worked at seven national fish hatcheries in six states. Originally from Massachusetts, and a graduate of the University of Massachusetts, he's had the opportunity to be a part of raising twenty-three species of fish and eighteen species of freshwater mussels, a salamander, and an endangered dragonfly. In his current position, he has the opportunity to mentor a number of future leaders of the U.S. Fish and Wildlife Service. He and his wife have five children and eight grandchildren. He hopes to retire in the great state of Wisconsin.

William Ardren, Ph.D., is a senior fish biologist at the Lake Champlain Fish and Wildlife Conservation Office in Vermont. He received the 2018 Rachel Carson Award for Exemplary Scientific Accomplishment for his work on restoration of landlocked Atlantic salmon in Lake Champlain. Before moving to Vermont, he was the regional geneticist for the Pacific Region of U.S. Fish and Wildlife Service. He has a Ph.D. in fisheries science from the University of Minnesota and conducted post-doctoral research at Oregon State University.

Bryan Arroyo, M.S., is the deputy director of the U.S. Fish and Wildlife Service, stationed in Washington, D.C. He has served as assistant director for endangered species, assistant director for fisheries and habitat conservation, and assistant director for international affairs. Bryan grew up in Puerto Rico, fishing both salt and fresh water. He instilled a love of fishing in his daughters who still fish with him. These days it is mostly his wife with whom he shares the boat. Bryan holds a B.S. in biology and M.S. in zoology.

Michael Bailey, Ph.D., is the national aquatic habitat coordinator for the U.S. Fish and Wildlife Service in Falls Church, Virginia. Much of his Atlantic salmon dissertation work at the University of Maine focused on Shorey Brook, a tributary of the Narraguagus River in Downeast Maine. Michael worked ten years at the Central New England Fish and Wildlife Conservation Office aiding in river herring and American

shad restoration. He and his wife, Jordan, have two children, Cora and Ellis.

Brett Billings, M.S., a native Kentuckian and U.S. Army veteran, received his B.A. in environmental broadcast journalism and M.S. in biology from Eastern Kentucky University. He enjoys fishing, fly-tying, and photography with his wife while educating their two sons about the natural world. He is a video producer at the U.S. Fish and Wildlife Service's National Conservation Training Center in West Virginia, where he can be found sampling fish and bugs in the Potomac River.

Ana Bode is a biological technician at Saratoga National Fish Hatchery in Wyoming. She graduated in 2015 from the University of Wyoming with a B.S. in fisheries and wildlife biology and management. Ana grew up in Deadwood, South Dakota, where her family introduced her to the outdoors. When she is not working you can find her fishing, camping, and hiking with her English setter.

Charles "Chuck" Bronte, M.S., is a senior fishery biologist at the Green Bay Fish and Wildlife Conservation Office, Wisconsin. He founded and directs a large-scale coded-wire tagging and data recovery program on the Great Lakes that assists states and tribes with managing sport, commercial, and treaty fisheries, and evaluates progress toward lake trout restoration in the Great Lakes. Chuck has published nearly one hundred scientific papers on fishes of the Great Lakes, primarily dealing with the biology and recovery of lake trout. He has served for the past twenty years on research boards of the Great Lakes Fishery Commission, and on editorial boards of the *Transactions of the American Fisheries Society*, the *North American Journal of Fisheries Management*, and *Journal for Great Lakes Research*. He began his federal career in 1988.

Doug Canfield is a video producer at the U.S. Fish and Wildlife Service's National Conservation Training Center in West Virginia. He grew up in New Jersey where he spent his weekends at the Great Swamp National Wildlife Refuge and his summers at Swartswood Lake. Photography is a family tradition started by his grandfather. Doug's interest was triggered by his father's collection of old cameras. He now enjoys filming and photographing fish of all sizes from Florida to Alaska.

Jeff Conway grew up in northwestern Pennsylvania, where he developed his appreciation of the natural world, fostered by his father. He earned a B.S. in fisheries from Mansfield University of Pennsylvania, where he met his wife of twenty-three years. Jeff has an eclectic array of interests including rebuilding Toyota FJ40s, home remodeling, building computers, reading, and spending time with his wife and miniature dachshunds. Jeff is the manager of Inks Dam National Fish Hatchery in Texas.

Robert F. Elliot, M.S., is a fish biologist at the Green Bay Fish and Wildlife Conservation Office in Wisconsin. He and his wife and son live near Sturgeon Bay on Wisconsin's rocky finger of the Niagara Escarpment that divides Green Bay from Lake Michigan. The clear Great Lakes waters enticed Rob as a child and have sustained his twenty-eight years with the U.S. Fish and Wildlife Service. He earned academic degrees at the University of Wisconsin–Eau Claire (B.S. and B.E.) and at Michigan State University (M.S.), and continues to seek enlightenment aboard aging wood vessels plying the sweet water seas from Deaths Door to the Manitou Passage.

Brian Fillmore is a twenty-year veteran fish biologist with the U.S. Fish and Wildlife Service. He supervises the Oklahoma Fish and Wildlife Conservation Office in Tishomingo, Oklahoma. His wife, Rebecca, works for the Oklahoma Department of Wildlife Conservation at the Durant State Fish Hatchery. The two met at the University of Idaho. They spend their free time mostly outdoors, fishing and kayaking with their young daughter, Vivien.

Jeff Finley is a fish biologist with the Columbia Fish and Wildlife Conservation Office in Missouri. A native of New Mexico, Jeff joined the U.S. Army to earn money for college and earned a B.S. in fisheries and wildlife from the University of Missouri. He worked with the Missouri Department of Conservation before taking his current position. Between deployments as a lieutenant colonel with the U.S. Army Reserve as an environmental science officer, Jeff enjoys working on the Missouri River and spending time with his wife of twenty-eight years and their three children and one granddaughter.

Wade Fredenberg, a fisheries biologist educated at Montana State University, considers himself fortunate to have been born and raised in the bull trout country of northwest Montana. He worked there for the U.S. Fish and Wildlife Service and now he plays there in his retirement. He considers it a great honor to have served a small role in the recovery of his totem fish, the bull trout.

Catherine Gatenby, Ph.D. began her studies of freshwater mussels at the University of Minnesota and later completed graduate studies at Virginia Tech. She developed feeding regimes, diets, and mussel propagation technology for more than twenty years, and built one of the U.S. Fish and Wildlife Service's first endangered freshwater mussel facilities at White Sulphur Spring National Fish Hatchery, in West Virginia. She is a coauthor of *Freshwater Mussel Propagation for Restoration.* Catherine works in communications for Fish and Aquatic Conservation, North Atlantic-Appalachian Region with emphasis on mussels. Most evenings you will find her dancing.

April Gregory is the curator of collections and exhibitions of the National Fish and Aquatic Conservation Archives in Spearfish, South Dakota. She oversees all aspects of the archival and museum collections, interpretive and educational displays, and design and outreach materials, and plays an important role in managing the care of the cultural resources on the historic site. April also serves on the U.S. Fish and Wildlife Service's Heritage Committee. She has been at the D.C. Booth Historic National Fish Hatchery since 2009, initially as an archives intern and serving as the Booth Society's executive director from 2011 to 2017. A Montana native, she earned degrees in photojournalism and art history from the University of Montana.

Ryan Hagerty was raised in the Appalachian Mountains of West Virginia and is an avid hiker, fisherman, and river explorer. He earned a B.F.A. in photography from Shepherd University. He is a photographer and video producer at the U.S. Fish and Wildlife Service's National Conservation Training Center, where he specializes in underwater photography and leads the Northeast Fish and Wildlife Service scuba team.

H. Dale Hall spent four years in the U.S. Air Force and more than thirty years with the U.S. Fish and Wildlife Service. His last three-plus years were as the director under President George W. Bush. He then spent nine years as the chief executive officer of Ducks Unlimited before retiring in June 2019.

Chris Hathcock received a B.S. in fisheries and wildlife from the University of Missouri and M.S. in biology from the University of Texas–Pan American. He has worked to conserve plants and ecosystems in southern and central Texas for the last seventeen years. He is currently the lead botanist at the U.S. Fish and Wildlife Service's San Marcos Aquatic Resources Center, San Marcos, Texas.

Kay Hively has volunteered for the U.S. Fish and Wildlife Service for almost forty years. She was co-founder of the Friends of the Neosho National Fish Hatchery and is a former newspaper reporter in Neosho, Missouri.

Rob Holm has worked for the U.S. Fish and Wildlife Service as a fish hatchery biologist for thirty-six years. He has worked with a multitude of fish species at several hatcheries throughout the Midwest including striped bass, black basses, trout, salmon, northern pike, and walleye. He finds the leading-edge conservation work at Garrison Dam National Fish Hatchery on the imperiled pallid sturgeon particularly gratifying. He and his wife, Brenda, are the parents of four daughters and grandparents of eight high-energy grandkids who also love their visits to the hatchery.

Stephen Jackson is a graduate of the U.S. Coast Guard Academy where he majored in marine sciences and biological oceanography. He started his U.S. Fish and Wildlife Service career in 1992 and has raised twenty-five different species at four national fish hatcheries, including as manager of Pittsford and Edenton National Fish Hatcheries in Vermont and North Carolina. He is presently the deputy assistant regional director for Fish and Aquatic Conservation in Atlanta, Georgia.

John D. Juriga, M.D., is a retired physician living in Salisbury, Maryland. He is the author of *Bob Hines: National Wildlife Artist*, Beaver's Pond Press, published in 2012.

George R. Jordan, M.S., completed his undergraduate studies at Montana State University–Bozeman before accepting his first position with the U.S. Fish and Wildlife Service in South Dakota. While there, he completed his M.S. at South Dakota State University–Brookings. He now resides in his hometown of Billings, Montana, where he is the supervisor of the Montana Fish and Wildlife Conservation Office. This station also has sub-offices in Bozeman and Lewistown, Montana, all of which focus on native species conservation on tribal, federal, and state lands.

Chris Kennedy is a fish biologist with the U.S. Fish and Wildlife Service's Colorado Fish and Wildlife Conservation Office. He earned a B.S. in biology at Buffalo State College. Chris has worked with cutthroat trout in Colorado for twenty-plus years, much of it in Rocky Mountain National Park, and was instrumental in developing a greenback cutthroat trout broodstock at Leadville National Fish Hatchery.

Chris's love of nature, history, and sports compels him to travel as much as possible outside of work.

Todd E.A. Larson, Ph.D., is a historian with degrees from the University of Minnesota (B.A.), University of Cincinnati (M.A.), and the University of Illinois (Ph.D.). He specializes in the history of American fishing and tackle and has written a number of books and several hundred articles on the subject. In 2006, Todd founded the Whitefish Press, the only press dedicated to preserving the history of fish and fishing. The press has since published more than 150 books. Todd serves on the selection committee for the Freshwater Fishing Hall of Fame and teaches history at Xavier University in Cincinnati, Ohio.

Katrina Liebich, Ph.D., grew up in northern Virginia and received a B.S. in biology from Virginia Tech University. Since then she's moved north, first to Michigan where she received an M.S. and Ph.D. in fisheries, then to Maine to study and work on Atlantic salmon conservation, and now Alaska where she's spent the past ten years as the fisheries outreach coordinator and now digital media manager for the U.S. Fish and Wildlife Service. From the early years of dinking around in streams with a net, that is still her favorite type of fishing: dip-netting the Copper River in Alaska for salmon to live off the land with her husband Trent, daughter McKay, and son Ragnar.

Mark Madison, Ph.D., is the U.S. Fish and Wildlife Service historian and manager of the Branch of Heritage and Partnerships at the National Conservation Training Center. He has degrees in history, biology, and the history of science, and previously taught at Harvard University, the University of Melbourne, and Shepherd University. He fly fishes the Potomac River every day, a few steps from his office in Shepherdstown, West Virginia, and sometimes even catches a fish.

Carlos R. Martinez, M.S., is the director of the D.C. Booth Historic National Fish Hatchery and the National Fish and Aquatic Conservation Archives in Spearfish, South Dakota. He is the U.S. Fish and Wildlife Service's national broodstock coordinator and serves on the regional scuba dive team. Carlos started his fisheries career with the Army Corps of Engineers at the Snake River's Lower Monumental Dam in Washington. He has been with the U.S. Fish and Wildlife Service since 1999 and arrived in Spearfish in 2008 after serving as the assistant manager at the Leadville National Fish Hatchery in Colorado. He received a B.S. in wildlife and fisheries biology and management from the University of Wyoming and an M.S. in fisheries ecology from West Virginia University.

Jim Mogen, M.S., is a fish biologist at the Montana Fish and Wildlife Conservation Office in Bozeman, Montana. During Jim's twenty-three years with the U.S. Fish and Wildlife Service, he has worked with Montana's imperiled native fishes, including Arctic grayling, bull trout, Yellowstone cutthroat trout, westslope cutthroat trout, and pallid sturgeon.

Chris Olds, M.S., is a fish biologist on Lake Huron based out of the Alpena Fish and Wildlife Conservation Office, Alpena, Michigan. He has spent more than a decade of his career involved in research of diets, parasites, and early life history traits of lake whitefish around the Great Lakes. He received a B.S. in fisheries management from Lake Superior State University and an M.S. in biology with a concentration on aquatic science from University of Wisconsin–La Crosse. He lives in Alpena with his wife and their four children.

Wes Orr was raised along Spearfish Creek in Spearfish, South Dakota, by parents who nurtured a love of the outdoors. He worked summer jobs for South Dakota Game Fish and Parks, Alaska Department of Fish and Game, and McNenny National Fish Hatchery until graduating from Colorado State University in 1962 with a degree in fisheries science. Wes served ten years in the Army National Guard and thirty-eight years for the U.S. Fish and Wildlife Service, retiring in 2000. Since then he has been chest-deep culturing westslope cutthroat trout as a consultant, to restore them to their native range in Montana and Wyoming.

Henry Quinlan, M.S., is a fish biologist at the Ashland Fish and Wildlife Conservation Office, on Wisconsin's Lake Superior shore. His brook trout work takes him to Isle Royale National Park and the Apostle Islands and Pictured Rocks National Lakeshores. He caught his first brook trout in the early 1970s in the tiny Jennings Creek, near his home in Beaver Dam, Wisconsin, and then many more as a graduate student at University of Wisconsin–Green Bay. He and his wife, Kristin, spent two years in the Peace Corps and they have two children.

Angeline Rodgers is a fish biologist and supervises the Lower Mississippi River Fish and Wildlife Conservation Office in Tupelo, Mississippi. She began her career with the state of North Carolina, where she kept her head underwater surveying fish and rare mussels. She took advantage of an opportunity to work with the U.S. Fish and Wildlife Service nine years ago, and returned to her home state, working with a variety of partners to further aquatic conservation. She is married with two daughters and enjoys spending as much time outdoors as possible.

Tait Ronningen, M.S., is a fish and wildlife biologist at the Missouri River Fish and Wildlife Conservation Office in Bismarck, North Dakota. He specializes in fisheries conservation planning through geospatial tools to guide research and management. Tait earned a B.S. and M.S. at South Dakota State University. He and his wife, Samantha, are parents of a son and two daughters and enjoy hunting, fishing, birding, and camping.

Will Ryan teaches expository writing at Hampshire College. He is a columnist with *Gray's Sporting Journal*, and his stories appear regularly in *Field & Stream*, *Classic Angling*, and other publications. His most recent book, *Gray's Sporting Journal's Noble Birds and Wily Trout*, explores the origins of American hunting and fishing traditions.

Ralph Simmons is the assistant manager of Tishomingo National Fish Hatchery in Tishomingo, Oklahoma. A graduate of Missouri Southern State University, he started his career in 1990 at the nearby Neosho National Fish Hatchery. Ralph has worked with more than twenty species of fish, reptiles, and mussels at federal fisheries facilities in three states. He and his wife, Christa, and their daughter raise registered Texas longhorn cattle on a small ranch.

Tim Smigielski was born and raised in Michigan and earned a B.S. in fisheries biology at Michigan State University (Go Spartans). After a twelve-year stint with the Michigan Department of Natural Resources, he joined the U.S. Fish and Wildlife Service where he has been a fish biologist for eighteen years. Tim is the outreach and communications coordinator for Fish and Aquatic Conservation in the Department of the Interior's Unified Region 3–Great Lakes. He is proud of his family: he and his wife, Janet, have been married for twenty-eight years and have two adult children, Luke and Jill. Tim enjoys walleye fishing and deer hunting and is a former high school football coach.

Craig Springer, M.S., M.A., is the son of a decorated Korean War soldier. Craig and his wife, Felicia, have three anglers, Carson, Willow, and Ava, and a not-so-mellow yellow Lab. He is a fish biologist with the U.S. Fish and Wildlife Service-External Affairs stationed in New Mexico, where Rio Grande cutthroat trout in the southern Rockies have succeeded smallmouth bass as his favorite fish. Craig earned a B.S. in fisheries science from New Mexico State University (Go Aggies); an M.S. in fish ecology at the University of Arizona; and an M.A. in rhetoric at the University of New Mexico.

Sam Stukel, M.S., is a fish biologist at Gavins Point National Fish Hatchery in Yankton, South Dakota. In addition to handling education and outreach for the facility, he also provides photographs for the U.S. Fish and Wildlife Service. Sam is a father of three, a part-time photographer, and holds a graduate degree from South Dakota State University.

Jeff Trandahl is the CEO and executive director of National Fish and Wildlife Foundation in Washington, D.C. He is a former clerk of the U.S. House of Representatives.

Jeremy Voeltz is a supervisory fish biologist in the Columbia River Fish and Wildlife Conservation Office in Vancouver, Washington, where he works primarily with salmon in the Columbia River basin. In third grade, he decided to be a fish biologist. That led to a degree in biology and fish and wildlife management from Northern Arizona University and stints with the Arizona Game and Fish Departments and then encounters with Apache trout at the Arizona Fish and Wildlife Conservation Office in Pinetop. An avid homebrewer and amateur chef, Jeremy enjoys time in the garden and outdoor adventures with his wife and twin son and daughter.

Aaron von Eschen, M.S., is a fish biologist at Valley City National Fish Hatchery, North Dakota, his third federal fisheries facility assignment in nine years. South Dakota's Lake Francis Case, his home waters, afforded angling experience that led to a career. He is a graduate of South Dakota State University where he researched new fish diets for yellow perch. Aaron is grateful to his wife, his parents, and his brother for their encouragement toward a career in fisheries conservation.

Christina Wang, M.S., is a supervisory fish biologist at the Columbia River Fish and Wildlife Conservation Office in Vancouver, Washington. Originally from St. Paul, Minnesota, Christina earned a B.A. in biology from Drake University and M.S. in marine biology from California State University, Long Beach. She has worked on lamprey conservation for her entire career. She lives in Portland, Oregon, with her husband, three kids, and their cat. Their favorite fish is a Pacific lamprey.

Nathan Wiese, M.S., is the fisheries and aquatic conservation geographical supervisor for the Missouri Basin Region of the U.S. Fish and Wildlife Service. He lives in Lakewood, Colorado, with his wife, Amber, two young daughters, and their middle-aged black Labrador retriever. The Wieses enjoy camping, fishing, and hunting and return annually to northern Wisconsin.

Aaron Woldt, M.S., grew up near Green Bay, Wisconsin, and completed undergraduate studies at the University of Miami and graduate studies at the University of Michigan. He is the U.S. Fish and Wildlife Service's assistant regional director for fish and aquatic conservation in the Department of the Interior's Unified Region 3–Great Lakes. He resides with his family and rescued Siberian husky just south of the Twin Cities, Minnesota, and remains an ardent Packers fan.

Charles "Charlie" Wooley is the regional director for the U.S. Fish and Wildlife Service in the Department of the Interior's Unified Region 3–Great Lakes, encompassing eight states. In 2018, President Donald J. Trump appointed him to serve a six-year term as the federal commissioner representing the United States on the Great Lakes Fishery Commission. Charlie was honored by Department of the Interior Secretary Gale Norton in 2001 with the department's Meritorious Service Award and was again honored in 2012 by Secretary Ken Salazar with the department's Distinguished Service Award, the department's highest award. When not working, he enjoys catching walleye with his wife near their home in Lakeville, Minnesota.

Kirk Young is a fish biologist who has worked to conserve fish in Arizona for more than thirty years. Kirk spent the majority of his time with the Arizona Game and Fish Department, including stints as wildlife manager, native fish program manager, and fisheries branch chief. Kirk left the state agency in 2012 and has since worked at the Arizona Fish and Wildlife Conservation Office in Flagstaff, on fishes of the Grand Canyon.

Jaclyn Zelko is a fish biologist at the Warm Springs Fish Technology Center in Warm Springs, Georgia, where she has worked since 2003. She is the Cryopreservation Lab manager, responsible for conserving the sex products of more than twenty species of fish and freshwater mussels. She is a graduate of Roger Williams University in Rhode Island, and lives near Warm Springs with her future fish biologists, Eva and Henry.

Index